Negotiating Ac
to Higher Edu

SRHE and Open University Press Imprint
General Editor: Heather Eggins

Current titles include:

Mike Abramson *et al.* (eds): *Further and Higher Education Partnerships*
Catherine Bargh, Peter Scott and David Smith: *Governing Universities*
Ronald Barnett: *Improving Higher Education*
Ronald Barnett (ed.): *Learning to Effect*
Ronald Barnett: *Limits of Competence*
Ronald Barnett: *The Idea of Higher Education*
Tony Becher (ed.): *Governments and Professional Education*
Hazel Bines and David Watson: *Developing Professional Education*
John Bird: *Black Students and Higher Education*
Jean Bocock and David Watson (eds): *Managing the Curriculum*
David Boud *et al.* (eds): *Using Experience for Learning*
Angela Brew (ed.): *Directions in Staff Development*
Ann Brooks: *Academic Women*
Frank Coffield and Bill Williamson (eds): *Repositioning Higher Education*
Rob Cuthbert: *Working in Higher Education*
John Earwaker: *Helping and Supporting Students*
Roger Ellis (ed.): *Quality Assurance for University Teaching*
Maureen Farish *et al.*: *Equal Opportunities in Colleges and Universities*
Shirley Fisher: *Stress in Academic Life*
Sinclair Goodlad: *The Quest for Quality*
Diana Green (ed.): *What is Quality in Higher Education?*
Susanne Haselgrove (ed.): *The Student Experience*
Jill Johnes and Jim Taylor: *Performance Indicators in Higher Education*
Ian McNay (ed.): *Visions of Post-compulsory Education*
Robin Middlehurst: *Leading Academics*
Henry Miller: *The Management of Change in Universities*
Jennifer Nias (ed.): *The Human Nature of Learning: Selections from the Work of M.L.J. Abercrombie*
Keith Noble: *Changing Doctoral Degrees*
Gillian Pascali and Roger Cox: *Women Returning to Higher Education*
Graham Peeke: *Mission and Change*
Moira Peelo: *Helping Students with Study Problems*
John Pratt: *The Polytechnic Experiment*
Kjell Raaheim *et al.*: *Helping Students to Learn*
Tom Schuller (ed.): *The Changing University?*
Tom Schuller (ed.): *The Future of Higher Education*
Peter Scott: *The Meanings of Mass Higher Education*
Michael Shattock: *The UGC and the Management of British Universities*
John Smyth (ed.): *Academic Work*
Geoffrey Squires: *First Degree*
Ted Tapper and Brian Salter: *Oxford, Cambridge and the Changing Idea of the University*
Kim Thomas: *Gender and Subject in Higher Education*
Malcolm Tight: *Higher Education: A Part-time Perspective*
David Warner and Elaine Crosthwaite (eds): *Human Resource Management in Higher and Further Education*
David Warner and Gordon Kelly: *Managing Educational Property*
David Warner and Charles Leonard: *The Income Generation Handbook*
David Warner and David Palfreyman (eds): *Higher Education Management*
Graham Webb: *Understanding Staff Development*
Sue Wheeler and Jan Birtle: *A Handbook for Personal Tutors*
Thomas G. Whiston and Roger L. Geiger (eds): *Research and Higher Education*
Gareth Williams: *Changing Patterns of Finance in Higher Education*
Jenny Williams (ed.): *Negotiating Access to Higher Education: The discourse of selectivity and equity*
John Wyatt: *Commitment to Higher Education*

Negotiating Access to Higher Education

The Discourse of Selectivity and Equity

Edited by Jenny Williams

The Society for Research into Higher Education
& Open University Press

Published by SRHE and
Open University Press
Celtic Court
22 Ballmoor
Buckingham
MK18 1XW

and
1900 Frost Road, Suite 101
Bristol, PA 19007, USA

First Published 1997

A catalogue record of this book is available from the British Library

ISBN   0 335 19678 0 (Pbk)   0 335 19679 9 (Hbk)

Library of Congress Cataloging-in-Publication Data
Negotiating access to higher education : the discourse of selectivity
    and equity / edited by Jenny Williams.
        p.   cm.
    Includes bibliographical references (p.   ) and index.
    ISBN 0–335–19679–9 (hb). — ISBN 0–335–19678–0 (pb)
    1. Universities and colleges—England—Admission.   2. Universities
and colleges—Wales—Admission.   3. Universities and colleges—
Entrance requirements—England.   4. Universities and colleges—
Entrance requirements—Wales.   5. Educational equalization—
England.   6. Educational equalization—Wales.   7. Politics and
education—England.   8. Politics and education—Wales.
I. Williams, Jenny, 1938–   .
LB2351.4.G7N44   1997
378.1′61′0941—dc21   96–49719
                                                                CIP

Typeset by Graphicraft Typesetters Ltd., Hong Kong
Printed in Great Britain by St Edmundsbury Press Ltd., Bury
St Edmunds, Suffolk

Contents

List of Contributors   vii
Foreword by Gareth Parry   viii
Preface by Sue Webb   x
Acknowledgements   xii
List of Abbreviations   xiii

1   Access to Higher Education in the late Twentieth Century:
    Policy, Power and Discourse   1
    Pat Davies, Jenny Williams and Sue Webb
2   The Discourse of Access: The Legitimation of Selectivity   24
    Jenny Williams
3   Number Crunching: The Discourse of Statistics   47
    Pat Davies
4   Alternative Students? Conceptualizations of Difference   65
    Sue Webb
5   Institutional Rhetorics and Realities   87
    Jenny Williams
6   Gatekeeping: Inclusionary and Exclusionary Discourses
    and Practices   108
    Anne Thompson
7   Student Voices: Alternative Routes, Alternative Identities   130
    Pat Green and Sue Webb
8   Conclusions   153

Appendix 1: Alternative Entry to Higher Education Project:
    Summary Information   162
Appendix 2: Summary National Data   165
References   174
Index   187
The Society for Research into Higher Education   195

This book is dedicated to Philip Jones, for his tireless work in the cause of Access and for the intellectual stimulation and support which guided our original project. It is particularly for his humour and friendship that we will remember him.

List of Contributors

The authors came together as a research team in 1991 to conduct a study of alternative entry to higher education. They currently occupy a range of positions in further and higher education and have been involved in the research and practice of access for many years.

Pat Davies is Director of the Continuing Education Research Unit, City University, London.

Pat Green is a lecturer in Women's Studies in the School of Humanities and Social Sciences, University of Wolverhampton.

Anne Thompson is Head of the School of Arts, Language and Teacher Training at Waltham Forest College.

Sue Webb was a development officer for the Manchester Open College Federation and since 1993 has been Course Director for Women's Studies in the Adult Continuing Education Department, Sheffield University.

Jenny Williams is Head of the Division of Women's Studies, School of Humanities and Social Sciences, University of Wolverhampton.

Foreword

The achievement of 'mass' levels of participation in a system retaining and rewarding 'elite' characteristics has been one of the distinctive features of the rapid expansion of British higher education in recent years. Both the doubling of student numbers since the early 1980s, and the increase in the participation rate for young people to nearly one third of the age group, were able to be accomplished without major reform or revision of the traditional qualifications for entry and without the creation of new or alternative institutions to accommodate this growth. Although identified with policies for increased access and widened participation, expansion was to be conditional upon competition and selection for places: with individual establishments continuing to determine who should be admitted to their courses, and with individual candidates continuing to hold their qualifications as a basis for eligibility, not as a right to entry.

While the policy and machinery of selective entry has continued under mass conditions, the question of who should have access to higher education has assumed major significance in the debates and struggles which have marked this transition. In the British case, this has focused on two key issues: reform of the academic and vocational qualifications studied by young people in upper secondary and further education; and action to advance the participation of adults in all types and styles of higher education. The two are firmly linked, but it was with reference to wider opportunities for adults, especially those not in possession of 'standard' qualifications, that issues around access and equity were to find their strongest expression in higher education. Indeed, it was a whole series of initiatives aimed at excluded and disadvantaged groups in the adult population which were to give rise to a self-conscious 'access movement' during this period.

Access to higher education, as a realm of discourse and field of practice, is the subject of the present book. In analysing the different understandings, shifting meanings and divergent positions absorbed in the notion of access, the authors point to the essential ambiguity of the language of selectivity and equity in British higher education. The key elements in this discourse, along with the power of different players to manage its ambiguities and omissions, are explored at various policy moments and at different levels of the system: from national debates through to institutional practices, in research agendas and official statistics, and with reference to qualifying routes and student identities. Furthermore, by placing access for adults at the centre of their analysis, the contributors engage directly with sets of distinctions and assumptions – about the admissibility of applicants, about the acceptability of their qualifications and backgrounds – which have served to legitimate patterns of inclusion and exclusion in a selective system. Although contested more sharply and interpreted more variously in recent years, these separations continue to manifest themselves in the new hierarchies of post-binary higher education.

The vocabularies of access, especially their capacity to disguise divisions and conceal contradictions, provide a rich source of material for the kind of discourse approach adopted in this volume. For the domestic commentator as much as the international observer, the complexity and volatility of the British encounter with mass higher education has, understandably, proved difficult to narrate and interpret. An ability to get behind the confusion of categories which have accompanied this episode is critical therefore to an understanding of the uneven, unstable and uncertain nature of the shift to more open forms of access and admission. The political geography of the book – referenced to England and Wales – is important in this regard, permitting an appreciation of the specificities which feature in these territories, and inviting comparison with regions and states where 'noise' about access has been equally strong (or distinctly more muted) in the public and private lives of universities and colleges.

A focus on England and Wales is also significant in the light of proposals for new forms of certification for young people between the ages of 16 and 19. Unlike in Scotland where a unified curriculum and assessment system will be introduced, the arrangements recommended for England and Wales distinguish between academic, applied and vocational tracks, with little disturbance to the specialist and subject-based qualifications which have served as the main channel of entry to higher education. How these recommendations might translate themselves into the current inquiry into the future of higher education in the United Kingdom is by no means clear, but the processes and outcomes of this exercise will provide researchers with fertile sources to build on the analysis presented in the pages which follow.

Gareth Parry
Institute of Education, University of London

Preface

This book covers a range of issues concerning the discourse about access in higher education. It arises from our interest in what access to higher education is and what is meant by accessibility, which we, the five women authors, have shared for at least a decade. Over this period, we have been involved as researchers and practitioners at a range of institutional and organizational levels with movements to widen access. We first came together formally in 1991 to work on the 'Alternative Entry to Higher Education' project initiated by Gareth Parry at City University and later at the University of Warwick, and this research has provided the stimulus for this book.

The 'Alternative Entry to Higher Education' project was set up with funding from CNAA, FEU, TEED and UDACE to explore the meaning of the growth in numbers of entrants to higher education who did not use the qualification route of two A levels or their vocational equivalents. The project was developed in the growing awareness of an increasing focus of attention by institutions, government departments and accreditation bodies, on local arrangements for entry for those who were qualifying for entry in alternative ways. We perceived at that time that little was known about these entrants or what these alternative ways of entering higher education might include in terms of qualifications, learning and experience, and it was this knowledge gap that the project was designed to remedy. The project, therefore, has been a trigger for many of the issues and questions we set out to explore in this book and it is a major source of the materials used (see Appendix 1 for a summary of the research population and methods used).

This collective research and our differing professional biographies provided the context for our increasing understanding of how policy is constructed and shaped across organizational levels and sectors. In our readings, observations and interactions, we 'heard' access being discussed differently and we began to focus on the language of access and the processes of negotiation and accommodation around meanings. The research findings helped to identify disparities in the discourse about access at different levels in the system and the contexts in which these ambiguities occurred. For example, we identified four issues: first, there was some confusion around the construction and use of national and institutional data; second, there were examples of a mismatch between policies and practice at the national and institutional levels; third, the access research agenda appeared to be dominated by a less than open policy agenda associated with conceptualizations of the mature student as a social species; and fourth, there were examples of a mismatch between the ways organizations categorized and identified students and the identities of these students. Ambiguity seemed central to the ways that access to higher education was framed in the policies, practices and papers of various key people and organizations. Consequently, this book has been conceived as a way of exploring further the existence and base of these ambiguities and the ways that they may have been used and manipulated.

Finally, the book has been written collaboratively and reflects our common concerns. It is more than a collection of individual chapters and it can be read as a whole because the argument develops sequentially. However, the chapters can each be read independently. Readers can make their own selections and follow their interests in the knowledge that each chapter reflects the diversity of our experiences and views and has been authored separately.

Sue Webb

Acknowledgements

The editor and contributors wish to acknowledge the members of the Steering Committee for the original research project which generated many of the ideas in this book: Philip Jones, Chris Duke, Susanne Haselgrove, Stephen McNair, Chris Parkin and Ros Seyd.

Thanks are also due to the researchers who assisted in the collection of that data: Peter Weller, Tessa Lovell and Soraya Shah; and to Diana Mullmier for her administrative and secretarial support.

Thanks too, to Geoff Williams for his technical and other support.

Particular thanks go to Gareth Parry for his continuous interest and for his incisive comments on early drafts of this book. The final version is of course the sole responsibility of the authors.

List of Abbreviations

ACACE	Advisory Council for Adult and Continuing Education
ACRG	Access Courses Recognition Group
ADAR	Art and Design Admissions Registry
A levels	General Certificate in Education Advanced level
APEL	Accreditation of Prior Experiential Learning
API	Age Participation Index
APL	Accreditation of Prior Learning
AVA	Authorised Validating Agency
BTEC	Business and Technology Education Council
CAT	Credit Accumulation and Transfer
CATS	Credit Accumulation and Transfer Scheme
CBI	Confederation of British Industry
CCCS	Centre for Contemporary Cultural Studies
CDP	Committee of Directors of Polytechnics
CNAA	Council for National Academic Awards
CRCH	Central Register and Clearing House
CRE	Commission for Racial Equality
CSR	Continuous Student Record
CVCP	Committee of Vice Chancellors and Principals
DES	Department of Education and Science
Dip HE	Diploma in Higher Education
DfE	Department for Education
DfEE	Department for Education and Employment
DoE	Department of Employment
EHE	Enterprise in Higher Education
ETPM	Education and Training Parliamentary Monitor
FAST	Forum for Access Studies
FEDA	Further Education Development Agency
FEFC	Further Education Funding Council
FESR	Further Education Statistical Record

FEU	Further Education Unit
GCE	General Certificate in Education
GCSE	General Certificate of Secondary Education
GNVQ	General National Vocational Qualification
GSVQ	General Scottish Vocational Qualification
GTTR	Graduate Teacher Training Registry
HEFC	Higher Education Funding Council
HEFCE	Higher Education Funding Council for England
HEQC	Higher Education Quality Council
HESA	Higher Education Statistical Agency
HNC	Higher National Certificate
HND	Higher National Diploma
LEA	Local Education Authority
MASN	Maximum Aggregate Student Numbers
NAB	National Advisory Body for Local Authority Higher Education
NCVQ	National Council for Vocational Qualifications
NIACE	National Institute of Adult Continuing Education
NOCN	National Open College Network
NVQ	National Vocational Qualification
OCN	Open College Network
Ofsted	Office for Standards in Education
ONC	Ordinary National Certificate
OND	Ordinary National Diploma
O level	General Certificate in Education Ordinary level
OU	Open University
PCAS	Polytechnics and Colleges Admissions Service
PCFC	Polytechnics and Colleges Funding Council
RSA	Royal Society of Arts
SCAVA	Standing Conference of Authorised Validating Agencies
SCOTVEC	Scottish Vocational Education Council
SCUE	Standing Conference on University Entrance
SRHE	Society for Research in Higher Education
SVQ	Scottish Vocational Qualification
TEED	(The Employment Department) Training, Education and Enterprise Division
UCAS	Universities and Colleges Admissions Service
UCCA	Universities Central Council on Admissions
UDACE	Unit for the Development of Adult Continuing Education
UFC	Universities Funding Council
UGC	Universities Grants Committee
USR	Universities Statistical Record

1

Access to Higher Education in the late Twentieth Century: Policy, Power and Discourse

Pat Davies, Jenny Williams and Sue Webb

Introduction

Our concern in this book is to describe and analyse one particular aspect of the shift towards mass higher education in England and Wales in the period from the 1960s to the 1990s. The focus is upon who has access to the system: who can legitimately claim a right to publicly funded resources leading, potentially, to enhanced lifetime status and earnings, and how selection and equity interact, particularly for adults. In all advanced industrial societies the transformation from an elite to a mass system of higher education has involved continuing debate and struggle: over the purposes of higher education, who should control it, how and where it should be organized and provided, what should be taught, and how it should be financed. This case study can be read as illustrative of trends and debates in very many countries. The specificities of the answers vary, but the questions are common ones. As Trow (1974) pointed out massification implies more than an increase in numbers; it involves *inter alia* more open access and a more heterogenous student body and therefore struggles over who it should be for and how the worthy should be identified are integral to these wider debates. The contestations are about what can be said and thought about higher education, who can speak, when, where and with what authority, and about who has the power to translate argument and policy into practice and to determine the shape, size and access to higher education.

Our prime focus concerns how the debates about the nature of access to higher education are being constructed and what are the political, economic, academic, institutional and personal contexts which give those debates their specificity and meaning. It is the incoherence and the state of flux we wish to examine, the interplay of alternatives, coming together at the time of writing, in a significant policy moment: the establishment of a national committee of inquiry into higher education in the UK (the Dearing Committee).

In trying to map this shifting reality, six key questions have guided our work:

1. What does access to higher education mean to the differing players in the system and what would access to a mass system entail?
2. What is defined and counted as higher education? Access to what?
3. Who controls the access process? What means of rationing are used and why? How are these legitimated?
4. Who is worthy of access? Who are the 'new' students? How are they labelled and why?
5. What are the academic histories of the 'new' students? How are their identities and subjectivities manifested?
6. How are these questions and answers articulated at different levels within the education system and with what consequences?

Such questions are usually posed separately and left unconnected; the strength of the approach we take here lies in our attempt to provide an integrated account.

Many writers on educational policy have attempted to provide the conceptual tools useful in understanding such contexts and processes (see for example, Ball and Shilling, 1994; Raab, 1994; Dale, 1994; Ball, S.J., 1994c; Hatcher and Troyna, 1994; Maclure, 1994). Among these writers a key debate has been between structuralist (or materialist) approaches and those labelled post-structuralist, particularly the version which uses Foucault's concept of a discourse. We do not wish to engage with this debate in detail, or comment on the precise articulation of the differing positions; this would take another and different book. Instead we wish to use and combine what we see as the strengths of both positions to illuminate the ways in which debates concerning access to higher education, particularly those focusing upon adults, have been articulated over the past decade. We accept that power is historically institutionalized in particular ways in the organs of the state, and that contemporary struggles over educational policy 'take place on a terrain already structured by power and above all by the power of the state' (Hatcher and Troyna, 1994:167). By implication the power to determine events is not static or unique to particular groups but is located to the structural advantage of some key players. But such power is exercised partly through the construction of a discourse which constitutes both the goals and subjects of policies, which legitimates such constructions and which frames, but does not completely control, forms of implementation. Therefore we are conceptualizing discourses as institutionalized structures of meaning that have symbolic and manipulative power (Ball, S.J., 1990a; Troyna and Vincent, 1995).

The rest of this chapter has two distinct but complementary sections, linked in a way that reflects our attempt to combine the two conceptual approaches. The first section provides a brief historical summary of developments in higher education over the past 30 years, a necessarily selective mapping of the key policy moments in the development of access debates and discourse from our perspective as players within the system. It looks at the historical institutionalization of forms of control, patterns of provision and the labelling of these in particular ways by significant players. It is intended to provide a succinct overview both for those who have lived through the changes and for those unfamiliar with the specifics in England and Wales. For the latter, it will highlight the key dates, documents, players and patterns which, although located in one country, can be found in the general thrusts of policy in many other educational systems (see for example Lemelin, 1994, on Australia, North America and India; Gale and McNamee, 1995, on Australia; Davies, 1995c, on various European countries; Boehm, 1995, on Canada). For both groups of readers it will provide the context for the current debates and will historically locate alternative ideologies and practices.

The first part of what follows then, identifies the key dimensions and moments which in our view have impacted on activity in access to higher education and which are problematized throughout the book; the second part sets out the framework of analysis we employ to explore the relationship between power, structural position, policy discourse and discursive practices at the various policy moments. It introduces the intellectual origins and conceptual tools that have informed our thinking and which are used and developed further in the rest of the book.

Thirty years of change

Since the early 1960s, the structure, size and shape of not just higher education but the whole education system in England and Wales has changed fundamentally. The post-compulsory sector – further and higher education and the interface between them which is the focus of this book – has seen the most dramatic and fundamental change in the late 1980s and early 1990s. It is not the intention here to write the history of that change in detail, but rather to identify the broad thrusts of policy, practice and debate in order to provide a context for the detailed analyses which follow. It is acknowledged that such a broad brush approach inevitably involves a process of selection and a judgement about the significance of particular events. The basis of that selection is those events which represent key reference points in the development of the discourse of access and key 'moments' in policy and practice. In particular they highlight those developments which have influenced or were influenced by the question, who is higher education for? Such a question necessitates other prior questions, in particular, what constitutes higher education and who controls it?

What constitutes higher education?

The 'old foundations' – the universities of Oxford and Cambridge in England and Glasgow, St Andrews, Aberdeen and Edinburgh in Scotland – were all established before 1600. The main development of the system took place in the nineteenth century with first, the creation of the University of London (a federation of colleges), the University of Wales and 11 'civic universities', and later a further seven university colleges initially teaching external degrees of the University of London. Subsequently, mostly at the end of the Second World War, these latter institutions became universities in their own right. In the 1960s, following the Robbins Report (Committee for Education, 1963), nine new 'green field' universities were built and ten Colleges of Advanced Technology (CATs) became universities, and in 1969 the Open University (OU) was established (see Duke, 1992, for a more detailed description of these developments). The polytechnics were established between 1969 and 1973, awarding degrees of the Council for National Academic Awards (CNAA) and managed by the Local Education Authorities (LEAs). In the 1970s, some of the colleges of education (the teacher training institutions) were incorporated into the polytechnics and others became Colleges or Institutes of Higher Education, offering a wide range of degrees which were validated by others, usually universities. Thus from the early 1970s higher education in the UK was a binary system based on universities and polytechnics, although there continued to be a significant number of colleges and institutes of higher education which did not fit neatly into this system, especially the smaller specialist colleges, of music, agriculture, theology and so on. In addition, the Open University, while technically part of the 'university sector', was quite distinct in terms of its structure, academic year, provision (almost entirely distance learning) and student body, and was separately funded.

From 1987 polytechnics began to be authorized by CNAA to award their own degrees and in the Education Reform Act of 1988 they were removed from LEA control and incorporated as independent institutions. In 1992 the Further and Higher Education Act finally abolished the binary system and enabled the polytechnics to be renamed universities. The colleges of higher education mostly became affiliated or associated in some way to a university, offering degrees validated by that institution, although many continue to be funded as separate institutions. In 1996, there were 177 institutions of higher education financed by the funding councils of England, Wales and Scotland and by the Education Department of the Northern Ireland Office, of which 93 had the title university (including the colleges of the federal institutions of London and Wales as separate institutions). In addition, higher education level study was provided in many of the further education colleges through various formal arrangements with universities.

The binary system was more than a structural division. It was supported by separate, unequal funding of the two sectors, and a different purpose which both reflected and promoted a public perception of differential status: the polytechnics largely focusing on local students, local needs and vocational education while the universities were national, often international institutions focusing on research and academic and postgraduate professional education. These were however stereotypes: many polytechnics were in fact national centres for specialist professional education, for example particular engineering fields, and many universities had large programmes of trade union and community education. In addition, within each sector there were hierarchies: the language of 'old foundation', 'civic', 'green field' and 'ex-CAT' in relation to the then university sector illustrates the labelling which underpinned such differentiation. The unification of the system has not involved giving all institutions the same formal authority: only 90 of the 177 institutions have full and autonomous degree-awarding powers. Rather it has focused on the development of a single funding methodology, so that it has not abolished past differentiation but provided the opportunity for a reshuffling of the hierarchy. Those institutions previously called 'new' – the green field and ex-CAT universities – are now called 'old'; the term 'new' now refers to the former polytechnics. Since age and tradition are closely associated in British culture with higher status, these are not neutral labels but indicate a new ranking. In addition, institutions are beginning to be identified (by themselves and others) as research, research and teaching, or teaching only institutions; some are developing strong institutional relationships (including mergers) with further education colleges and identifying themselves as access institutions, blurring institutional boundaries. What constitutes higher education both institutionally and intellectually is being questioned; and what was called a binary system in the 1970s and 1980s and formally became a unified system in the early 1990s, is rapidly becoming a restratified system in the mid-1990s (Scott, 1995).

Alongside this structural mutation, there has been a major change in the size of the system (see Table 1 in Appendix 2). Expansion, although recognized as a need and under discussion in government and academic circles in the 1950s (Blackburn and Jarman, 1993) was nevertheless, both in terms of the number of institutions and the student population, given a major push in the early 1960s by two key documents. The first was the Anderson Report (Ministry of Education, 1960) which recommended mandatory awards covering full fees for all those accepted on to a full-time first degree, with means tested maintenance grants for all undergraduates, so that higher education was no longer dependent on the ability to pay. The second was the Robbins Report which recommended a large expansion of universities based on demand: 'courses of higher education should be available for all those who are qualified by ability and attainment to pursue them and who wish to do so' (Committee for Education, 1963:8), frequently referred to as 'the famous Robbins principle'.

The early 1970s saw the plans for expansion made explicit by government with a proposal for a ten-year programme of expansion for further and higher education (although with a lower unit of resource) which envisaged that the non-university institutions would eventually have similar numbers to the universities (DES, 1972). The introduction of maintenance grants and the expansion of the non-university sector reflected the spirit of the 1960s and early 1970s and as such has been called the 'era of social democratic expansion' (Smith and Saunders, 1991:4). Although numbers expanded in the 1970s, the age participation index (API) remained stable; not until the major expansion of the late 1980s did the index reach 15 per cent. In 1991, the DES set a target to increase the API for 18–19-year-olds from 20 to 30 per cent by the year 2000 (DES, 1991b). In the event, the expansion raced ahead of these forecasts and it became clear that not only would an API of 30 per cent be reached several years before the target date (in fact it was reached with the 1993 entry), but that demand from adults had continued to increase. A period of 'consolidation' was therefore announced (DfE and Ofsted, 1993) with plans to reduce the number of entrants by 3.5 per cent, accompanied by changes in the funding arrangements to ensure an effective response from the institutions. Thus the demand-led policy enunciated in the Robbins principle, with weak state control over the number of admissions, finally came to an end in official discourse.

Precisely how this change from expansion to consolidation was implemented by the institutions is still not totally clear, particularly, as we shall see in Chapter 3, since time series comparisons of data are highly problematic because the definition of higher education and of a student have not been static. What counts as 'higher' education is clearly fundamental in measuring any increase. However, since expansion in admissions impacts on the system progressively over a number of years, the total number of students continued to rise beyond the announcement of consolidation, to 1,625,000 in 1995/6 (HESA, 1996b) (see Table 1 in Appendix 2).

Who controls higher education?

While the purposes of higher education are embedded in policy statements of the various players (as we shall see in Chapter 2), the way in which they are operationalized is influenced by where power, authority and responsibility lie within the system. The question of who controls higher education is therefore a key one in understanding who it is for.

Control is closely linked to funding and to the management of supply and demand in the system. This link between the management of demand on the one hand through changes in the interpretation of who higher education is for and how their suitability is judged, and of supply on the other hand through funding policy, can be seen clearly in the post-Robbins period. Johnes and Taylor (1990:31) pointed out that 'the acceptance of the Robbins principle meant that total expenditure on universities became demand driven in the mid 1960s', but Parry (1995:116) has argued that the Report also 'encouraged a restrictive interpretation of the word "qualified" (a minimum pass in two General Certificate in Education (GCE) A levels)'. Thus while the determinants of the level of expenditure shifted from supply to demand, nevertheless demand continued to be managed through selection.

As alternative routes to higher education began to emerge in the early 1980s, the government attempted to hold to A levels as the 'gold standard' and singled out Access courses in particular for scrutiny and criticism (see, for example, DES, 1985a). When it shifted its position in the 1987 White Paper (DES, 1987) and endorsed vocational qualifications as the second and Access courses as the third official routes into higher education, this was accompanied by a tightening of the funding arrangements through the introduction of contract-based funding and performance indicators. 'By making institutions' income dependent in larger measure on their ability to attract and satisfy student demand, this funding approach will both promote effectiveness in marketing and teaching, and enhance the scope of institutional independence' (DES, 1989:2). Thus funding and the management of demand were explicitly linked.

The 1992 Act unified the system and established the new Higher Education Funding Councils (HEFCs) (for England, Wales and Scotland; Northern Ireland continued to be funded through the Northern Ireland Office), changes which have been represented (Brown and Scase, 1994) as a shift from an underfunded version of the German dual system to an underfunded version of the North American system. The funding formulae which rapidly emerged were certainly based much more closely on market principles: a per capita sum which varied according to the subject and level; in addition, funding for research was separated from funding for teaching. Thus despite the fact that admissions and curriculum were specifically excluded from the jurisdiction of the Secretary of State in the 1992 Act, a mechanism had been put in place through the funding arrangements which facilitated considerable government control over the numbers recruited in broad subject areas, more recently operationalized as MASNs. Since not only university costs but student financial support were directly dependent on admissions decisions, this was obviously a key point at which to act if public expenditure was to be controlled. Nevertheless, it represented a radical departure from previous funding arrangements: no longer could the system be described as demand-led; rather it was tightly controlled, complete with penalties, from the centre. The announcement of 'consolidation' requiring a reduction in planned admissions by many institutions confirmed the shift back towards supply-led funding and was particularly difficult since it came when the admissions cycle had already begun.

Some universities (Richards, 1996) have responded to the funding constraints with a once taboo idea – that students should pay towards the cost of tuition. To some extent a fee-paying system had already appeared: as the number of full-time undergraduate (free) places has been consolidated, the number of part-time (fee-paying) places has grown.

While the government claims a non-interventionist position in relation to higher education, it is clear that considerable centralization has taken place (Jenkins, 1995) and state funding is more tightly controlled both in terms of the overall amount and of the mechanisms, formulae and criteria, albeit at arm's length through the Funding Councils. Since the tradition of universities as independent and autonomous institutions is strong and jealously guarded, particularly by the 'old' universities, and admissions and curriculum were specifically excluded from the Secretary of State's jurisdiction in the 1992 Act, funding is the only formal and explicit mechanism for influencing higher education. It is, however, a powerful one, not unrelated to admissions and selectivity, and has been the focus of much debate in the 1980s and 1990s.

The other arm of the government's 'non-interventionist' strategy is accountability – hence the increase in attention paid to quality audit, quality assessment, and performance indicators. While there is agreement on the principle of public accountability, there is also disagreement about the measures and mechanisms, and a possible relationship with funding. One element of these debates around quality has been the qualifications of the students on entry as a relevant factor in making judgements about both the systems and the curriculum. Current plans for the future of quality assurance arrangements and proposals to make admissions policy and practice a more important focus of attention within them, are likely to make this link more explicit and more contested.

Alongside the changes in the funding of higher education has been a parallel set of changes in relation to further education, the key provider for adults of courses and qualifications for entry to higher education. The Further and Higher Education Act of 1992 established the framework for the incorporation of the further education colleges and new funding arrangements to be managed by the Further Education Funding Council (FEFC). Again, radical new arrangements were put in place, based on a combination of core, additional and demand-led funding to maintain stability, to encourage growth and responsiveness and to monitor provision. In terms of access and progression to higher education, the expansion targets embedded in the new funding arrangements constituted new opportunities both for young people and adults in the three years 1994–97, although it is not clear what effect the end to growth in 1997 will have on these opportunities or how they can be exploited fully at a time when higher education is 'consolidating' its recruitment.

Government funding of both sectors and its policies to ensure accountability are therefore clearly linked to questions about what higher education is for and what kind of students should be there.

 ## Who is higher education for?

Robbins (Committee for Education, 1963) set out a model of higher education which incorporated a number of purposes: personal development, social cohesion, and learning for its own sake. In the late 1970s and early 1980s, a number of important reports (see for example the Leverhulme Reports, SRHE, 1983) showed it as primarily excluding and dividing rather than including and integrating large numbers of people, in particular working-class and ethnic minority groups. In response, its function in promoting social cohesion rose up the policy agenda both as a means of bringing into a common culture those who were excluded but also as 'one of the rights of citizenship in modern democratic societies' (Fulton, 1981:10). In addition, and perhaps more significantly, addressing 'the real and pressing needs of our economy' (Ball, C., 1984:81) became an important purpose since it was here that the manpower required by a technologically-based economy could be produced. It is these two imperatives: social justice and economic efficiency which have informed the debate of the 1980s and early 1990s around the question: who is higher education for?

It was clear in the 1970s that the pressures for social equity and economic competitiveness, alongside the predictions of falling numbers of suitably qualified 18- and 19-year-olds (DES, 1978b) meant that expansion would require the recruitment of different kinds of students: 'more means different' (Ball, C., 1990). Much of this notion of difference centred around adults or mature students who represented a key target group for policy-makers and practitioners. As Parry (1995:107) has pointed out, mature students were frequently constructed as 'returners' – those who missed out on earlier educational opportunities, highlighting 'acknowledged deficiencies and inequities in the system of compulsory and post-compulsory education.' Mature students were also key players in the economic life of the nation, either as workers who needed continuing education or skills upgrading, or as unemployed people who required retraining in the new technologies. Constructing adults as mature students therefore constituted a response to both the social justice and the economic imperatives of the late 1970s and 1980s as well as providing a way of meeting the (wrongly as it turned out) predicted major shortfall in demand from the 18- and 19-year-olds. Thus they became and have remained a prime focus of the policy debate and the key target group not only for those with a specific interest in the education of adults (ACACE, 1979; UDACE, 1985, 1988; NIACE, 1989, 1993), but also the representatives of industry (CBI, 1989, 1994) and of institutions (CNAA, 1978, 1987; CVCP, 1995), the planning and funding bodies for higher education (NAB, 1984; UGC, 1984), and more recently the HEFCs (see, for example, HEFCE, 1995) as well as the DES (1978b, 1987, 1991b) and Department of Employment (1990). Alongside these policy bodies, the academic community has also focused much of the research into higher education on issues surrounding adults in higher education, as the publications list of SRHE and Open University Press reveals. Across the complete spectrum of players and positions, 1988 has been seen as a watershed: the year in which mature students (defined as over 21 on entry to undergraduate, and over 25 on entry to postgraduate programmes) constituted more than 50 per cent of all entrants to higher education for the first time (DfE, 1992a), although as we shall see later in this book this overall average conceals significant differences.

Within this overarching concept of adult or mature students has been a focus on the recruitment of particular target groups. While in part driven by the economic argument and the notion of wasted talent (see Fulton,

1981, for a fuller discussion of this issue), the main thrust of this approach has come from the social justice argument. Thus in many of the documents referenced above, attention has also been drawn to the need to recruit from groups under-represented in higher education: women, ethnic minorities, manual and unskilled occupational classes and, somewhat more recently, people with disabilities; and a range of policy debates and initiatives was launched to address their needs. While it is clear that there are now many more women and ethnic minority students in higher education (see Tables 1 and 6 in Appendix 2), the situation is much less clear in relation to the lower socio-economic groups. In addition, women are still under-represented in the physical sciences and in engineering and technology, and not all ethnic groups are represented in proportion to their presence in the general population, so that the extent to which the initiatives have been successful is still debated (see Chapters 3 and 4). However, there seems to be a growing assumption in the policy discourse that expansion has taken care of most of these groups with the exception of people with disabilities: this is the only group referred to specifically in a recent paper from NIACE (1993), and the Advisory Group on Access and Participation set up by HEFCE in 1994 focused its initial discussions on people with special learning needs and disabilities.

The question of who higher education is for is clearly related to the qualification routes available. Young people entering higher education for the first time have conventionally done so by 'matriculating' with a minimum of two passes at GCE A level in relevant subjects. Despite mounting concern that such a preparation was far too narrow, the government rejected proposals for reform, including the Higginson Report from a committee which it had set up to review the examination (DES, 1988b). A levels were held to be the 'gold standard' against which the academic standards of all students were assessed, reflected too in judgements about institutional practices and reputations. The establishment of a points system (based originally on 1–5 and later 2–10 for grades E to A respectively) facilitated the measurement of standards of entry and these soon became proxies for the standard of the course, the department and thus the final degree (Davies, 1986; Parry and Davies, 1990) and by extension the quality of the institution. The resistance to reforming A levels and the institutionalization of point scores as measures of quality emphasized the importance of the academic over the vocational and the young over the adult student. It also meant that in order to achieve higher levels of participation from under-represented groups, particularly adults, it was necessary to develop alternative or 'non-standard' entry qualifications and routes into higher education. Broadly speaking these alternatives can be divided into three groups: vocational routes, access routes, and the accreditation of prior learning.

The development of the vocational routes was clearly linked to the economic imperative of educational policy. In part it was brought about by the establishment of the Business and Technology Council (BTEC) qualifications as a recognized vocational route in further education (the BTEC First and BTEC National Diplomas) with clear progression to similar courses at higher level (the BTEC Higher National Diploma, HND). The latter have also led into degree programmes in many institutions, particularly in some subject areas (see Webb *et al.*, 1994b, for an illustration of this pattern in one case study institution). However, alongside the increasing respectability of the BTEC qualifications was the more significant, albeit gradual, development of a new national framework of vocational qualifications (NVQs) and general national vocational qualifications (GNVQs) (DoE with DES, 1986; DoE, 1981, 1984). The 1986 White Paper (DoE with DES, 1986:23) explicitly stated, in italics for emphasis, that '*from the outset, there should be recognition of the National Vocational Qualification at appropriate levels in entry procedures and regulations for degree courses and for entry to the professions.*' Thus in the White Paper in the following year (DES, 1987), vocational qualifications were officially recognized as the second route into higher education.

Parry (1996) has usefully charted the development of the access routes since the early 1970s and suggested that the period up to 1982 was characterized by 'pockets of activity', stimulated by a letter of invitation from the DES (1978a) to seven LEAs to set up special Access courses. This was rapidly followed by 'discourses of derision' in the early 1980s emanating primarily from government (see especially DES, 1985b). As indicated earlier in this chapter, there was a key change in that position in 1987, when Access courses were officially recognized as a third route into higher education (DES, 1987). This was accompanied by the setting up of a national framework for quality assurance of such programmes (Davies and Parry, 1993) managed centrally and jointly by CNAA and CVCP through the Access Courses Recognition Group (ACRG) and locally through a network of some 40 local Authorized Validating Agencies (AVAs), usually consisting of consortia of higher and further education institutions. These local consortia were often Open College Networks with a remit to develop wider credit accumulation programmes, from basic education to entry to higher education level. Together these measures paved the way for a significant increase in the number of Access courses so that by 1995 there were almost 1,300 registered with the Higher Education Quality Council (HEQC), which took over responsibility for the national framework following the demise of CNAA.

The third group – the accreditation of prior learning (APL) – is a much more ad hoc collection of arrangements with a varying degree of activity both within institutions and nationally. It has been much influenced by the work of the Learning From Experience Trust, encouraged by NIACE, and supported by CNAA and the Department of Employment (see for example Evans, 1988; Duckenfield and Stirner, 1992; DfEE, 1995). It is difficult to assess the extent to which it is employed formally in admissions to higher education but it undoubtedly remains rather marginal as an alternative route. Nevertheless, it is significant because it tends to overlap other types of alternative route, having one foot in the access tradition, particularly the accreditation of adult (especially women's) experience in domestic and personal life and in voluntary or community work, and one foot in the vocational route, through the accreditation of work-based learning. It has also connected with the development of credit-based and outcome-based systems of learning at a number of levels and has therefore had an indirect influence on the curriculum.

In addition to the formal use of APL, there is another form of entry, which is a function of the discretion available to institutions to admit 'others' if they are satisfied of their capacity to benefit (Parry, 1995). While not a 'route', it appears to have been significant, particularly in the former polytechnic and colleges sector, but largely unknown and unrecognized. The lack of information about this form of entry and the possibility that it might constitute an informal process of assessing prior learning, was one of the triggers for the research study in which this book has its origins (Webb *et al.*, 1994b).

None of these alternative routes is universally accepted across the system; all continue to be resisted or embraced differentially within and between institutions. In addition, alongside these attempts to widen and expand participation has been a somewhat contradictory movement to reduce the level of financial support for students. The mandatory grants for tuition fees and maintenance for students on full-time first degrees' established following the Anderson Report (Ministry of Education, 1960) were extended to include those on two-year full-time diploma courses in 1976, and in 1975 the necessity of prior educational qualifications was removed. Mature students (defined for this purpose as those over 26) were in certain circumstances eligible for an additional allowance, and all students were entitled to apply for other social security benefits. However, in the late 1980s these began to be eroded. In 1987 the entitlement to housing benefit and income support during the vacations were removed; in 1990 the maintenance grant was frozen and subsequently reduced by 10 per cent per year from 1993/4; the loss of grant was replaced by the entitlement to a loan up to a maximum in a full year of £1375 for students living away from home in London; and the supplementary mature student allowance ceased with effect from the 1995 entry. In addition, for those on courses of preparation for higher education, the discretionary awards paid by LEAs to targeted groups, particularly in the metropolitan areas, gradually disappeared as restrictions were placed on local government spending. These, and the entitlement to other benefits, were replaced by an Access Fund, for full-time students only, administered by further and higher education institutions; the fund totalled £21.6m for higher education and £6.4m for further education in 1995/6; given the number of students in the post-compulsory sector, the sums available to individuals were inevitably small.

What constitutes study at higher education level?

The notion that 'more means different' implies a change not only in the student profile but also in the curriculum offer of higher education. The key change here has been in the structure and organization of the curriculum and awards, with a recent increase in the numbers and proportion of part-time students to more than 518,000 in 1995/6 (including the OU), representing a ratio of full-time to part-time overall in the UK of 2.2 to 1 (HESA, 1996a) and 2.4 to 1 among first-year undergraduate students in 1994/5 (see Table 2 in Appendix 2), suggesting that as these entrants work through the system the ratio overall will increase further.

At postgraduate level, there has been a large increase in the number of Masters programmes, particularly part-time and particularly those of a professional rather than an academic kind. At undergraduate level, many universities are now offering joint honours and/or modular degree programmes, some which operate across the whole institution, some as separate modular schemes, some only in particular departments or schools. While many of the 'new' universities have taken these developments further than the 'old' ones, nevertheless it is a growing trend across the system and often associated with the establishment of credit accumulation schemes (Robertson, 1994). In addition, some degree programmes have become four years full-time (rather the norm of three years) by incorporating an initial foundation year (sometimes called year 0) (DfE, 1992b).   — ▷

Another significant trend has been an increase in study beyond the physical confines of the university buildings, partly in response to the need to accommodate increased numbers of students. This has taken two forms: franchising and distance education. Many universities have franchised parts of degree programmes (usually the first year of a three-year course or the first two years of a four-year course) to further education colleges, in addition to the many vocational undergraduate and sub-degree-level diplomas which are offered there. In 1992, 11 per cent of all higher education students were studying in further education colleges (Smithers and Robinson, 1995) and this appeared to have risen to more than 12 per cent in 1993/4, based on figures which exclude the Open University (USR, 1994; DfE, 1994b). In addition, and less developed than franchising, is the gradual introduction of independent study materials and elements of distance learning into the curriculum for both part-time and full-time students.

The types of courses available have also changed: for example, initial nurse training is now an undergraduate programme; much of the 'liberal adult education' offered by the 'old' universities has been 'mainstreamed'; and there are many more interdisciplinary degrees in the social and physical sciences and many more vocational oriented programmes related to business and management. The Enterprise in Higher Education Initiative (EHE) has also focused attention in all disciplines on the development of skills which are transferable to and within the world of work.

Although patchy across the system as a whole and relatively recent (mostly in the late 1980s and early 1990s), with some institutions having engaged very little with these ideas, overall these developments constitute a shift away from the concept of a cohort of students taking a single subject honours degree full-time over three years in the same place. Thus the focus moved during the late 1980s from access to accessibility (Wright, 1991) and to a greater concern with the edifice that students enter, with 'redesigning the interior, giving it more storeys with lower ceilings and more sets of stairs between them' (Schuller, 1991:7).

Patterns and players

The 1990s can be conceptualized as the decade of the individual and the market; access and accessibility have given way to consumer choice; input, process and academic disciplines have given way to guidance, outcomes and vocational relevance. While the 1980s was a decade of expansion and an interest and concern about the increasing *total* cost of higher education, the 1990s is the decade of consolidation and of an interest and concern with the models and mechanisms by which the total cost is distributed among the stakeholders. Such interests now include a focus upon individual responsibility (particularly financial responsibility). Recent years have seen the government become a much more important player (albeit somewhat indirectly through the funding councils) in determining who and what higher education is for and thus the numbers and profile of students and their routes into institutions. In the same period some key players have disappeared: UDACE, CNAA, FEU, UGC, UFC, NAB, PCFC, DES, DfE, TEED; new ones have appeared: HEFCs, HEQC, FEDA, FEFC, SCAVA, NCVQ, NOCN, DfEE; and others seem to have increased in significance: NIACE, CBI. This list illustrates the changing nature of the context and framework within which the discourse of access has developed but also conceals an underlying continuity through many of the individuals involved in the policy process and in practice within institutions. Many of these players have also developed a professional voice through the groupings identified above; for example, around the access route the Forum for Access Studies (FAST) and SCAVA have developed a newsletter, *Access Networking*, and an academic journal, the *Journal of Access Studies*. Thus the groups have constructed and been constructed by an emerging discourse of access.

The end of an era?

In May 1996, the Secretary of State for Education and Employment established a national committee of inquiry into higher education (the Dearing Committee). Its terms of reference are 'to make recommendations on how the purposes, shape, structure, size and funding of higher education, including support for students, should develop to meet the needs of the United Kingdom over the next 20 years'.

One of the principles to which the Committee 'should have regard, within the constraints of the Government's other spending priorities and affordability' is:

there should be maximum participation in initial higher education by young and mature students and in lifetime learning by adults, having regard to the needs of individuals, the nation and the future labour market;

students should be able to choose between a diverse range of courses, institutions, modes and locations of study.

(Education and Training Parliamentary Monitor, 1996:3)

Thus while maximum participation is clearly signalled, so too are financial parameters – a clear shift from the famous Robbins principle (Committee for Education, 1963). In addition, through clear references to adults and the world of work it challenges what Trow (1989:55) described as the 'values and assumptions that define the English idea of a university' which were affirmed by Robbins. The Dearing inquiry therefore heralds a key policy moment in the development of the discourse of access to higher education.

Why discourse analysis?

The previous section has indicated that, particularly since the 1980s, the size, shape and governance of higher education have changed considerably. The rest of the book is particularly concerned with this period, and with who are defined as worthy participants in this changing and enlarging system. As indicated earlier, it was felt that an approach which prioritized discourse analysis would be most appropriate to examine the complexities and contestations of the present higher education scene.

Discourse is the central concept in Foucault's analytic framework which he used to show how knowledge can determine and define meaning, representations and reason and that the organization of a discourse is an exercise of power because of the ways it controls and constrains what can be said as well as the right to speak. For Foucault (1977:49), discourses are 'practices that systematically form the objects of which they speak. Discourses are not about objects, they do not identify objects, they constitute them and in the practice of doing so conceal their own intervention.' In other words, it is through discourse that social meaning is constructed, subjectivity is produced and power relations are maintained. The consequence of this is that in order to consider questions about the meaning of higher education, we need to examine not simply the language through which it is presented but also the institutional practices and the social and political positions of those who 'speak' about higher education. Such an analysis also needs to include a consideration of the way that power and position interconnect with knowledge construction, since for Foucault the study of the emergence of a discourse, its genealogy, demonstrates how particular 'regimes of truth' develop and gain their hold over institutional settings such as education. The manufacture of consent, the control over 'common sense,' the 'uncritical and largely unconscious way of perceiving and understanding the world' (Gramsci, 1971:322) are processes which illustrate such an exercise of power: 'the common-sense normalcy of mundane practices as the basis for the continuity and reproduction of relations of power' (Fairclough, 1993:139).

Foucault argued that:

> Power produces knowledge. Power and knowledge directly imply one another. There is no power relation without the correlative constitution of a field of knowledge, nor any knowledge that does not presuppose and constitute at the same time power relations.
>
> (Foucault, 1989:93)

> There are manifold relations of power which permeate, characterise and constitute the social body, and these relations of power cannot themselves be established, consolidated nor implemented without the production, accumulation, circulation and functioning of a discourse.
>
> (Foucault, 1986:229)

This argument about the nexus of power/knowledge was elaborated in his paper on 'Governmentality' (Foucault, 1979) in a way that has particular relevance to this book. In the analysis of governance, he traced a shift in the relations between the ways that sovereigns commanded obedience of their subjects through the exertion of force justified by divine authority, to the ways that the modern state maintains order by relying on its subjects' (or citizens') acceptance of a social contract and the concept of self-governance. More specifically, Foucault argued that institutions such as education play a significant part in the development of self-governance by identifying what constitutes a legitimate object of government intervention and in shaping how these objects can be made 'thinkable and calculable' and therefore 'amenable to deliberated and planful initiatives' (Miller and Rose, 1993:77). One way that this is achieved is through the construction of discourses that define the purposes and practices of education institutions and in so doing categorize and classify the subjects and outcomes of such institutions. It is here that the justification of our use of discourse analysis in this book lies, since it enables us to examine one aspect of how power works, what Hacking (1991) called the technology of power.

How is discourse analysis used?

Foucault has been particularly influential on later writers in a range of disciplines, including the social sciences, literary theory, philosophy, and social linguistics. Potter and Wetherall (1994) provided an overview of some of these disciplines, illustrating the very different ways in which 'discourse analysis' is used within them. It seems to us that these differences in use stem from the concerns of particular disciplines, from the 'object' being studied, whether it is a piece of conversation, a written text, or the processes of policy formation, and from the nature and purposes of the research, from what it is that is being explained. Because of this variety and complexity in the use of the term 'discourse analysis' we will provide a brief outline of the model we have used, not in order to claim exclusivity or correctness, but rather as a guide to our thinking, particularly for readers unfamiliar with this approach.

Our model does not stem from influential work in the field of semiology and theories of language, but rather from a 'critical social policy' or 'policy sociology' approach, as illustrated in the work of S.J. Ball (1990a, 1990b, 1994a, 1994c), Edwards (1993); Epstein (1993); Robbins (1993); Ball and Shilling (1994); Rabb (1994); Dale (1994); Maclure (1994); Halpin and Troyna (1994); Dwyer (1995); Gee and Lankshear (1995), among many others, and from the earlier writings of the Centre for Contemporary Cultural Studies (Finn *et al.*, 1978; CCCS, 1981) and others (Donald, 1979). Within this approach particular aspects of educational policy and practice are scrutinized in terms of a struggle to define what constitutes a legitimate arena of policy, over what forms policy interventions should take and their effects within particular institutions.

Three important facets of this approach are illustrated in the writings cited above. The first is a detailed analysis of features within specific policy arenas, for example speeches, acts, White Papers or professional reports. The second is an emphasis upon revealing the process of policy formation and its practice which is frequently complex and contradictory, since there is no simple straightforward correspondence between ideological aims and policy texts, between economic and educational contexts. Third, this emphasis upon struggle suggests no simple top-down or necessarily linear model of policy formation and implementation. Though, as we have outlined earlier, the notion of a discourse embodies power relations, there are different sets of power relations involved in policy implementation at different organizational levels. The diversity of actors at each level means that a range of discourses are available; rarely is there one 'regime of truth' – 'within the policy process there are disjunctures between the corporatist economic frameworks used to set the agenda of educational discourse and the diversity of interests at the local level' (Dwyer, 1995:475). Dwyer criticized Foucault for failing in his own studies to give enough weight to these differential levels of power. We have borne this criticism in mind when undertaking our own study.

This then is the framework we are using, the academic models we are drawing upon. The discourse which is our central focus is the discourse of access to higher education. Although there is no single discourse of access, for simplicity and coherence within this analysis we suggest it is useful to develop such an abstraction, a way of bringing together a theme which is important within a range of other discourses about higher education. There are many differing positions within this discourse of access, taken by differing actors; positions which are contested and which change over time. We use position to mean a clustering of language use and patterns of behaviour around sets of elements integral to the discourse. We talk about differing positions within the one discourse of access and within each position a number of elements combine and recombine in numerous ways. The concept of a 'mature student' is an example of such an element, the notion of a 'qualifying examination' or 'entry qualification' another. Through a discourse position which integrates these elements in particular ways, many students are conceptualized as 'different' or as 'special' and as necessitating different and special admissions procedures; typifications of mature students are developed to identify and characterize them in particular ways. The players who contribute to the development of these typifications and therefore to this discourse include, at institutional level, admissions tutors, institutional managers and policy-makers and, at the cross-institutional level, politicians, pressure groups, academic researchers and political activists.

'Discursive practices' is the term we use to describe and analyse the patterns of behaviour and the use of language by actors within the discourse. Written admissions policy statements for example are products of and formal representations of the discursive practices of institutional policy-makers and admissions tutors. Such practices are not fixed or unchanging even within one institution. Contestations can be seen in a range of practices, in the ways in which admissions policy statements are articulated or admissions selection interviews carried out within and between institutions. Admissions tutors and applicants may account for their experiences in different ways.

The final component of the framework for analysis is the notion of a 'subject' and the way individual and group subjectivities are constituted through discourses. The discursive practices of one set of actors position the subjects of those practices within the discourse. For example, the way in which an admissions tutor behaves in interview may position the mature student as a problem for the institution, drawing for justification upon a range of wider discursive practices (departmental policy on A level grades, institutional concerns about national competitive ranking or published statements by professional associations). The mature applicant may or may not accept the validity of this position; may position him or herself as grateful supplicant or as a worthy candidate and so construct the position adopted by the admissions tutor as a problem. Subjects within a discourse usually have less power to influence the nature of that discourse, but they are not simply passive recipients. They participate to some degree in the construction of their own, often changing, subjectivities and may draw on other discourses where these are available.

How will discourse analysis be used in the study of access?

This book argues that access to higher education in the UK over the last two decades has been an essentially contested concept. Various chapters will focus on the competing understandings surrounding access and will attempt to tease out the relationship between these understandings and particular players, and the positions they hold in institutions locally and nationally. More specifically, the book will explore how access principles are defined and promoted in particular types of higher education institutions, drawing primarily but not exclusively on our research study of 13 institutions (see Appendix 1). Finally, the consequences this contestation over access has had for the subjectivity of the players and participants in universities will be examined. In other words, how are the players and subjects positioned by the discourse and how do they position themselves within the emerging 'mass' higher education system?

The initial research questions outlined on page 2 can now be reformulated within this discourse framework:

1. How is the discourse of access constituted in the 1990s? What are the key positions within it and the elements of which it is composed? How are these used or available for use by particular groups of players?
2. What constitutes higher education and legitimates the selectivity of its entry procedures? Who should have access to it?
3. What is 'known' about the system? What intelligence is available to frame these debates and positions? How does this operate to constitute higher education as a legitimate object of government intervention?
4. What is the nature of the articulation of an access discourse with other key discourses (economic, political, institutional) in particular contexts; for example with the discourses of massification, of quality and accountability, of research and monitoring?
5. What discursive practices illustrate the alternative understandings, the positions within the discourse? Who are they associated with? What is their relationship to and how are they articulated with, different loci of power? What is the relationship of discursive practices to action? How does agenda control become operationalized in different contexts?
6. How are subjectivities constituted within different discourse positions and within a range of discursive practices? Who is included in and who is excluded from a discourse position? How do the subjects of the discourse position themselves?

Our analysis of the material in response to these questions has been supported and enhanced by Marshall (1990) who derived from Foucault five key processes which help to unpack the complex ways in which discourses work in the context of education: differentiation, normalization, institutionalization, compliance, and rationalization.

Differentiation or 'dividing' practices are carried out by members of educational institutions and government agencies to distinguish differing groups of students or potential students from non-students, 'those procedures, which through classification and categorisation, distribute, contain, manipulate and control people . . . giving them an identity which is both social and personal' (Kenway, 1990:174). Dividing practices in the recent history of access to higher education have informed the dispute over whether expanding access is contingent on the furtherance of equal opportunities policies and necessitates widening access, or whether it is primarily a response to demographic changes and funding policies.

Normalization is the 'naturalisation of a discourse type' (Fairclough, 1989:92), that is to say the processes through which power-holders use labels and phrases in such a way that they appear neutral, and in the best interests of all concerned. Normalization focuses therefore on the types of objectives being pursued by those with power and the language through which these objectives become regarded as normal, acceptable and legitimate. For example, we might consider how selectivity in recruitment becomes normalized around notions of 'a good student' or 'the best' students.

Linked to this process of establishing the prioritization of the objectives of institutions are the third and fourth processes: the forms of institutionalization which translate objectives into practice and the means through which compliance is ensured – the manufacturing of consent (Fairclough, 1989). For example, individual institutions engage in a process of ranking and grading qualifications and examination results and this is encouraged and supported by government agencies concerned with admissions, data collection and funding. The data that are produced by such processes can be manipulated statistically and so appear to provide notions of 'objective merit' to rank order students and institutions. This results in a hierarchical differentiation of universities that is documented and institutionalized through the admissions literature and statistical bulletins.

Finally, the fifth process, rationalization, can be illustrated in the way in which particular forms of merit are legitimated, made acceptable, indeed laudable, as signifiers of higher education potential. Another example can be seen in the way that the elements of the discourse are used to justify the particular form, including the size and shape that higher education takes, and the ways that the system is assessed and evaluated. It is at this point that access discourse aligns with other educational discourses such as 'quality'. Since quality is predicated on diversity to ensure fitness for purpose, it promotes difference, and thus a divergent discourse around access can be sustained. These five processes will be exemplified in their contextual specificity in different chapters, highlighting the discontinuities, contradictions and coherences across policies and practices.

To conclude, this book focuses upon differences in the discourse around expanding and widening access to higher education, on who is promulgating such ideas and how. It will examine the range of justifications for the diverse and various access policies, the resistances to them, the changing notions of selectivity which they necessitate and the institutional practices which follow from such commitments or resistances. It also looks at the subjects of the access discourse, the students, those labelled as 'new', 'non-standard', or 'non-traditional', and how their personal identities match with the institutional discourses which allow them to become students, even if hyphenated ones. The book interweaves a micro and macro analysis. It begins at the macro level, at the level of government debates and policies. Institutional policies and practices are then scrutinized and we end with the students themselves. Thus there is an attempt to use the framework provided earlier, to focus upon and interlink quite different levels of description and analysis. The breadth of this study has clearly posed particular problems and could be seen as over-ambitious. However, it is the emphasis upon the inseparability of the power-knowledge complex, upon the intimate configuration of debates, policies and practices, which allows for, indeed demands, differing levels of analysis. These levels can then both be treated separately and later interlinked and recombined in particular ways.

Plan of the book

This chapter has provided an introduction to the study, comprising both the historical context to present day debates and positions and the conceptual approach to be taken when looking more closely at this contemporary scene. Chapter 2 begins the analysis at the macro level. The central theme is the construction of a typology of five divergent discourse positions around the nature and purposes of higher education which imply quite differing legitimation practices and definitions of the boundaries between 'normal' and 'abnormal' students. Common sense understandings of abnormality as illegitimate difference and contestations around the nature of this difference are illustrated in government documents and ministerial statements, and in academic and institutional practices, professional debates and pressure group rhetoric. Discourses of derision, using stereotypifications and ridicule are counterposed to those using idealizations and exaggeration. Differing access positions manipulate the ambiguities of the language of selectivity and equity. The expansion/contraction in student numbers, the institutionalization of the binary system and its subsequent removal, changing controls over and of the source of institutional and student funding and the establishment of centralized quality systems, provide the crucial frameworks within which access policies and practices emerge and flourish or wither and die. The complexity of these processes is the focus of Chapter 2.

Because government policies, particularly those concerned with higher education, are expected to take cognisance of 'facts' and statistical evidence, Chapter 3 looks at the nature of the numerical data used to justify labels and policies. The discourse of numbers, the nature and purposes of data collection and official statistical presentations are subject to scrutiny. 'The "numbers game" has been a central issue in political and ideological debate' (Bhat *et al.*, 1988). What kind of numbers game has been played and by whom in this arena? One reason that ambiguities around access and equity can be manipulated by different players in the discourse is that there are many contradictions and inconsistences in the data available. Detailed research, undertaken as part of a research project on alternative entry (Webb *et al.*, 1994b) is used to illustrate the confusion, ignorance, unreliability and invalidity built into data collection at governmental and institutional levels.

As a particular example of both systematic and random errors, the 'dividing practice' – the processes of categorizing students encapsulated within the practices and publications of the various data collection agencies – are unpacked as an element within policy discourses. How, for whom, and for what are higher education statistics formulated?

Chapter 4 raises a linked but different set of issues. How different are the 'abnormal students'? The focus here is upon the academic discourse of research. The structural locations, social and educational, of students are defined as the elements of difference in empirical and theoretical studies. Sex, age, 'race', social class and educational qualifications are the constituents of standard/non-standard divisions, not just in the common sense of admissions tutors, but in the discourse of research. Admission and progression studies attempt to provide legitimacy for one or more categorizations. Do alternative entry qualifications provide a basis for theorizing difference? If not, can we move beyond the current orthodoxies, or recombine the current divisions in different ways? Does most current research simply reinforce and 'normalize' divisions useful to political and institutional rhetoric?

Chapter 5 shifts the focus of policy-making to the level of the institution. Does an analysis of mission statements and strategic plans enable us to understand differential practices which encourage accessibility? Do the different types of institutions vary in their accessibility to differing groups of students, as some discourses of derision and idealization suggest? How does the language of 'responsiveness', 'flexibility' and 'equal opportunities' translate to policy and practice at institutional and subject level? What, if any, are the processes of accountability at institutional level through which mission rhetoric impinges upon the practices of departments and subjects? An institutional case study provides some insights to answer these questions.

The discourse of selectivity and equity makes sense in differing ways to those at differing levels within an institution. A range of discourses are intelligible to, are interpreted and used by actors in differing positions within a hierarchy. This theme will be taken up in more detail in Chapter 6 which looks at admissions tutors as gatekeepers, focusing in particular on the nature of their exclusionary and inclusionary discursive practices. Who controls entry and how? It is at this point that the categorization of potential students as 'normal', 'special' or different impacts directly upon the lives of individuals.

This is the theme of Chapter 7: how do alternative entry students make sense of their own educational careers, their own lived experiences of the educational policies and practices outlined earlier? At this level an individual educational career can be encapsulated as a changing discourse of subjectivity and identity. The personal biographies of students provide the raw material where meanings are contested, where resistance to or compliance with labels is manifest, and where official languages of achievements and entitlements are reinterpreted or incorporated in individualistic forms. How do personal discourses articulate with available public ones? The negotiation of access is an individual journey, set within the context of institutional and government policies and practices. How rational or idio-syncratic, planned or accidental, is this negotiation?

Finally, Chapter 8 returns to the key questions and asks how they are articulated at different levels within the system. What are the relationships between debates at a national level, the contexts within which commissions are constituted or policy texts produced, the contexts of practice (national and local) and the contexts of outcomes? What options do current policy discourses provide for widening access? How are notions of equity being redefined and institutionalized? Is a mass education system predicated on particular forms of institutional differentiation or restratification? What would it mean to say that we have developed a mass system?

2

The Discourse of Access:
The Legitimation of Selectivity

Jenny Williams

University for dunces
Fiasco of the dunces joining university.
(Daily Express headlines 28 August 1995)

'Standards and quality at all levels are among my highest priorities.' Gillian Shepherd (Secretary of State for Education and Employment, response to the above press stories).
(Education and Training Parliamentary Monitor, 1996)

Introduction

These headlines and statements illustrate the furore in the press in August 1995 over A level standards, the increasing percentage of first and upper second class degrees awarded and in particular over the admittance to some new universities of students who had failed their A levels, showing the continuing, bitter and largely incoherent debates over who has a legitimate right of entry to higher education and why. The changing political, financial, organizational and institutional contexts of these debates have been highlighted in Chapter 1. The purpose of this chapter is to explore differing positions and elements within the contemporary discourse on access, and the nature of their articulation by different players. It concerns itself with the discourse of the relatively powerful: government ministers, other politicians, political think tanks, educational reports and White Papers, key pressure groups, academic leaders and researchers; and it summarizes both political and academic discursive practices and the use made of these in the 'common sense' of newspapers and journals. What is of interest here is what Fairclough (1989) called the manufacture of consent through the control of 'common sense' (Gramsci, 1971). It is the available, public, written texts which have been examined for this chapter, not rationales elicited privately by interviews with elite policy-makers. Rather, the texts chosen, for example the academic press or speeches by government ministers, were written to influence either the general political climate within which policy decisions are taken, or more directly the opinions of academics and/or policy-makers. There are many competing and conflicting voices (positions within the overarching access discourse) attempting to control the agenda of access to higher education, attempting to define 'normal' students, i.e., those who have a legitimate right to scarce and expensive public resources. In defining the normal, such voices also define the 'abnormal', the 'special', the 'problematic' students who should either not be in higher education at all, or who need quite particular entry routes, or courses, teaching or even institutions.

It is this shifting and complex division between the normal and abnormal, legitimate and illegitimate students and in consequence between the acceptable and unacceptable ways of defining merit, particularly in the context of increasing student numbers and debates around massification, which are explored in this chapter. A brief initial section looks at the ways in which the contemporary discourse of access operates at a very general level through an exploration of the polarizing categories, the 'condensation symbols' which frame alternative understandings. The final section explores the complexities of current debates through the construction of a model of five positions within the discourse which can be compared, contrasted and used to understand particular contemporary trends.

Polarizing categorizations

The power to define legitimate access to the most expensive and prestigious sector of publicly funded education is likely to be contested. Contradictions and conflicts are numerous and public debates are constructed around 'icon words' or 'condensation symbols' (Edelman, 1977). Words such as access, standards, academic excellence, mature students, consumers, enterprise, quality, are used as shorthand descriptors of who should or should not be let into what sort of academia and on what terms. Such 'icon' words have become embedded in 'polarising discourses' (Ball, S.J., 1990a); the simplistic opposition of alternative understandings:

elite v. mass
standard v. non-standard
traditional v. non-traditional
quality v. access
academic v. vocational
qualified v. unqualified
academic freedom v. government control
research v. teaching

What is important is the way such polarizations around key icon words work. Clearly they simplify debates and issues. But more importantly, by using one or two key words, the unacceptability of the opposite, the alternative, is assumed. The processes of categorization, of differentiation do not have to be spelled out in detail. Meanings are constructed through explicit or more often implicit contrast; a positive rests upon the negative of something antithetical. The normal, the worthy student and the acceptable processes of admission are legitimized by reference to the abnormal, the unworthy, the unacceptable. The silences are as important as what is said; by implication the abnormal can be derided or ridiculed. Discourses of derision and idealization are intimately connected. 'Letting the Gold Standards Slip' (headline, *Birmingham Post* 29 August 1995) illustrates this connection. The complexities and ambiguities of the 'gold standard', i.e., high A level grades, can be hidden by such a headline. It is both the norm and the ideal and must be protected from alternatives, the non-standard, lower alternatives. Those institutions which had responded to the shortage of scientists and mathematicians by providing non-A level routes into their degrees, with government and HEQC support, can be pilloried through such simple headlines.

Polarizations around elite/mass, access/quality are frequent and widespread. Increasing access is associated with a lowering of standards.

> On the question of access the time has come for a period of conscious consolidation, in order to prevent any further dilution of quality. It strains credulity to hear claims that the academic standards of all universities are as high today as they were within the smaller sector in 1979 when there were half as many newly qualified graduates gaining first degrees.
>
> (Nigel Forman MP, former Minister for Further and
> Higher Education, 1996)

> The high quality of British Universities is threatened by growth.
> (*Independent on Sunday* headline, 25 February 1996).

More is constructed as worse, not just different.

> The argument that wider access leads to lower standards is essential to maintain the privileges of the elite. The notion of what is meant by 'standards' and whether we are referring to 'adequate' or 'high' is so vague that the word is capable of a range of meanings to suit any argument. This issue will never be resolved because whenever evidence is provided to refute the proposition that access leads to lower standards, the meaning of standards will be redefined.
>
> (Wagner, 1989:36)

The linguistic link between standard students, i.e., 18-year-old school-leavers with three good A levels taken at one sitting and notions of 'standards' is not accidental. The non-standard student becomes the 'other', the threat to quality. Bargh *et al.* (1994:37) suggested that non-standard students are perceived in different ways, depending on who they were being compared with, for example whether with young students with good or indifferent A levels, and that such comparisons will change with institutional contexts. So it is necessary to unpack the discourse of access very carefully; polarizations are not fixed and unchanging. Their meaning shifts sometimes subtly, sometimes more dramatically, as they are used within alternative discourse positions or within different sets of discursive practices (Gee and Lankshear, 1995). Within differing political or educational contexts the positive and negative evaluations, the valorization or ridicule of particular elements, changes. As Robertson (1994:8) suggested,

> terminology and institutional behaviour appear to be at best in the process of formation. Even the most basic concepts remain contested; principles and practices which pass as commonplace in some quarters remain largely unfamiliar or disputed elsewhere.

How do debates based upon polarized and simplistic dichotomies and upon a lack of clarity in terminology and evidence operate within higher education and why might this happen? Clearly they link with much wider educational and political discourses upon which they draw and into which they feed. One of the key points about 'condensation symbols' is that they can allow for contradictory policies and practices to appear to be reconciled. People who may express quite diverse views on higher education in one context may in another context accept that mature students or under-represented groups should have more access to higher education, because they are not spelling out the meaning given to those symbolic labels and their policy consequences. Ambiguity allows government ministers or heads of institutions to claim virtue by deft slippage in the terms used. Of course they are providing an accessible system of higher education: look how many mature students are entering!

The discussion so far has not yet either described or adequately explained the complexities of the debates and their resonance within wider political and educational discourses. Salter and Tapper (1994) have argued that universities are the 'custodians of selection'; that they define the context of individual social mobility, certificate professional knowledge, influence occupational mobility and provide the autonomy to promote particular sets of values. The terrain being fought over is therefore a crucial one. The positions taken concerning the meaning and salience of selectivity are developed in the rest of this chapter.

Discourse positions: access and equity

In the remainder of this chapter I have drawn heavily on the work of Ball, S.J., 1990a, 1990b; 1993; 1994a, 1994b; Dale, 1989; Whitty, 1989; Robbins, 1993; Skeggs, 1994, all of whom have focused particularly upon compulsory education and the consequences of the Education Reform Act of 1988. Some of these insights are applied to higher education. The discourse of access can only be understood as one aspect of wider political and educational discourses. It has elements within it which stem from these wider contexts, which are recombined in particular ways. In order to explore these elements further, I will outline a typology of 'ideal type' positions on access to higher education, focusing particularly upon notions of selectivity and equity, in order to illustrate how access is constructed within competing discourse positions and illuminate how similar language can produce different meanings by stemming from and being embedded in different discourses. 'Words and concepts change their meaning and their effects as they are employed within different discourses' (Ball, S.J., 1990a:17).

I am aware of the problems inherent in the construction of such typologies. The labels I have attached to particular educational positions may be contentious. This is not the intention. They provide an academically neat blueprint for a messy reality.

> Abstract accounts tend towards tidy generalities and often fail to capture the messy realities of influence, pressure, dogma, expediency, conflict, compromise, intransigence, resistance, error, opposition and pragmatism in the policy process.
>
> (Ball, S.J., 1990:9)

However, development of such a typology provides a way of understanding the access debates, mapping the parameters and highlighting particular elements. Five positions within the discourse and their associated discursive practices are compared and contrasted; the academic traditionalists, the marketeers, the utilitarian trainers, the liberal meritocrats and the access movement. Three of these positions have an affinity with S.J. Ball's (1990a, 1994a) typology of positions in the discourse of compulsory education: the neo-conservatives, neo-liberals and industrial trainers. I have added two further voices, because they are important within the higher education arena.

Certain key questions which are indicators of the way access and equity are framed have influenced this analysis. They will be posed in turn for each position. How and by whom should the numbers of students admitted to higher education be determined? Who should be admitted, on what terms and to do what? How is their selection justified? Who are the normal and who are the abnormal, and where should the boundary between the two be drawn? What is defined as the problem; who is the enemy and who or what is being attacked? What is the meaning of mass education? Clearly the answers to these questions are part of a wider debate concerning the purposes of higher education in the late twentieth century. It is not just how those questions are answered directly which provides us with comparative data: it is the silences, the hidden agendas which are crucial. The abnormal constitutes the normal by implication. In unpacking these contrasting positions and subjecting their discursive practices to scrutiny, the five processes of differentiation, normalization, institutionalization, compliance and rationalization outlined in Chapter 1 can also be illustrated.

Academic traditionalists

S.J. Ball (1990a) suggested that this label can be attached to the neo-conservatives, the elite descendants of the nineteenth century humanists, and used the Hillgate group as exemplars. Certain aspects of this position are central to many academic cultures particularly highlighted in terms of academic standards, merit, excellence and intellectual freedom. Who should determine the nature of higher education and the number of students admitted? Within this position the answer is clear: academics should. Academic freedom is intertwined with the institutional freedom to determine who is admitted to study what academics determine is on offer. It is those students who can demonstrate *in advance* of entering that they have the capacity to benefit who should be admitted. The academic traditionalists place enormous emphasis upon the gold standard of A level points scores which symbolize and reinforce notions of academic merit and are presented as neutral, fair and a just selector of the suitable. A normal, acceptable student is one who has undergone a quite particular form of academic socialization, designed for 16–18-year-olds in schools. A higher education institution can, on this basis, take for granted the preparation that the individual has received and build upon it. The abnormal student is one for whom this preparation, this academic and cultural socialization, cannot be taken for granted. The gulf is a wide one.

Why is there such a preoccupation with A levels? Importantly they were historically controlled by University Examination Boards, and so exemplifed university power over content and standards. Also, and equally importantly, the academic quality of a department or institution is deemed to be reflected in the quality of its entrants and the selective nature of its entry criteria, because such entry standards are seen to be unambiguously related to the quality of the output. All forms of league tables, internal and external, include entrants' points scores as one key comparative feature (Parry and Davies, 1990). The merit of the individuals gaining access has become interlocked with that of the institution, in competition with others. Research by Fulton and Ellwood (1989) showed the strength of these particular designations of standards and merit, held by the majority of admissions tutors. Chapter 6 will explore this further, looking at the use made of this particular form of public discourse within our sample of institutions.

Who and what are being attacked? At one level it is government control. Increasing student numbers and a public acceptance of the inevitability of mass higher education are at fault in the sense that they undermine an elite system based on personal knowledge of students. The government has replaced the buffer UGC by the UFC and established mechanisms to determine the size of full-time undergraduate courses in particular subjects (by institution contract funding) and to monitor the quality of what is on offer through complex and time-consuming external accountability processes. So the battles continue at a national level over the extent of governmental intrusion into academic decision making (see Salter and Tapper, 1994, for an excellent review of these developments). Universities, it is held, should not be instruments of such social engineering (Kedourie, 1988). Lal (1989) entitled his pamphlet for the Centre for Policy Studies, 'Nationalised Universities'.

At another level, the enemy are those who try to establish the equivalence of other qualifications to those of A levels, particularly vocational qualifications, and so undermine academic quality by undermining the notion of A level as the central determinant of academic merit (Kedourie, 1988). This argument had, in the early 1980s, some success in what Parry (1995) called the 'delegitimisation of Access'. The Lindop Report (DES, 1985a) gave voice to the fears that courses taking mature students, or those without the normal minimum entry qualifications, might lead staff to be tempted to lower standards. Altering the nature of entry to degree-level study was thus framed as lowering the quality of the degree on offer through a change in the *content* of the degree (Parry and Davies, 1990). The curriculum epitomizes *what* a university is, the admissions process who it is for.

Such arguments have continued. Nigel Forman MP (1996) restated the position that 'there should be no more adulteration of the A level gold standard.' GNVQs, he suggested, were suitable for employment or part-time students, but not as 'dilute alternatives to A level qualifications.' Beloff (1995) writing in *The Times*, deplored the demise of the old self-governing communities of scholars as government control had increased. He suggested that both the egalitarianism of the left, espousing the notion of wider access, and the philistinism of the right, were responsible for throwing away the priceless asset of independent universities. Similar arguments reasserted themselves in a different form during 1995 as an attack on the 'new' universities and their admissions practices. Such practices, i.e. not using A levels as predictors of academic success, might possibly have been acceptable when undertaken by polytechnics, but not once such institutions were absorbed within the category university. Nicholas Budgen, the MP for Wolverhampton South West, was quoted as arguing that universities and polytechnics were quite different, with different purposes and degrees of different value. 'They are turning our [*sic*] universities from centres of excellence into remedial institutions. The harsh but simple fact is that by mixing up winners and losers you hold the winners back' (*Wolverhampton Express and Star*, 31 August 1995). A spokesman for Birmingham University was quoted in the *Birmingham Post* (29 August 1995) as saying, 'Before, there used to be two sets of institutions, and people knew they were different and had a perception of what these differences were.' In case its readers were ignorant of the differences, the editorial in the same edition spelled it out:

> When the old polytechnics became new 'universities', anyone heard quibbling about their right to use the term was accused of snobbery and elitism. . . . Well now the cracks are beginning to show and all those who believed standards were being put at risk stand vindicated. It seems increasingly apparent that standards throughout the British educational system – from General Certificate of Secondary Education (GCSEs) to A levels to degrees – are being sacrificed on the altar of greater 'access'.

The discourse of derision was not confined to the provincial press or ordinary MPs. A pertinent example appeared in the *Education Guardian* (2

September 1995) in an unattributed interview with an admissions tutor. 'We do admit candidates who fail their A levels,' said one science don from one of the 1992 universities. But, he added, 'they must have failed the relevant subjects.' Even in an academic report for HEFCE, summarizing research on the effects of consolidation on the entry of non-standard students, a report which is very supportive of wider access, Scott and Smith (1995:64) wrote without quoting the evidence,

> one new factor that has emerged in 1995 is more blatant [*sic*] evidence that, as a result of the past decade's expansion, large parts of the higher education system have ceased to be seriously selective . . . doubts about the wisdom of creating a mass system, hitherto suppressed, have coalesced round the issue of non-A level recruitment.

Thus discursive polarizations around elite/mass, quality/access and academic freedom/government control are widespread. The government, it is argued, by encouraging expansion has devalued the currency of a degree. 'The high quality of British universities is threatened by growth' (Judd *et al.*, 1996:17).

What is not said within this discursive framework, the silences, are particularly important. The distribution of A level results may be published by schools in the new league tables, but their relationship to social class, ethnicity and geographical location remains largely hidden. The social as opposed to academic selectivity of A levels raises questions as to the neutral notions of merit embodied within their defence. If failures at 18 are redefined as successes three years later, then this undermines the rationale for A levels as unambiguous indicators of a fixed and permanent elite, and selection as a rational process. For example, more black Caribbean students are older, do not have A levels, attended further education and have working-class parents. The 'racial' selectivity of higher education is hidden within the discussions of entry standards and the unacceptability of particular routes into institutions. The failure of academic researchers and funding bodies to provide detailed evidence on the relationship between a range of entry qualifications and degree success illustrates the strength of the 'agenda control'. Where such research has been produced, suggesting a very complex set of relationships between entry qualifications and degree classification (Bourner and Hamed, 1987b; Gallagher and Wallis, 1992), it is frequently ignored or unknown. Thus there remains an idealization of standards as embodied in a particular way of assessing some disciplines which are taught in schools. Mass systems, it is suggested, by their very nature undermine the integrity, value and excellence of tried and tested elite provision. A moral panic around standards has been generated, which Dearing was asked to assuage in his review of the qualifications for 16–19-year-olds (1996a). The notion of 'mass' within this position resonates with labels of 'cheap and nasty', with a cultural discourse within which 'the masses' is a term of denigration and mass production cannot be quality production. Such a discourse also draws upon a nationalism which contrasts university provision in this

country with the 'degree factories' common elsewhere. The essence of excellence in higher education, unlike compulsory education, lies therefore in
the inability of the vast majority of the population to achieve its standards.
Differentiation (Marshall, 1990) between the normal and abnormal student
is very clearly portrayed within this position, as are the normalization processes which define merit on the basis of A level grades as fair, neutral, in
the best interests of all and an unambiguous measure of quality and equity.
The institutionalization of these processes within the UCAS selection system, where the design of the form and the timing of offers are predicated
on A level applicants and where the majority of offers of places are based
on A level points scores, is supported by academic staff and by student
compliance with such a rationing system. It is operated by admissions tutors
who use the language of merit and quality to protect their institutions' reputation and their subject's share of the 'best' candidates. The processes are
legitimated through the discursive practices outlined in this section. Their
strength is in the taken for granted nature of the assumptions upon which
they rest.

The marketeers

The labels neo-liberal, market liberal or Thatcherism are used by many
writers (Dale, 1989; Whitty, 1989; Ball, S.J., 1990a; Smith and Saunders,
1991; Letwin, 1992, for example) to identify an economic discourse, associated in particular with the writings of Hayek. Alternatively the term 'new
right' is used as a descriptor (Raab, 1993). From this wider discourse stem
the discursive practices of the education marketeers. The emergence of
ideas of a social market in education is linked by Salter and Tapper (1994)
to the Institute of Economic Affairs and by Raab (1993) to the Adam Smith
Institute. The icon words are consumer choice, competition, privatization,
and differentiation via the market. Extensions of market relationships are
defined as extensions of freedom and consumer choice. Though the government clearly has a residual role in deciding upon the size and purpose
of higher education through its control of finance, the proponents of this
position argue that it should leave academics to decide upon the nature of
the universities, and students to choose which of the competing institutions
they will attend (Lal, 1989). The market then becomes both an allocative
and rationing system and education a consumption good (Ball, S.J., 1994a).
Consumers demonstrate their preferences and resources follow these choices.
There is a contradiction at the heart of the market strategy which has become sharper as the 1990s have progressed. To what extent is the market
to be managed by government, so that student demand is managed, controlled and limited, or channelled in particular directions? The DES then
the DfE played a major role (see Chapter 1) in controlling the market
through differential fee bands for particular subjects and through the bidding system for student numbers resulting in lower unit costs. Such control

has led to terms such as 'quasi-market' or 'so-called market' being used (Troyna, 1994). Raab (1993) suggested that these contradictions reflect two quite different tendencies within the new right, the neo-liberal and the authoritarian strands. Consumers are not trusted by the second group to choose what they ought to choose in the national interest.

Who should be admitted to higher education within these controlled market constraints is clear. As education is seen as a private consumer good it is those students willing to purchase their own education and at the same time define it as an investment in their future life-chances. Cuts in maintenance grants and the emphasis upon loans define the educational consumer in quite particular ways. Dependency upon the state for support through grants or benefits has been lessened or removed. Consumers, if it is in their own interests, will, it is argued, accept a debt to be paid back later when earnings are higher. What Letwin (1992) called the 'vigorous virtues' of independence, energy and self-sufficiency are to be encouraged. League tables provide the information to underpin choice and student charters define the product available.

There is no assumption therefore within this position that all institutions should be the same. A differentiated range of institutions provides a wider choice for personal decisions. Institutions will seek a market position and target particular consumers, but may take 'rational' decisions that some students are easier to teach, more likely to succeed, need fewer special resources, etc. If there is a perception that mature students need more support they may also be perceived as less cost-effective. The line between the normal and abnormal student becomes blurred as they are all defined as consumers. The abnormal become the small minority who are worthy but who cannot invest in themselves; those for whom loans, tax relief, private endowments and employer grants are not enough. Special scholarships are needed for the few (Kedourie, 1988; Lal, 1989), the bright poor, in the interests of social justice. Tooley (1995:29) for example suggested that authentic marketeers take issues of equity seriously. 'For precisely this reason they propose a voucher-type safety net for those too poor or otherwise unable to provide educational opportunities for themselves and their children.'

Debates concerning difference and inequality tend to prioritize differences in *output*, i.e., the standards of the degrees on offer. Higher quality outputs cost more money and in a free market the consumer, whether student or employer, would invest according to their own perceived interests. But the market has not been allowed to operate freely. Vouchers are still a promise not a reality. According to Lal (1989) and Jenkins (1995) the government nationalized the universities rather than privatizing them. The Chevening Discussion papers produced by Jackson (1988) contained a blueprint for further moves to free individuals and institutions from government domination, by charging differential fees, providing vouchers and introducing student loans. Little of this, apart from loans, was in place when Jackson became a minister with special responsibility for higher education. He propounded similar themes in the *THES* in 1995, suggesting private sector finance would promote the autonomy of universities and reduce the extent of their dependence on the state. So even from within the Conservative party, the enemy has been defined as a particular sort of government control, which distorts the market, which attempts social engineering by linking access with economic and technical change, which assumes that the economic demand for particular sorts of skills can be predicted and planned, and which encourages the belief in the 'sameness' and equality of higher education institutions.

The silences and hidden agendas are clearest in this ideal market blueprint which has not yet been put into practice. But they are still important in those aspects which have been implemented. The notion of the student both as educational consumer and investor needs careful unpacking. There are social class, age and gender elements implicit within these labels which confer differential power. The poor may have neither the material nor cultural capital available to study. The young are a better investment than their elders despite the rhetoric of lifelong learning. Women, by and large, organize consumption for and on behalf of others. Differential purchasing power in all markets produces differential and unequal services. In education it is suggested that, 'Implementation of market reforms in education is essentially a class strategy which has as one of its major effects the reproduction of relative social class (and ethnic) advantages and disadvantages' (Ball, S.J., 1994a:103). Or, as Brown (1995:94) put it: 'the market is associated with the increased importance of material capital required to meet the escalating costs involved in acquiring the appropriate forms of cultural capital.'

The key concept within a market discourse is that of 'choice', a concept which is operationalized at all levels – choice of institution, choice of length, pace, mode of study, of programme, of form of study. Such a choice is not just that of a consumer but reflects individual financial calculations concerning lifetime returns, for example. There is an ambiguity in the discourse as the language shifts between consumer and investor as though they were synonymous. Theorists differ in their assessment of whether individual investment in higher education is financially worthwhile, and in whether decisions are in practice based upon such calculations. Keep (1996) for example, suggested that in an expanding higher education system, returns will not be particularly high as graduates may not obtain top jobs and that expansion rests upon political rather than economic arguments. Bowe, *et al.* (1994:43–4) argued that decisions to enter higher education are not made on 'rational' economic criteria. Education is a 'positional good', part of the cultural consumption of certain social classes and a site for the reproduction of social difference. Thus a commodification of higher education can only be partially successful. Ranson (1993) disputed the marketeers' central platform of consumer autonomy and empowerment. He suggested it was producers who were empowered, as they are enabled to select students according to a hierarchy of esteem within a segmented system.

The processes of differentiation and normalization formulated by the marketeers are therefore clear. The language of consumers and products has entered higher education together with the institutionalization of loans, competitive bidding for student numbers, and the separation of funding for teaching and research. A general acceptance of the notion of rationing based upon a student contribution to their own education illustrates the nature and extent of compliance here. We cannot, it is argued, afford mass higher education on any other terms (Tysome, 1995). Such claims become normalized through repetition and rationalized on the basis of competing demands on public expenditure. An idealization of the market as a neutral, rationing mechanism, based on consumer choice rather than government intervention frames the notion of massification. A mass market provides for entrepreneurial potential and a cheaper product but an elite sector can and should remain as differentiated consumers demand a differentiated product.

Utilitarian trainers

The assumption that national economic success is intimately linked with the production of highly skilled graduates has a long history, is widespread across the globe and is associated with all political parties in Britain. It is part of a wider economic discourse of international competitiveness and wealth creation. The discursive practices of trainers rest on icon words such as skills, economic relevance, enterprise, competencies, accountability, and fitness for purpose. The language of the business world was exemplified in the DfEE consultation document on lifetime learning (1995). It talked about customers, clients, products, core business and even an after-sales service. There was an increase in England in this rhetoric throughout the 1980s and 1990s. Key proponents have included government departments such as the DTI, particularly important ministers such as Lord Young, employers' groups such as the CBI, and key pressure groups such as the FEU, Council for Industry and Higher Education, RSA. The CBI for example asked for an age participation rate of 40 per cent by the year 2000 (*THES*, 4 November 1994) and the RSA, under the particular influence of Christopher Ball, produced three major reports (Ball, C., 1988, 1989, 1990), all emphasizing the link between higher education and economic needs. 'Competitive economies will in future depend on the success of the education system in producing a high average level of education and training, rather than a small leadership elite' (Ball, C., 1989:15). Government papers have reproduced these themes, (see especially DES 1985b, 1987; DoE, 1987). The most recent and vivid examples at the time of writing come from the parliamentary debates on the establishment of the Dearing Inquiry into Higher Education. 'Our economic success will increasingly depend on higher levels of knowledge, understanding and skills . . . We must ensure that they (graduates) are equipped with the skills and flexibility needed by the labour market in the 21st century' (Gillian Shepherd, Education Secretary, in *Education and Training Parliamentary Monitor,* 1996). The idealization presented is of the effects of higher education on the economy rather than the experience itself for the students.

The framing of the notion of wider access within this position is in terms of a widening of the skills deemed relevant to entry to higher education, to the content of what is on offer and to the destinations of graduates as employees. This is exemplified in the debates over the dominance of A levels as the gold standard of entry. Christopher Ball (1989:20) saw A levels as 'one of the most serious impediments to wider participation and to the solution of the problems of skills shortages.' Peter Morgan, Director General of the CBI, called for changes which would undermine the control of academics, and of those responsible for economic under-performance (1990); academics were portrayed as anti-capitalist. The development of NVQs and particularly GNVQs has been one way to bypass this impediment and the Enterprise in Higher Education Initiative was a mechanism for bringing change to the content/methods of teaching without confronting academic freedom head on. Government exhortation followed similar lines: 'The government will, in particular, expect institutions to concentrate on equipping students for working life, on encouraging entrepreneurial attitudes among students and staff' (DES, 1987).

The proponents of this position see a competency-based curriculum emphasizing transferable skills relevant to the requirements of employers as appropriate for higher education, just as for the training of 16–18-year-olds. Thus the issue of selection to higher education changes its format as it is linked with particular vocational purposes of study. Mature students bring relevant experience and skills. There emerges the possibility of 'reinterpreting the goals of quality and excellence, not in the old selective and exclusive way, but as the value added by the process and experience of higher education to achieve fitness for purpose' (Ball, C., 1989:24). Academic knowledge becomes instrumental, a way of understanding industrial and commercial problems, of developing the self as an employee; accessibility and occupational relevance pull in the same direction (Wright, 1993). The 'Enterprise' curriculum stimulated changes that are relevant to access because it attempted to change the nature of what is on offer in higher education. Expansion is important. If selection takes place within a framework of expansion in higher education, so new groups can be added without diminishing the access of the normal, the 18-year-old. The phrase 'more means different' is crucial. If there are more places then the different are more acceptable and less threatening.

The line between the normal and abnormal student is much less sharp when the abnormal are defined as merely different. If the economy requires different skills then difference is more positively framed. The discursive practices of this position have been particularly influential not just in the speeches of ministers and government officers but in administrative arrangements. The DfE was merged with the Department of Employment in 1995 and education and employment, learning and training became institutionally intertwined. The HEFC contains a high proportion of businessmen. The normal has been widened to include vocational and other qualifications. Progression to higher education was defined as an acceptable outcome in terms of TEC funding in particular localities. But who recruits these 'different students'? In the past it was overwhelmingly the polytechnics with their historical roots in vocationalism. This division, between the old and new universities, appears to be continuing, particularly at undergraduate level, according to Bargh *et al.* (1994) and Scott and Smith (1995), both in terms of who is recruited and the rationale for the curriculum on offer. At postgraduate level, particularly with the growth of MBAs, the division is less clear. Who is the enemy? Who is being attacked and for what? Certainly it is the academic traditionalists. This was most forcefully put by Robert Jackson when he described university academics as 'cartels of producer interests sunk in a rentier culture of wealth consumption, battening on the national economy' (quoted in Kedourie, 1988:10). 'Academic' is sometimes used pejoratively in opposition to economic relevance. Such polarizations became partially embedded in the relevant government departments. S.J. Ball (1994b) quoted from interviews with senior civil servants and politicians, detailing the way the DES attempted to marginalize and control the growth of vocationalism as a dominant theme, and saw the Department of Employment as a threat. This dominance of a discourse around liberal education within the DES led to alternative mechanisms to establish vocationalism as part of the agenda of higher education. The trainers and the marketeers form alliances around some aspects of vocationalism but disagree on others. The divisions between them move and blur as each attacks the other for using the market differently. Both positions centralize the element of the consumer. For the marketeers the consumer is primarily the student. For the trainers it is the employers or the economy as a whole or 'national needs' and the students are the products.

This leads us neatly to the hidden agendas behind the discourse of education as training. What sorts of employees do employers want? And more importantly, what counts as skills, both for entry and on graduation? The labour market continues to be gendered, horizontally and vertically, and this is mirrored in the acceptability of skills and their validation as transferable from personal to public life. Domestic/caring skills are only rarely included within the lists deemed appropriate in records of achievement. Yet where else do many mature mother students learn their time management skills? The social class agenda hidden within this approach can be seen in the hierarchy of personal qualities required by employers, and their association with particular forms of middle-class socialization. It is those students for whom this socialization cannot be taken for granted for whom 'the formal teaching of personal and social skills represents the latest version of "compensatory" education, for those who lack the personal qualities which come naturally through everyday social education within the middle class family' (Brown and Scase, 1994:170). It is the 'new' universities, the lower status ones they argued, who are providing this form of compensatory education. But employers continue to recruit their high fliers from the traditional, older universities who take such skills for granted. Thus a hierarchy in the graduate labour market is mirrored in the hierarchy of universities and the hidden processes embodied in 'fitness for purpose' are exposed.

Brown (1995) pointed to a further contradiction but does not develop it. The costs to the individual of going to university are increasing. While trainers were defining the widening of access as part of national economic needs, the Treasury and the Department of Social Security were limiting access to the benefits and grants required for study. As dependency on the state was defined as unacceptable, students were transformed into consumers. But the unemployed, women in low-paid jobs, those made redundant in middle-age for example, are rarely seen as important for training investment by employers. They are largely required to bear the costs themselves. At the same time, the student as future employee was presented as a key element in the discourse of widening access and a mass higher education system legitimized through a relationship between the demand for higher level skills and economic growth. If this link is questioned, either through a denial of the coupling itself (Hughes and Tight, 1995), or by illustrating the extent of graduate under-employment (Keep, 1996), then the justification for growth is removed. 'There should be maximum participation in initial higher education by young and mature students and lifetime learning by adults *insofar* as this can be shown to be consistent with the needs of the nation and the future of the labour market' (terms of reference of the Dearing Inquiry, 1996).

In conclusion, Marshall's processes can again be summarized. Differentiation with this paradigm is less clear cut. More individuals, particularly 'the mature', have experience defined as relevant to higher education. Their access is normalized through the acceptance of a relationship between output from higher education and economic growth linked to a discourse of wealth creation and economic competitiveness. Many elements have been institutionalized by providing 'alternative' routes, developing vocational qualifications defined as 'standard'. But compliance and legitimation are differentially manifest within and between institutions. A continuing hierarchy of worth which distinguishes the academic from the vocational, education from training, remains embedded and influential in higher education.

Liberal meritocrats

The historical origins and strengths of this particular discourse position can be found in the changes in compulsory education between 1944 and the 1970s. The move to mixed, comprehensive secondary schools was supported by a meritocratic discourse of considerable appeal and complexity. In higher education this is manifest in the Robbins Report (Committee for Education, 1963). The icon words remain as individual rights, merit, personal development, wasted talent, accessibility, and equality of opportunity/equal opportunities. There is a marked overlap with the discourse of the trainers at times, particularly for example in the writings of Christopher Ball. But the two approaches are distinguished here on the basis of their justification for entry to higher education; whether it is an individual right gained by virtue of being 'qualified', or whether it is a right to a particular sort of higher education linked to the requirements of the economy or society as a whole. A 'qualified' individual may, within the liberal meritocratic position, choose an education simply for its own sake with the added bonus that society may benefit as a by-product.

Who should be admitted to higher education, and how, revolves around the notions of 'qualified', 'accessibility' and 'under-representation', focusing upon the individual within the framework of these three factors. Historically certain social groups have sent a smaller proportion of their members to higher education; the working class, women (particularly to scientific and technological disciplines), ethnic minority groups, the disabled and the mature. The solutions to this under-representation have taken two forms in particular: a version of accessibility in terms of the 'packaging' of knowledge acquisition into semesters, modules and credits, and second, a widening of 'qualified' to include skills gained in different institutions and in contexts other than education. Three quite different sources highlight the strength of these discursive practices. Opacic (1994), writing as a representative of the NUS, argued that semesterization leads to widening access, improving individual choice and the increasing flexibility of learning suited to individual needs. Robertson (1994), writing at the behest of the HEQC, linked extending access, choice and educational mobility to the development of a credit-based assessment/certification system supported by a credit-based funding system. NIACE (1993), drawing upon a long liberal meritocratic tradition which in the past used the language of individual rights and the liberatory effect of education, presented its new vision in the language of the 1990s: learner entitlements, explicit learning criteria, credits and credit frameworks. The meritocratic vision has been re-framed in the 1990s within an institutionalized system of accessibility in terms of credits. 'Credit has become a proxy for the radical repositioning of learning in the lives of most people' (Robertson, 1995:3). This enables the concept 'qualified for entry' to be refocused also. Robertson (1994:14) provided a very good example of the subtleties of this discourse position:

> Credit systems may be usefully judged against the proposition that they may help to improve the efficiency of higher education by attracting a wider range of students with previously untapped potential. They assist the effectiveness of higher education by accepting that learning may be recognised in all its forms, by mitigating the consequences of non-completion and 'failure' and by facilitating greater flexibility in student choice and curriculum design. The effect is to make higher education more relevant to individual life career needs.

Modularity can be marketed as a way of increasing access to less specialized degrees more suited to older students and part-timers, while preserving standards through the development of a national credit framework which allows for comparability of outputs. The national framework for the recognition of Access courses similarly provided closure around particular sorts of courses deemed appropriate and the safeguards to protect standards and the currency of a kitemarked Access certificate (Davies and Parry, 1993). The division between the normal and abnormal student is again altered with this position. At one level the normal is widened to include those gaining entry by a range of different routes, gaining credits at different times in their lives. In another sense the difference is exacerbated by the complexity and bureaucracy associated with these alternative routes and the effort that is required to promote diversity and yet demonstrate comparability with the normal. The numbers using these alternatives remain relatively small and they are assumed to be for the different, in particular members of the under-represented groups (Benn and Fieldhouse, 1993). There is very little evidence as yet that this is necessarily the case (Davies, 1994, 1995a). The 'informed learner choice' (Robertson, 1994) may imply a shift in power relations between learner and provider, but structural inequalities in initial educational qualifications, in access to jobs providing training, and to information, in economic support and in ways of defining relevant skills illustrating academic potential, underpin and limit learner choice. If the 'normal' is to be widened in this way, we need to know how and who will then be included.

The tactics of the players within this discourse position have been to try to achieve particular goals without spending too much time overtly attacking the enemy. Clearly they are opposed to the dominance of a traditionalist academic position, defined as 'exclusionary standards' (NIACE, 1993). But the tendency has been to build alternatives. Access Federations, Open Colleges, National Open College Network, national and institutional credit frameworks, semesterization, modularization, experiments with a third semester, are seen as processes which bypass the traditionalists. The enemy cannot be ignored and the acceptance and legitimation of the above processes depend in practice upon a range of players and gatekeepers who may or may not be convinced by this version of a meritocratic order (see Chapter 6). But the institutional/national mechanisms which are defined within this position as those which will increase and/or widen access can be developed incrementally. In particular the development of a national credit system has been presented as a way of reconciling warring factions. A lengthy quotation from Robertson (1994:81–2) encapsulates the liberal meritocratic position of the 1990s:

> Those persuaded by the merits of the market place, the sovereign consumer, the individualisation of social and economic activity, and the erosion of professional privilege will find plenty to encourage them in the operation of credit systems. On the other hand those who are

interested to pursue greater social equity through wider access to a rare public good (higher education) or who believe that students from all backgrounds deserve an education that delivers good-quality employment, or who simply wish to extend the range of benefits of higher education more generally throughout society will also take comfort from credit systems as instruments to achieve this. We can find little to contest in the basic principles of credit based systems, which are: the promotion of democratic participation in higher education to all who can benefit; the enhancement of personal skills and effectiveness; the encouragement of individual initiative, critical thinking, good judgement and self reliance; the expectation of good quality in higher education and the delivery of successful employment prospects.

There are silences and hidden agendas which are only infrequently discussed. The term 'under-represented groups' presupposes collective rather than individual reasons for lack of entry to higher education. Yet the presentation of reform is in terms of the removal of individual barriers to entry, including the development of counselling systems to guide students through the maze of credits and modules established in their interests. Detailed questioning of liberal meritocratic solutions in other contexts such as comprehensive education have blunted the intellectual appeal of this position. Feminist critiques have also highlighted the problems with meritocratic approaches which do not take into account existing class and gendered structures within education and the labour market (see, for example, Miles and Middleton, 1995). If the new and alternative routes into the system highlighted in this position did widen access, if the data really were available for us to make judgements concerning strategies for the removal of under-representation, then claims could be verified. One of the silences of academic researchers has been in answering this question. Information systems which would enable collective forms of disadvantage to be highlighted have not been developed or if developed rarely used to achieve this purpose (see Chapter 3). Many Access courses target particular groups of students (see Benn and Burton, 1995) but there is little information on the success of this targeting, of who goes where and how.

Differentiation within this discourse position has been institutionalized as a different set of routes into higher education learning. A mass system is defined as one where lifetime learning should be available when it suits the individual, on a full- or part-time basis, with credits gained as building blocks to qualifications. Where the credits are gained is much less important than their national currency. Rationing and selection then become elongated over a lifetime, subject to complex funding formulas and possibly linked to a 'learning bank'. However, these processes are as yet only just beginning and some aspects of funding policy work against them. Part-time students receive no personal funding as of right. The legitimation of alternative standards has been attempted through complex bureaucratic mechanisms which rest on the institutionalization of the power of a different group of professionals – ACRG, CATS, NOCN and OCNs experts for example.

The access movement

The historical origins of the access movement (the fifth position), from the nineteenth century onwards, have been outside higher education in other forms of adult education. Within more recent access discourse this position prioritizes provision for groups historically excluded from higher education. Corrigan (1992) portrayed the access movement as a change initiated from below, outside central state sponsorship and concerned with the structural rather than individual nature of inequalities. It is this emphasis which distinguishes the access movement from the liberal-meritocratic position, though some elements of both positions clearly overlap. Access practitioners may subscribe to either position, as Benn and Burton (1995) discovered. In fact the majority (72 per cent) in their study subscribed to a liberal-meritocratic justification: increased individual opportunities for study. Bargh *et al.* (1994) distinguished between sponsored and open forms of access. The open form compensates for structural inequalities by focusing upon what is taught in higher education and how such knowledge is delivered. Friere (1972) is held up as an exemplar by many. Icon words include social justice, political literacy, empowerment, and community development.

The access movement has seen itself as heir to earlier movements in adult education and to the 1970s developments such as the construction and delivery of the Diploma in Higher Education. In 1986 a group of higher and further education professionals came together to develop the Forum for Access Studies, campaigning for alternative provision responsive to adult needs and aspirations. The purpose of providing alternative routes into higher education is not just to stimulate individual or even group mobility, but to act as a catalyst to both community developments and to change higher education itself (Parry, 1989; Connelly, 1991). Mason (1987:58) similarly suggested the key questions are to do with how adults access knowledge: 'What changes to pedagogical style, to the curriculum and to assessment techniques are necessary to achieve this?' Over the decade during which FAST has existed and expanded there have been many arguments as to its unifying rationale, illustrated in contributions to its journal, the *Journal of Access Studies*. The institutionalization and normalization of Access courses within further education and the formalization of recognition procedures described earlier has led the proponents of the access movement to encapsulate their position by polarizing 'Access' and 'access'. Enrolment on certificated courses within established frameworks (Access courses) are contrasted with courses designed to deliver community development and empowerment (see examples in Coats, 1994). Harrison (1993) for example, wrote that the domination of provision by higher education had emasculated and domesticated access provision. Smith *et al.* (1993) and Diamond and Kearney (1990) polarized Access (limiting) with access (good).

The origins of Access courses lie in a community development model which addresses itself to the empowerment of the local community at all levels while the more recent model focuses only on progression to higher education. This has been achieved . . . by relegating all non-HE access courses, which are still primarily located in the first model, to a different discourse.

(Connelly, 1991:41)

There has been a strong fight by the providers of Access courses to preserve the notion of a threshold competence pass, to argue against a grading system which mirrored A level points scores:

The A levelisation of Access represents a move which will reinforce the dominance of liberal definitions of equality of opportunity and undermine the effectiveness of measures which attempt to achieve wider participation. Those who take an 'equal treatment' view of Access in fact fail to recognise the essentially political nature of the access movement.

(Stowell, 1992:172)

The incorporation of some members of the early access movement into a liberal/democratic position has meant that the enemy tends to be ex-colleagues or people claiming similar goals and political ideologies. In particular there emerged an attack on credits and levels as measures of competence which 'through their hierarchical structure, reflect traditional educational categories and connive in the production of a relation to knowledge that is hardly progressive' (Avis, 1991:48). Edwards (1991:92) suggested that a particularized focus upon the individual learner was linked to the fragmentation of courses which modularization and unitization represented: 'The practices which are being developed to meet the needs of individuals reinforce the identity of persons as separate from one another, engendering autonomy within inequality, inequality as consumers of products.' The access movement draws upon a radical approach to education which asks for a fundamental shift in the distribution of cultural capital. The shifts in the organization and management of both compulsory and post-compulsory education in the 1980s and 1990s have undermined the energy of and space for such a radical movement. The dominance of the notion of credit in the mid-1990s, even if Robertson acknowledged his debt to his own earlier participation in the access movement (1995), demonstrates the shift both in the professional discourse and the positions of key players.

How is the abnormal student distinguished from the normal in this position? Clearly the abnormal of other discourse positions are normalized, indeed one may say idealized. The centrality of experience and motivation and the need for 'conscientization' are highlighted. The mature student is constructed as an ideal student, enlivening dull seminars, the saviour of many tutors struggling to motivate 18-year-olds. At the same time there is a designation of difference which highlights the problems and difficulties seemingly inherent in combining maturity with studenthood. Gallagher *et al.* (1993:37) suggested mature students were excessively disadvantaged by problems common to most students. Severe personal difficulties were stressed by, for example, Smithers and Griffin (1986) and Wheeler and Birtle (1993). These special difficulties necessitate special provision. Pascall and Cox (1993:174), in a very sympathetic account of the experiences of mature students in higher education, suggested 'the presence of Access students in large numbers does inevitably distort [*sic*] the curriculum and necessitate changes to the curriculum.' Bird, Yee, *et al.* (1992), again in a radical study of the experiences of black students, advocated particular support groups, special student advisers and special staff training. I am not arguing here that such provision is unnecessary. It is included in order to demonstrate the ways 'separateness' and 'difference' are constructed within this particular discourse position. Negative statements concerning the problems of particular groups of students and the 'excessive' investment of time and staff they need, presented as necessary to achieve social justice, then become part of the discourse of derision used to justify exclusion, as we saw in the language of some previous positions. Research showing that mature students do not lack the basic skills for studying (Richardson, 1995) or that 18-year-olds cost more to provide with housing, recreation and sports facilities (Maynard, 1992), can then be ignored.

The silences and hidden agendas within the discourse of the access movement mirror other situations where idealized categorizations bring together disparate groups. Mature students can rarely be treated as a unified category; nor can the class, 'race', ethnic and sex groupings highlighted in equal opportunities targeting practices. Feminist theorizations of difference (Brah, 1993; Mirza, 1993; Griffiths, 1995; Lennon, 1995) grapple with the ways in which individual lives are structured by societal categorizations. As Lennon (1995) suggested, the ideological content of forms of categorizations has material effects on the lives of those subject to them, and we need ways of explaining the distinctive consequences of being inserted into key discourses in particular ways. To be positioned as a student, or a consumer or a potential employee means something different when interlocked with categorizations around sex, social class, ethnicity or disability for example. This silence of the access movement, except in a few small-scale experiential accounts, has allowed a few simplistic categorizations to continue, and to be defined as those with virtue. As Edwards (1991:86) put it, 'different conceptions of the learner produce practices which reflect and reproduce ideological positions which are part of the wider processes of social development and reproduction.' Critiques of Australian initiatives, where equity targets attached to designated under-represented groups have been part of the institutional funding system since 1988, have highlighted the difficulties in institutionalizing the ideals of the access movement. Gale and McNamee (1995) illustrated the compensatory nature of many programmes, based upon cultural deficit models of the recipient groups. Clearly, widening access rather than simply increasing numbers is central to an access mission for mass higher education. But the term 'mass' does not fit into this vision.

The discourse of community empowerment enhanced by a changing higher education system encapsulates an entirely different set of images from the symbolism of an undifferentiated, passive and possibly unworthy 'mass'.

In conclusion let us return to Marshall's key processes. The valorization of difference within the discursive practice of the access movement is clearly distinct from the other four positions outlined. 'Ability to benefit' is repositioned and linked with structural inequalities experienced by groups or communities. However, the success at least in terms of discursive dominance, of the meritocratic version of access, the institutionalization of credit frameworks, the limitations on the funding of non-certificated adult education, have left little space for this alternative version. The eclipse of the radicalism of the political left is not confined to the access movement. As we have seen earlier, discourses of derision marginalize such a position throughout the educational system.

Concluding remarks

Salter and Tapper (1994) portrayed educational changes during the 1980s and 1990s as an ideological struggle between an economic view of higher education and a traditional liberal idea of a university, in the context of a bureaucratic drive by the central state for control over higher education and the influential position of the 'new right' in educational policy. My aims in describing educational policy and practice over a similar time span have been more modest; to make explicit the discourse positions taken by key actors with respect to access and equity in higher education. Academic models inevitably polarize positions which in practice are not so clear cut or coherent. Many of the actors switch positions, depending upon the audience, or use the language of one position to bolster the strength of another. Trainers and liberal meritocrats make alliances and appropriate each others' language. Gee and Lankshear (1995:11) put it this way: 'When we come into sites of social practice that bring together people from different discursive traditions and backgrounds we cannot assume that the meanings we associate with given words/concepts are the same as other peoples.' But it is the wider context of a discourse which enables us to make sense of it. Certain icon words are used across all positions: standards, quality, equal opportunities; others across most: economic needs, credit, learner choice, accessibility. This chapter has concerned itself with unpacking the differing deeper meanings beneath the surface of such words consequent upon their use within the different discursive practices by different actors. A leader in the *THES* (6 October 1995) claimed a bipartisan approach to higher education across all political parties, and political and educational responses to the Dearing Review of 16–19 qualifications and his appointment to look at higher education seem to support this, particularly around the integration and equal valuing of academic and vocational qualifications. In practice there is less consensus. Condensation symbols are designed to create symbolic stereotypes and metaphors which reassure supporters that their interests have been considered. But they are framed in ways that the proposed solutions may also be contradictory or ambiguously related to the way supporters originally viewed the issue.

(Troyna, 1994:73)

The renaming of vocational qualifications as 'applied A levels' is a good example of this process. Enhanced standards are symbolically attached to the changed name. Conflicts, however, remain and differing positions mean differing things by standards, excellence and equity. Tasker and Packham (1994) for example unpacked the incompatibility as they see it of academic and industrial values. They defined quality audits as part of a managerial ideology and practice which is used as a tactic of surveillance, as part of an attack by government and industry on academic freedom. Hughes and Tight (1995) exposed what they saw as the myths of the 'learning society' rhetoric.

What I have tried to illustrate in this chapter are the differing and often incompatible positions within the national debates on access and equity over the last decade. I have explored how the 'icon words' operate as part of polarized categorizations, how differentiating labels are normalized, dividing practices institutionalized and legitimating rhetoric used. The silences and hidden agendas have been highlighted. The remaining chapters will develop these themes in alternative contexts: academic, institutional and personal, moving from a macro to a micro focus. They will explore both the discourse and discursive practices specific to those contexts and the ways in which the national agendas outlined here impinge upon and are reworked by different actors in their different settings.

3

Number Crunching: The Discourse of Statistics

Pat Davies

Introduction

Different types of quantitative data are used in different ways by policy-makers and practitioners in this field. At the simplest level, raw numbers – of entrants, of students, of teachers, of institutions – have been used primarily to measure and demonstrate the expansion of recent years. At another level, quantitative data relate to cash and public expenditure, where inflation has become an issue with 'adjusted' comparisons needing to be made 'in real terms' and thus subject to differing interpretation and use. When the numbers of students, teachers and institutions are coupled with the data on expenditure, the debate tends to centre around concepts such as the 'unit of resource' as a basis of drawing comparisons over time and between institutions. At the same time there has been examination of some of the apparently simple categories of quantitative data and the relation between them, for example, the social characteristics and entry qualifications of students compared to the subjects studied, the performance and progression of the students, and the degrees awarded (see Metcalf, 1993, for a useful review of this literature), although these have been in some ways more problematic methodologically, a point which will be explored more fully later in this chapter. Each of these layers of complexity has provided the opportunity for different quantitative models to be developed and differing interpretations to be placed on the resulting comparisons by the various players in the policy arena and to be marshalled in the political and ideological struggle around the purpose of higher education – who is it for? Who should benefit? On what basis should selection be made? In addition, in a new market-oriented policy regime, such data have the potential to influence the operation of the market in a number of ways, since they have begun to form the basis of institutional performance indicators which may not only inform the choices made by the consumers of the system, but also may be used as a means of rewarding 'success' and penalizing 'failure' through the funding formulae employed by government.

Positions in the numbers discourse

As we have seen in Chapter 2, the choices and uses of terminology represent the discursive practices of different positions in the discourse of access. Most positions at some time reflect the assumption that statistical data are somehow objective or neutral in a way that qualitative data are not, but government in particular has a long established preference for the quantitative paradigm (Finch, 1986). As Salter and Tapper (1994:16) have pointed out, this has been a particular feature of the new ideology of the 1980s which has adopted 'objectively necessary' goals such as economic growth, using the 'impartial' sciences of economics and statistics in the construction of educational policy and, in this way, legitimizing itself by claiming to be value-free and indeed, non-ideological. However, there have been differences in the preferences for certain types and sources of quantitative data and in the way in which they have been used within the official and academic policy communities.

An examination of these discursive practices reveals the positions and the underpinning ideologies of the various players. For example, the relationship between entry and completion of a programme of study might be referred to as the 'retention rate' – a measure of the success (or failure) of an *institution*, depending on its relation to some (usually unstated) norm; or it may be known as the 'wastage rate' – a measure of the wastage of investment of *cash* and/or of *human capital*. Alternatively, it might be referred to as the 'completion rate', a positive term; the 'non-completion rate', a relatively neutral term; the 'withdrawal rate', usually negative but active; or the 'drop-out rate', again usually negative but passive; or the 'failure rate', the most negative – all measures of *students'* success or failure to stay the course. All these terms might be used to describe the same number and all are (usually tacitly) assumed to be related in some way to entry qualifications – 'standard' or 'non-standard' entry – and/or the social characteristics of the students – 'traditional' and 'non-traditional' entrants. Thus there is considerable divergence in the way data have been interpreted and presented and in the terminology used, which reflects different interests and perspectives – social, individual, systemic – and hints at different views about the purpose and beneficiaries of higher education. The use of 'completion rate' or 'non-completion rate' is rather like choosing to describe a glass as half full or half empty and those interested in flexible models of higher education in which students move in and out of the system depending on their circumstances and needs have long sought a terminology which would convey 'non-completion' in a more positive light.

If we take the positions proposed in Chapter 2 – academic traditionalists, marketeers, trainers, liberal meritocrats, and the access movement – it is possible to elaborate these in terms of their use of numbers and quantitative data.

The academic traditionalists eschew numbers at one level, particularly as performance indicators and measures of institutional and staff quality since they represent an attempt to undermine intellectual freedom and impose bureaucratic and managerial measures of effectiveness rather than academic or professional ones. At another level they defend the traditional use of numbers as a measure of student quality – at entry (the A level score), during the course (the percentage grade) and at graduation (the degree classification) – since these are all seen as rooted in academic and professional judgements. The notion of value-added, which depends crucially on measures of input and performance, is therefore not a relevant concept in this position.

The marketeers and trainers on the other hand view numbers – quantitative rather than qualitative data – as hard rather than soft data and as neutral or objective facts, often in opposition to professional or subjective judgements. Marketeers might take this position for example, in the use of retention rates and A level entry scores in the construction of performance indicators or measures of institutional quality rather than more qualitative statements by academic professionals about the student experience. In addition, the fact that a higher education market based on vouchers would require extensive data systems to monitor spending of the voucher is seen as unproblematic. Trainers often use labour market studies and studies of economic competitiveness couched in quantitative terms as part of the argument for vocational routes into and pathways through higher education with a focus on monitoring and measuring skills in the aggregate. Both thus work with a concept of economic value-added in higher education. However, despite their preference for numbers, both these positions in the discourse attack the traditional measures of academic standards – percentage marks and degree classifications – on the basis that they are not rooted in objective and measurable criteria.

Liberal meritocrats at one level reject quantitative measures, particularly in relation to the assessment of students, arguing instead for learning outcomes, records of achievement and so on, and percentages and grading have become part of their discourse of derision in relation to the academic traditionalists. However, the individualized notion of value-added which they embrace, framed and supported by institutional and national credit accumulation and transfer schemes, requires sophisticated data systems if they are to be credible and effective. In addition, institutional and national data are required to argue that present arrangements have failed to deliver a democratic higher education and to suggest a more managerial approach to admissions based on a central operation. What is under attack here is the elite professional academic culture, and numbers are used to expose the weakness of such a position. There is on the one hand a silence about the problematic nature of the data on which this attack is based, while at the same time offering a critique of the system of national data collection for failing to provide the kind of statistics for properly informed policy decisions (Robertson, 1994).

The access movement is concerned with empowerment as an individual concept and value-added which, if measured, or indeed if measurable at all, would be in qualitative terms. Here, institutional and national data are somewhat irrelevant and are sometimes seen as counter-productive since quantitative data can only measure aggregate features of a system and only in ways which construct and classify individuals and their position in the system in inappropriate ways. Nevertheless, since players in this position also embrace a concept of social value-added in relation to under-represented or disadvantaged groups, they frequently use quantitative data to attack the academic traditionalists, marketeers or the trainers for their failure adequately to address questions of participation and equity.

Just as the words and images adopted by the various players illustrated in Chapter 2 represent the discursive practices of different positions in the discourse of access, so too do their choices and uses of different kinds of data. However, as those who seek a new terminology recognize, the statistical classifications and categories used in quantitative approaches are not passive labels but actively shape the way people – policy-makers and practitioners as well as students – think of themselves and of the actions that are open to them; they are part of the bureaucratic machinery, itself part of the technology of power in a modern state (Hacking, 1991) and while possibly less overt than in the debates surrounding immigration and race (Bhat *et al.*, 1988), the 'numbers game' has nevertheless been significant in the political and ideological debates around higher education.

The rest of this chapter seeks to explore in more detail the data on access to and participation in higher education as part of the 'numbers game' and the 'technology of power'. It does not seek to ask why certain people wish to dominate the discourse but rather to explore 'how things work . . . at the level of those continuous and uninterrupted processes which . . . dictate our behaviours etc.' (Foucault, 1986:233). It illustrates the fragmented, inconsistent, incompatible and unreliable nature of the data which has made possible many of the divergences and contradictions in the discourse and seeks to explain why, even though a key area of policy interest and attention, this weakness has persisted and how the policy community has managed the problem. It explores the pressures which have brought about change and analyses the adequacy of the new arrangements.

What data are there?

The recent past

Prior to the 1994/95 academic year, data on entry to and participation in further and higher education were collected through a number of different systems by different agencies: PCAS; UCCA; CRCH and GTTR; ADAR; BTEC; FESR; USR; and the Open University. These data were collated and published sometimes by the agencies themselves (for example, PCAS and UCCA) and sometimes by the DES (subsequently the DfE, and currently the DfEE), either in large annual volumes of statistics for the whole of higher education or in the form of statistical bulletins focusing on particular aspects of the system or the students. The former were comprehensive but slow to appear; the latter also took time to arrive in the public domain and were less comprehensive but usually provided time-series data. Of particular relevance here and often used in policy debates on access and participation were the bulletins published every two years on mature students (DES, 1988c, 1991a; DfE, 1992b, 1994a).

Even without further elaboration, this list indicates the complexity of the data and suggests some of the difficulties of reliable, comprehensive quantitative analysis of higher education and of changes in policy and practice. Comparisons between types of institutions, modes of study, participation of particular groups, in any given year as well as over time, and often merely defining the population (for example England only, England and Wales, Great Britain, UK, including or not the Open University) were fraught with difficulty. Even single data collection agencies did not produce data which were stable enough over time for valid time-series comparisons. For example, PCAS data were based on member institutions and, as I have pointed out elsewhere (Davies, 1995a), the membership changed from year to year so that direct year-on-year comparisons were not possible.

The published data of particular relevance to issues of selectivity and equity – age, sex, social class, ethnicity, entry qualifications – have been problematic. While one might expect age to be a straightforward category, the current definition of a mature student – 21 or over on entry (at 31 August prior to September or October start) to undergraduate or sub-degree level study or 25 or over on entry to postgraduate study – did not become the common definition for all institutions until the end of the 1980s. Prior to that individual universities used ages ranging from 19 to 26, with 23 being the most frequent (Liggett, 1982). Measures of social class and the population from which they were sought or obtained have varied between all the data sets so that a valid and reliable aggregate was not available in published sources. The two main admissions agencies, PCAS and UCCA, collected information on ethnic background from home applicants for the first time in relation to the 1990 entrants, although again this was not published for all applicants or tabulated with entry qualifications in the published data. Information on entry qualifications has been particularly problematic in all the data sets and associated published data. The FESR for example, had no category for 'not known' so that a large proportion of entrants were classified as 'no formal qualifications'. This distorted the representation of students in two key ways. First, it clearly overstated the number and the proportion of 'non-standard' entrants in the 'no formal entry qualifications' category and second, the fact that such students were incorporated in a named category meant they were not identified as queries or tagged as 'missing' and therefore were locked in that category. Any measurement of value-added or of the relationship between entry qualifications and retention rates or of the access of 'non-standard' students based on these figures was therefore likely to be seriously flawed. The research study which stimulated the writing of this book (see Appendix 1) found that this factor accounted for an error of 20 per cent in the classification of students' entry qualifications in one institution.

In addition, in the published data the detailed categories were grouped together in a way which had no clear rationale: it mixed academic with vocational qualifications and different levels of qualifications together (see Webb *et al.*, 1994b for further details). While it was possible to obtain more specific analysis from most of the agencies on request, this was by no means straightforward as the fields and definitions were not easily available so that it was inevitably a long and slow process to develop aggregate data.

In all data sets it was easier to collect entry qualifications for young students entering direct from school with A levels, since the whole applications system was geared to this group – the 'standard', 'traditional' entrants – particularly since both UCCA and PCAS passed on much of the information as part of their service to institutions and it was thus able to be imported centrally. However, this did not mean that the data was 'clean' for all under-21-year-old entrants with A levels, since we found that in some universities students who took a year out after A levels were classified as 'other qualifications' at entry, thus turning them into 'non-standard' or 'non-traditional' students.

Much of the national data, particularly the FESR and USR, was derived from institutional returns and an examination of the institutional procedures and processes which produced the information revealed further layers of ambiguity and inconsistency. Our study (see Appendix 1) revealed margins of error in the data on highest entry qualification ranging from 8 to 20 per cent across the seven then polytechnics involved in the first phase of the project. The origins of these miscodings lay in a number of key factors. First, the data might be derived from different sources: PCAS (or other clearing system), the institution's central registry, the students' entries on the application and/or enrolment form, or some combination of these. Second, there were different organizational arrangements for the collection and recording of information: at central registry level, at school or department level, by a central team or by individuals dispersed around the (sometimes multisite) institution. Third, institutions ranked qualifications differently for the purpose of determining the highest educational qualification: for example, it might have been on the basis of 'most relevant' or of 'common sense' perceptions of what actually constituted the 'highest'. These 'common sense' perceptions were both more important and more variable in the absence of clear national or institutional coding guidelines. In one respect this is understandable and justifiable: different departments and courses have different kinds of links for recruitment and different requirements in terms of qualifications, skills, personal characteristics and experience. Thus they have different interests, needs and priorities in relation to data for monitoring and evaluation: what is highest for one department may rank much lower for another. This development of an internal but nevertheless differentiated consensus based on common sense perceptions and differing interests then tended to become formal or informal rules of coding and categorizing which maximized compliance and continuity of practice. In this way the labelling of students in particular ways is rationalized and institutionalized at local level and embedded in the discursive practices of the institution. Such classifications are seldom challenged and subtle but frequent changes in departmental or central practices often go unnoticed. The data may therefore progressively lose their validity and reliability as a representation of the institution and its population. When institutional data produced in this way are aggregated at national level, it is not surprising that they tend not to stand up well to rigorous scrutiny.

An important consequence of the fragmented and problematic nature of published data has been an inevitable reliance on interpretations and presentations by interest groups. Routine, in-depth scrutiny, analysis and commentary by the academic community has not in general been possible since it inevitably required external project funding to support the more complex and time-consuming work involved. While some work has been carried out on the relationship between entry qualifications and performance (see for example: Tarsh, 1982; Wilson, 1982 in relation to A levels; Davies and Yates, 1987; Bourner and Hamed, 1987a; Malloy and Carol, 1992 in relation to other qualifications), it has generally been fraught with methodological problems, particularly those associated with aggregation, and therefore has focused only on part of the system. The alternative longitudinal studies are by definition long term and thus expensive. Much academic work has therefore been small scale (the *Journal of Access Studies* for example, has carried many reports of case studies and analyses of institutional data), partial or methodologically problematic, or it has been commissioned by the higher education community itself (see, for example, Taylor, 1992; Metcalf, 1993). The notable exception in recent years was the Leverhulme Study (see especially Fulton, 1981; Warren Piper, 1981) which produced a large amount of data as a basis for judgements and recommendations for the future. Perhaps one of the reasons for its impact – Robertson (1994) for example, likened it to a Royal Commission – was the evidence and in particular the quantitative data it collected and presented. However, the general absence of a substantial and rigorously critical academic literature based on quantitative data (see Chapter 4) has further facilitated a presentation and treatment of very problematic data as an 'objective' reflection of the system and of the impact of expansion on selectivity and equity issues.

Current and future developments

The key recent development has been the unification of the data collection systems and a major revision of policy in relation to the publication of the data and access to them for research and analysis purposes. With effect from the 1994 entry to higher education, there are two key agencies involved: UCAS, which includes the ground previously covered by PCAS, UCCA, CRCH and GTTR (and from the 1996 entry has also incorporated ADAR);

and HESA, which includes the ground covered by USR, FESR and the Open University. Some information relating to students studying at higher education level in further education institutions is also collected by the FEFC. This streamlining presents improvements, possibilities and problems for the future since, although it deals with many of the difficulties of aggregation, for example, retrospective time-series comparisons will be more rather than less difficult for some years to come. In addition, since the classifications are consistent they have the potential to shape perceptions more effectively: the technology of power is more comprehensive. It is therefore important to explore the strengths, weaknesses and differences in the new systems of data collection and analysis.

In many ways the UCAS data represent a compromise between the PCAS and UCCA arrangements and although data in relation to all institutions are now collected on the same basis, they are still only partial in that they only cover applications to full-time degrees and HND programmes. There are no other substantial improvements in relation to the annual published statistics and although there is an intention to publish bulletins on particular themes, which is a welcome addition, the data are not currently available on-line and free to the research community (as is the case with HESA). It is hoped that this may be possible in the future.

A number of features are particularly relevant here. First, 'comparisons with previous years are exceptionally difficult and little attempt has been made to construct time series' (UCAS, 1994:18). This means that much of the interesting new data, for example in relation to Access entrants, which became available for the first time from PCAS for the 1992 entry (PCAS, 1993) and revealed interesting comparisons with the 1993 entry (PCAS, 1994) (see Davies, 1994, 1995a) are now lost in terms of continuing comparisons.

Second, PCAS previously conducted an operation called 'mustering' which collected information on student registrations in higher education so that adjustments could be made to the applications and acceptances data for 'direct entrants' (those students who had applied directly to the institution without using the PCAS system). 'Mustering' has been discontinued; instead there is a procedure to 'encourage universities and colleges to register those accepted very late in the admissions process who have not previously completed a UCAS application form' (UCAS, 1994:23). While this means that the data can be published more quickly – about three months following the point of entry rather than around nine months in the past – it also means that there is a loss of what UCAS officers have referred to as 'the integrity of the UCAS scheme.' The data are less comprehensive since late registrations can be lost and 'direct entrants' who do not apply through the UCAS procedures are not included. In addition, there is some evidence (UCAS personal communication, 1996) that it is not simply a question of late applications but that some institutions see no need for their applicants to go through the UCAS procedures. This is particularly the case for further education institutions who see their students progressing to higher education level courses in the same college as 'their students already', and only 'natural progression', and 'anyway there is no point' since the students do not wish or cannot go to an institution further afield. It may also represent a shift in behaviour towards more local compact arrangements in which the arguments for not using the UCAS system are similar. However, in terms of data (and of course UCAS income) the numbers are significant – UCAS estimated about 30,000 direct entrants in addition to the 291,000 recorded acceptances for 1995 entry, about 10 per cent overall (personal communication, 1996).

Third, there seems to be at best a lack of clarity in the presentation of entry qualification data. The introduction to the relevant section in the report on the 1994 entry (UCAS, 1994:126), used a number of different phrases to describe the data: 'the qualifications obtained'; 'the highest qualification'; and 'the main (best) qualification' [*sic*]. The tables which followed were referred to as 'main qualifications', although in practice this meant 'best' according to a ranked list used by coders. This ranking, what is called 'precedence' for the highest qualification, was:

UK degree
Other degree
BTEC/SCOTVEC higher
Partial degree credits
Certificate of Education
Two or more A levels/four or more Highers (Part 1)
GNVQ
BTEC/SCOTVEC lower
Baccalaureate
Other UK qualification
Other overseas qualification
Certificate of Sixth Year Studies (CSYS)
Access course
Fewer than two A levels (Part 2)
Previous A/AS levels
None

(UCAS letter to Scottish Institutions 1 March 1995)

Like rankings used elsewhere in the past, for example the FESR (Webb *et al.*, 1994b), there is no clear rationale for this hierarchy. Why, for example, should 'Access course' (which included foundation courses in, for example, art and design) be ranked lower than BTEC National or First? Why should three A levels taken two years previously for example, come at the bottom of the list under 'Previous A/AS levels', only one step up from 'None'? Despite the dubious basis of such rankings, they send out strong messages to institutions about the way in which the value of particular qualifications are differentiated and subsequently construct the data output in ways which define 'normal' entry routes.

Fourth, in published data (UCAS, 1994), the 'main qualifications' were grouped together into broader categories (inevitably since otherwise the

tables would be unmanageable) but in ways which are not particularly useful and in fact are similar to the practice adopted in relation to the FESR
data which we have criticized elsewhere (Webb *et al.*, 1994b). The groupings are problematic in a number of ways. For example, 'Access and Foundation qualifications' included Access courses, art and design foundation
courses, and foundation courses which are at higher education level (Year
0 of four-year programmes for example). It therefore comprised a number
of different types of programme at different levels. Similarly, the category
'BTEC/Scotvec' included awards at First, National and Higher level; and
the category 'Other' still included a wider range of academic, vocational
and professional qualifications at very different levels. While detail is available very promptly on request, the published data give no information on
these groupings. Thus, although specialist interest groups might probe such
classifications, the general discourse tends not to treat the data as problematic
but to take them at face value and pay little or no attention to the, largely
hidden, confusion beneath the labels.

Fifth, key fields for issues of selectivity and equity are further weakened
by other problematic classifications and/or non-response rates. For example,
social class was based on the standard occupational classification of parent,
step-parent or guardian who has or had the highest income or, if the applicant was over 30 on 30 September prior to entry, on the person contribut-
ing the highest income in the household (UCAS, 1994:170). Therefore, in
relation to mature students, the data were a mixture of the occupational
classification of parent/step-parent/guardian/highest income earner in the
household; the occupation of the applicants themselves (if they were not
the highest earner) seems not to count even if they are aged 50. Further,
the data are not available for all students and, perhaps not surprisingly
since most are adults, they are weakest for those not taking the A level route.
For example, the percentage of Access/foundation students for whom these
data were missing was possibly as high as 30 per cent for the 1994 entry
(UCAS, 1994).

Interestingly, on ethnic origin the situation was better: around 4 per cent
were missing from the data. However, again this was higher for Access/
foundation students and has to be added to the 10 per cent direct entrants
who were missing entirely from the data. Information on ethnic origin is
now related to entry qualifications, which was not the case previously with
PCAS data (Davies, 1994), but again this improvement is offset to some
extent by the problem identified above on the categories of qualifications.
It is clear, therefore, that there remain problems with the data and UCAS
has consulted with interest groups – for example with SCAVA and HEQC
in relation to Access and foundation courses (UCAS, 1995) – and is seeking
ways of resolving such problems. Nevertheless, the danger is that because
the system of collection and analysis is unified, the data will be seen as more
reliable and valid and will therefore carry more weight in the discourse.

The HESA data-collection system represents significant improvements on
previous arrangements in some ways but also a similar compromise, both

between the differences of the past and the wide range of demands for the future, and between an ideal national data set and the practical constraints at institutional level where the main task of collection is undertaken (see Davies, 1995b, for more detailed discussion).

The improvements are substantial. First, the coverage is comprehensive: it includes information on all higher education institutions in the UK, including the Open University, all students, staff and finance. Second, the existence of a unique student identifier, a continuous student record (CSR) and a new structure to the data will permit (in time) new ways of monitoring student performance. Third, there has been considerable development and rationalization of some fields. Of particular interest here is 'highest qualification on entry' which now includes 'not known' and a much more realistic, comprehensive and useful set of categories, although there are still significant problems with the ranking guidelines and a continued reliance on the varied and variable decisions of institutions. There is, however, one striking exception: there is only one code for A levels so that it is not possible to distinguish between entrants with two, three or more A levels and those with only one. The absence of the one A level entrant in the data set is of particular interest here: it means that students who were previously included in a category defined as 'non-standard' since they possessed less than the 'normal' two A level qualification have now been reclassified as 'standard' and are included in the 'normal' category of A level entrants. By such means, the proportion of 'standard' entrants will be increased and the proportion of 'non-standard' will fall; and a previously differentiated group of students will disappear – they have been normalized through an apparently technical adjustment. The discursive practices around admissions will be significantly changed since a whole group of 'non-standard' students have disappeared from the discourse: it is no longer possible to talk about them because they do not 'exist'. In addition, the discourse of the future will be constrained and shaped by this apparently minor administrative adjustment to the coding frame. It will be interesting to observe the extent to which this is made explicit or noticed by the policy players and practitioners, particularly since these categories are the outcome of consultation not only with higher education institutions and other interested players but with the key government departments which usually use two A levels as the basis of equivalence with the new vocational qualifications (NVQ and GNVQ). A new ambiguity and difficulty has therefore been introduced into the counting of these equivalences which form the basis of the national education and training targets.

The way 'highest qualifications on entry' has been presented in published data remains generally problematic and an examination of the way in which groupings have been constructed provides a further illustration of how numbers play a part in shaping the discourse. The three key sources of this data for 1994/5 (HESA, 1995, 1996b, 1996c) used a category 'GCE A Level, SCE Highers and equivalent' which included 'ONC or OND (including BTEC and SCOTVEC (Scottish Vocational Educational Council) equivalents.' This ONC/OND category (code 41) included 5.5 per cent (36,406) of all first-year students who thus were subsumed in the larger group. However, the separate grouping 'A Level equivalent vocational qualifications' comprises GNVQ/GSVQ (General Scottish Vocational Qualification) level 3 (code 37) and NVQ/SVQ (Scottish Vocational Qualification) level 3 (code 38) which represented only 0.2 per cent (799) of all first-year students (HESA, 1996c:12). Thus in all the tables, apart from the introductory frequency count, the larger group of students with vocational qualifications (at what has long been recognized as equivalent to A level) are invisible, while the small group with different kinds of vocational qualifications, those being prioritized by government, are clearly visible. While it is possible to identify the larger group, as I have done here, it is not possible to examine them in any detail since they do not 'exist' in the tables which provide more information.

The way in which students whose highest qualification on entry was an Access course have been considered is also interesting. In the first summary report (HESA, 1995), the categories 'Accredited ACCESS course' (code 44) and 'Unaccredited ACCESS course' (code 45), were both included in the group 'Other qualifications' rather than 'GCE A levels, Highers and equivalent', despite the government's own recognition of Access courses as the third recognized route to higher education (and by implication equivalent to A levels) in 1987 (DES, 1987). In addition, despite having established a national framework of quality assurance to allow the difference between kitemarked and other Access courses to be distinguished, those which are 'accredited' have been aggregated with those which are 'unaccredited' in all the published tables where Access courses were separately identified (HESA, 1996b, 1996c).

Since none of these features of the data is immediately obvious, the possibility of false assumptions or misleading interpretations remains strong and the data may (continue to) be used in inappropriate ways. Indeed HEFCE has itself fallen into this trap, claiming that 'A levels remain the most important entry route for students to HE, representing 50 per cent of all entrants (HEFCE, 1996:10). However, the 50 per cent referred to included ONC/OND/BTEC/SCOTVEC qualifications, the vocational equivalent, and as the data in Table 4 in Appendix 2 showed, these comprised 6 per cent of the first-year students on first degrees, 12.8 per cent on other undergraduate courses and almost 8 per cent overall. It also included entrants with one A level, two AS levels or one A level and one AS level, all of which are less than two A levels and would in the past have been counted as non-standard. While Annex B of the Report lists the HESA code numbers which have been used to arrive at the grouping 'A level and equivalents', the categories are not spelt out so that the presence of the vocational qualifications is obscured.

I am not suggesting conspiracy theory here, but I am arguing that the practical and technical requirements to condense data for publication, coupled with the requirements to monitor the development of government and institutional policy priorities, shapes the data in particular ways. What is published is not objective in any neutral sense but an outcome of the interplay of these interests and the practical constraints and compromises around both the collection of data at institutional level and their analysis and publication at national level.

There is one key feature of the new system which is of very great significance: the data are (mostly) open and freely available in electronic or printed format not only to individual higher education institutions but also to the research community, through an association with the SRHE and through a genuine interest on the part of HESA to support it. Consequently, there are easier and more effective opportunities to scrutinize and rework data for the purposes of policy analysis and evaluation and thus to challenge, as I have done here, the basis of published analysis. At the time of writing the data available are limited, since the quite proper concern to protect students' identity and the more practical pressures of the first cycle with a new system have created some limits on the usefulness of what has been available through these arrangements. However, the arrangements have been reviewed and major improvements are planned. Although there is still considerable work to be done on methodology and on improving the data set, and of course time-series comparisons will be more rather than less difficult for some years to come, the prospects for the future are much improved and a much greater potential exists for the development of new categories, new terminology, and new ways of talking about the system – in short, new discursive practices. It remains to be seen how that potential will be exploited.

Why have the data been so weak? Why has it taken so long to establish a comprehensive national data-collection system?

At first sight there appear to have been frequent references to the inadequacy of the data from both the academic and policy communities. Fairly simple data on participation have long been identified as important and missing (see, for example, Little and Robbins, 1981, in relation to black and Asian students). More recently, data on the relationship between institutional characteristics and student profiles have been noted for their absence: 'The most serious gap is in quantitative studies, which enable the influences of different characteristics and institutional circumstances to be assessed' (Metcalf, 1993:25). The policy community has noted the problem: 'Monitoring remains a weak point in the system. Many of the critical issues for the new higher education remain undervalued or ignored in monitoring and statistical systems' (NIACE, 1993:58). This is particularly a problem for those seeking change. Robertson (1994) for example, repeatedly pointed out that the absence of data relevant to credit accumulation, and even more so to credit transfer, stifles change since it precludes the evaluation of the impact of policy and practice on students and institutions and it inhibits the development of predictive and planning models. In other words, it shapes what can and cannot be said about the system as a whole and affects how institutions think about themselves and the image they present to the wider world.

Despite the widespread recognition of the absence of data in key policy areas, there appears to have been a general lack of awareness of the problematic nature of the data which did exist. For example, the data on mature students published in 1992 (DfE, 1992b) have been quoted widely by commentators and analysts of access to higher education but generally treated as unproblematic. At a seminar presenting the findings of a recent research project (Webb *et al.*, 1994b), senior policy-makers, while previously aware that national data on access and entry were questionable, nevertheless expressed surprise at the extent of the difficulties uncovered in relation to the FESR. This lack of awareness, or failure to alert readers to the complex nature of the data, often compounds the problem. For example, Coffield (1995:22) in seeking to challenge the CVCP's unproblematic assertion (CVCP, 1995) that mature students constitute the majority of those in higher education, pointed out that this is 'technically correct' but 'only when part-time and non-traditional students are added to the totals of full-time students.' It is difficult, however, to sort out what this means since what would adding 'non-traditional' students to 'full-time' students actually involve in terms of quantitative data? While it is appropriate to challenge the statement, a lack of consistency in the terminology and use of data weakens this case and serves to reinforce the idea that 'part-time and non-traditional students' are not normal. Discursive practices of this kind arise in large part because the data have been so ambiguous: apparently straightforward statements are in practice very seldom so and yet to explain and unpack the ambiguity around them is both time-consuming and complex. The result is that caveats and explanations are seldom presented, the impression is given that the data are straightforward and compliance with their classifications are reinforced and their significance rationalized.

The alternative to the use of routinely collected data inevitably involves large-scale, expensive, longitudinal research. Policy and practice in this field are often seen as too urgent for such time-scales: Little and Robbins (1981) argued that the under-representation of black and Asian students was so urgent that measures to correct it could not wait for comprehensive research. Government attitudes tend also to take this view, and while there is no strong tradition of governments using social science research in policy-making, this was particularly true during the 1980s when policy was based overtly on conviction and ideology rather than research or rationality. This approach to policy was reinforced by an ideological opposition, of the New Right in particular, to the idea of strong central (or local) planning and indeed it has become clear that many of the statistical models for planning were not adequate. The outstanding example of this in relation to entry to higher education was the 'Model E' projection (DES, 1978b) of the effect on demand for higher education arising from the decline in the numbers of 18-year-olds, which turned out to be inaccurate because it failed to take account of the differential birth rate and participation rate of different social classes. More recently, as late as May 1991, the government (DES, 1991b) was predicting an API for 18–19-year-olds of 29.7 in 1996; in fact this was reached in the 1993 entry (DfE, 1995).

Despite a widespread recognition of the problems, a comprehensive national data-collection system was only possible when a number of other structural changes had taken place: the abolition of the binary system; the merger of UCCA and PCAS; the merger of UFC and PCFC; the merger of CDP and CVCP; the merger of USR and FESR; and the incorporation of teacher training and art education into the common framework for admissions. Together these constituted a major reordering of vested interests – not something which could be achieved quickly or easily.

There has also been a lack of demand at institutional level. The absence of a managerial culture, particularly in the 'old' universities, means that there has been no routine collection and use of quantitative data of the kind relevant to access and participation, at the centre of the institution for management purposes. Not only do selection and admission lie at the heart of departmental autonomy and the culture of the 'academic tribe' (Becher, 1990), but as Fulton and Ellwood (1989) pointed out, institutions have frequently seen no need for data to monitor their policy and practice. In addition, as discussed above, the wide range of different departmental practices in terms of alternative routes and links into higher education programmes within a single institution, means that departments may have very different needs in relation to appropriate data. These factors help to explain why there has been little faith in or commitment to support central data systems at departmental level, even among the former polytechnics with a stronger managerial culture (Davies *et al.*, 1994). Institutions also understand very well the political uses to which such data may be put and have thus been 'understandably wary of crude indicators, which may mislead when taken out of context' (NIACE, 1993:59). The long lead time in the production of national data, coupled with rapid change at institutional level, particularly in the late 1980s, has also meant that the data were out of date by the time they became available, thus further undermining the commitment necessary to produce valid and reliable data. All these factors were also reinforced by the weakness of institutional computer systems and the cost of improving and upgrading them in a climate of financial pressure.

Overall, therefore, it has been possible for departments and the central administration within institutions, and for institutions and government agencies at national level, to hold the other(s) responsible for resolving the problem or for inhibiting the reforms necessary to do so. This resembles the mutual assumption that the other side owned the problem resulting in 'permissive or collusive inertia' which has been noted elsewhere (Parry and Davies, 1990) in relation to change in the admissions to higher education.

The lack of evidence, or ambiguous evidence, about the nature and extent of the changes which have taken place or the impact future changes might have, can work to the advantage both of those wishing to preserve the status quo and to those seeking to bring about reform, especially radical reform. Radical change is likely to generate conflict and conflict inhibits the implementation of change either through direct confrontation or through more covert resistance and subversion. Therefore a key task for those wishing to bring about change is to manage or suppress conflict and one way to do this is to maintain a silence about the extent of the change, at least until it is well established. Thus by failing to create the systems necessary to provide the data or to produce them quickly (the data for 1988 which demonstrated that adults were the majority of the entrants for the first time did not appear until 1992), creates a space in time and debate during which the change can be implemented beyond the point of no return. Players in various positions in the discourse of access have recognized this space and used it in their different ways to bring about the kind of change they desired. Some were able to demand more because there was not enough, while others demanded less because there was too much – of the same thing. For example, references to 30,000 Access students, without any clear data to support the claim (see Davies, 1994) were used to justify the demand for changes to the UCAS form, for consideration and attention in the institutional policy processes and to justify the existence of a national framework. At the same time, USR and UCCA, and until 1992 entry PCAS, could argue that there were not enough Access students to justify a separate category of entry qualifications in their data analysis because the data from higher education (but not further education) suggested that the numbers were much lower. Similarly, tutors could claim that Access courses were important because they targeted under-represented groups, and policy-makers could claim that equal opportunities policy and practice were in place, without any clear data showing that the representation of working-class students or ethnic minority groups had significantly changed. The absence of clear data has therefore been a significant tool in what Croft and Beresford (1992) have called the 'manipulation of ambiguity', a feature of this terrain not unique to England (Davies, 1996).

Ambiguous and problematic data can also foster uncertainty, insecurity and even contribute to the engendering of a sense of crisis. As Neave and van Vught (1991) pointed out, higher education has a tendency to equate change with crisis and at the same time to use crisis as a tactic of negotiation to regulate and mediate the pace of change. The recurring moral panic around GCSE and A level results and around admissions practices, illustrated in Chapter 2, and the ways in which various positions in the discourse use quantitative data, constitute an example of such negotiation around the massification of higher education and represent a strategy for the management of change.

Why is it happening now?

It has been part of the general thrust of government policy in all fields of public sector activity to put in place systems and procedures for the tighter control of public expenditure and for greater accountability, often expressed as an increased use of, mostly quantitative, performance indicators and measures of quality. While higher education was a small system for a fee-paying elite with no maintenance grants, it represented a relatively low level of public expenditure supported mostly by those who benefited from it. Therefore there was little demand for numbers to plan or evaluate the system or to control the behaviour and activities of institutions or students. The rapid shift to a mass system has meant expansion in raw number terms, a more heterogeneous student body and more diverse types of institutions. Thus the demand on public expenditure has risen and the concern with the nature of the student body has increased.

At the same time the logic of a market in higher education generates a number of pressures for comprehensive and more reliable data. First, the emphasis on consumer choice offers at least the potential for a loss of control of the behaviour of individuals. The idea of a free market tends to undermine the perception of order within the system (there is much talk of the need for individual and institutional discipline – almost a moral imperative) and quantitative, 'objective' data are seen as a way of imposing some sense of order and rationality on an increasingly diverse system. They also facilitate the reordering, the restratification which tends to follow unification of national systems (Scott, 1995), since the positioning of an institution in the market place is frequently supported by average A level point scores on entry, percentages of mature students, and so on. In the context of higher education in particular, the loosening of control over the behaviour of individuals and institutions threatens the tight control of public expenditure, hence new funding mechanisms which in turn demand more data. At the same time, technological developments have obviously also made larger national data-collection and processing systems significantly cheaper and easier to establish and to maintain.

At institutional level, there has also been a growing recognition that unless institutions 'are prepared individually or collectively to address the need for sufficient comparative information to enable informed choice, others will take on the role, from a less well informed base' (NIACE, 1993:59). In other words, in a competitive market place, institutions need to take the lead in developing data which will influence student choices and form the basis of funding formulae. The acceleration in the speed of data-processing which has taken place in recent years also means that it is now possible to reflect developments in policy and practice more quickly and therefore to be more useful in the management of change. Thus on the one hand the manipulation of ambiguity has become less useful, at least in private, and possibly a more risky strategy and, on the other hand, the need for reliable and valid data for new managerial purposes (especially marketing and accounting) has become more pressing. The demand for more data has also come from the research community. As Willenborg *et al.* (1995:1) pointed out, this is 'mainly due to the great power of modern PCs which enable researchers to analyse large data sets by themselves, whereas in former days only the statistical offices were able to analyse such data sets.' In addition, there has been a growing recognition that both further and higher education are relatively under-researched and a corresponding increase in interest in these sectors as a field of study.

Finally, the agenda of many individual participants in the discourse – marketeers, trainers, liberal meritocrats and adherents of the access movement – has been about radical change and there is a growing recognition that the ground has shifted, that the debates and issues of the past are no longer relevant in a mass system. Thus they now need to be able to demonstrate the impact of change and develop future strategies. In short they need new kinds of information on which to base new discursive practices and to reposition themselves in a changed discourse.

Concluding remarks

Large-scale data-collection systems, by definition, need to impose a consistent and reliable means of 'objectively' measuring and understanding the profile of the student population and the performance of the system as a whole. However, technical and administrative decisions about categories and rules of classification are not neutral, since they differentiate students, and by extension institutions, in particular ways which shape the discourse. At both national and local levels, the classifications and categorizations which take place enable or promote certain kinds of agendas and debates and inhibit or prevent others. Since compliance with rules is a central tenet of the bureaucratic procedures necessary to achieve reliability and validity, such classifications are institutionalized at various levels – course, department, university, national system. The inconsistencies and differences embedded in these practices are often hidden and their political nature obscured. The categories which emerge are normalized and rationalized; the need for data stability in order to measure change over time embeds these processes and further legitimates the data definitions. The need to simplify and generalize about the system as a whole inevitably obscures the diversity within it and hence further reinforces the definitions of 'normal' or 'standard'. The constructions which emerge then provide the only available way of talking about students; other definitions are at best difficult and in some senses excluded.

The new unified systems which have been put in place in the UK represent in many ways a major improvement on previous arrangements. However, problems have yet to be resolved and new methodologies have yet to be developed before the system can be fully exploited and a more open and dynamic discourse of access can emerge.

4

Alternative Students?
Conceptualizations of Difference

Sue Webb

Introduction

In this chapter the focus shifts to encompass the academic discourse of research on access. This is because researchers are some of the key actors in developing and maintaining particular agendas about access to higher education. Researchers help to define how access has been thought about, spoken about, and made a subject that can be planned for by policy-makers and practitioners. They help to frame the answers to questions about who has access to higher education. Therefore, in order to explore further the issue of who is selected for entry and how this compares with notions of equity, I will examine the ways that the scope, form and scale of access research have been informed by and constrained by a discourse of access, and vice versa. Researchers' questions and the kind of data they work with will be reviewed to consider how they have used national and institutional data constructed (although frequently for other purposes) by government agencies and others. I will discuss whether or not research has posed different questions from those of policy-makers and government agencies and the extent to which researchers have developed different methods of classifying and naming students in the access discourse.

Researchers' decisions about collecting and analysing data about students in higher education have involved dividing practices which have categorized and differentiated between types of students. Most often researchers have worked with the same categories as the policy-makers, practitioners and government agencies. They have classified students as either standard and non-standard or traditional and non-traditional, using the polarizations that have become familiar within the discourse of access. Similarly, researchers have conflated categories such as non-traditional, non-standard and mature in the way that national statistics have done and have failed to problematize divisions by age, qualification, gender, 'race' and social class. My intention is to show how access research has contributed to the construction of intelligence about the system and in turn has contributed to the creation of material that can be used by politicians and institutional managers to rationalize and legitimate their practices. In sum, the focus is on deconstructing the research material that is used in policy debates.

More specifically, the recognition that ambiguities in the data can be manipulated by different positions in the access discourse leads me to pose the following questions about research practice. What does widening access mean? Is a 'mass' system a more inclusive system recruiting different types of students than previously? If so, what categories of social and demographic difference are used and what are ignored? Furthermore, in what ways are the categories that are used regarded as evidence of social equity? Is the assessment of the impact of expansion and the categories developed to measure the system informed by different positions in the discourse of access? If so, in what ways is it informed? How does research on access position the subjects of the research, the students, whose participation is measured, and the policy-makers and practitioners whose performance and strategies are described and perhaps assessed? And finally, how have these research questions and categories been generated; what is the relationship of these to other discourses within higher education such as those of quality and standards, and in what contexts has access research been conducted?

The research context

In broad terms, access research practice is carried out in an institutional and national context which imposes constraints on what may be done by limiting funding and by developing a culture of what questions are important and what form they should take. Within these contexts, however, there is a complex interplay of forces operating from different positions. Research on access is being conducted within policies and practice which are contested. Researchers, policy-makers, access providers and students interconnect in different ways and have different *entrées* to funding resources and publication channels to voice their concerns, raise questions and shape the system.

Consequently the process through which the research discourse is developed could be described as a functioning network in which the actors and subjects in the discourse have different loci of power. Miller and Rose (1993:84) outline the operation of a functioning network in the following way:

> This involves alliances formed not only because one agent is dependent upon another for funds, legitimacy or some other resources which can be used for persuasion or compulsion, but also because one actor comes to convince another that their problems or goals are intrinsically linked, and that their interests are consonant, that each can solve their difficulties or achieve their ends by joining forces or working along the same lines. . . . Hence persons, organisations, entities and locales can be brought into a loose and approximate, and always mobile and indeterminate alignment.

Language and position play an important part in establishing these functioning networks and in enabling policy and practice to be determined in an indirect manner. A range of agencies, government departments, policy organizations with funds for research, academics, pressure groups, teachers and employers may come together through shared vocabularies, theories and explanations. However, if in the discourse of access, the agreements between these diverse groups, who occupy different loci of power, are based on the manipulation of ambiguity as was argued in Chapter 2, we may expect that some voices will have a greater role than others in shaping the language to be adopted and key elements in the system. Chapter 3 has argued, for example, that policy-makers and planners tend to take more notice of quantitative rather than qualitative research (Halpin and Troyna, 1994). It is more likely then that research on access will be funded if it focuses on quantitative questions and answers, and as a consequence such work is likely to be one of the more influential voices if it is presented in the language of disinterested truth.

The main focus of this chapter is to explore how researchers' practices have enabled particular 'truths' to be developed and sustained about the students who have access to and participate in higher education. Such an approach will contribute to an understanding of how research data can be used as evidence both to support and undermine diverse claims about the system: for example that the participation of particular groups has been widened, and that social equity has either been achieved or not. In the discussion I will show that only a few access research studies locate themselves in the discourse of empowerment or feminist research (Lather, 1991) and make explicit their commitment to radical social change. In other words, there is, as Foucault has suggested, a 'politics of truth telling' and research studies are part of the production and institutionalization of 'regimes of truth' suppressing alternative discourses and reducing their credibility (Foucault, 1980).

Conceptualizing access: muddles and misunderstandings

Interconnections between access research and practice encourage a professional discourse to develop and become incorporated into many parts of further and higher education. Frequently though, the academic debate, the research studies and the policy statements from institutions fail to use language consistently or to define terminology carefully. As a consequence the data generated in these ways fail to answer crucial questions and so can provide 'evidence' for rationalizations of very diverse policies and practice. Examples of these conceptual muddles can be seen in four elements of the access discourse: increasing and widening access; the labelling of students as standard/non-standard or traditional/non-traditional; the relationship of student input quality to degree output; and the notion of maturity.

These four elements might appear to be diverse ways of conceptualizing the students who have access to higher education because they focus on different aspects of their biography, social position and experiences, but there is considerable overlap in the ways that criteria to identify features in these elements are spoken about. The ways that researchers have used these elements of difference and the extent to which they have contributed to or reflected the muddles in the discourse of access are therefore critical to an understanding of the ways that different voices are able to exert their influence over the practice of higher education. For example, student numbers have certainly increased, as Chapter 3 has demonstrated, but the extent to which access has been widened is more controversial. At times the two are treated as synonymous. The argument rests on what counts as 'widened', and this depends on how the different positions identify and divide normal and abnormal students. As a consequence the discussion about 'more' students in the system is almost always embedded within a debate about how similar or different they are. The research question that follows from this then, is how is difference understood and investigated?

Elements of difference: standard/non-standard and traditional/non-traditional labels

In access research, difference is nearly always conceptualized in terms of identifying the features of the 'access' or 'new' population of students and comparing these with the features of those who have entered previously as of right, representing the norm against which the others are judged and may be found wanting. For example, one of the comparators frequently used has been qualifications on entry, with A levels constituting standard entrants and everything else defined as non-standard. Consequently the debate about widening access has become polarized by policy-makers in terms of the numbers of standard and non-standard entrants (HEFCE, 1996a). Alternatively, other attributes such as maturity or the social characteristics of gender, 'race' and class are segmented schematically into the categories traditional and non-traditional. Importantly, these terms are then used interchangeably with standard and non-standard labels. The FEU (1987:2) for example, defined non-traditional students as 'all those who do not follow the traditional route to university through the acquisition in the sixth form of the required A levels *at 18.*' Similarly, Bargh *et al.* (1994) included in a study of non-standard students all those who had qualifications other than A levels, applicants without formal qualifications, all mature applicants irrespective of their qualifications, and all ethnic minorities, again whatever their qualifications. Such a definition which constructs a population as 'other' using both social characteristics and qualifications, and does not differentiate, even according to government definitions of 'standard' qualifications, makes assessing the impact of increasing numbers on selectivity and equity complex if not impossible.

Scott and Smith (1995), in a follow-up study to their work with Bargh *et al.* (1994) removed the ethnic category from the inclusive label 'non-standard', but similar problems with the aggregate data remained. They justified their definition of non-standard in terms of the common sense designations of admissions tutors who, they argued, tended to group together all these types because they saw them as untypical of the 'normal' student body. I do not question the prevalence of this perception and indeed in Chapter 6 further evidence is provided of this type of dividing practice by admissions tutors. However, in constructing their research sample in this way, a sub-species of student is created who appears to lack any of the attributes associated with 'standard' or 'normal' students. Moreover, the complexity of cross-cutting categories is lost. Students who may have qualified for entry in the same ways as 'standard' students are positioned as abnormal because of an attribute such as their age or their ethnicity. Consequently, such research can provide legitimacy for a range of understandings about the impact of policy-makers' and practitioners' strategies for access. Because of the double or treble counting involved, it is impossible to know how many students overall are included. It also means that difference is exaggerated and notions of abnormality are 'normalized', taken for granted and assumed to be the necessary basis for policies and practices. The power of the discourse is particularly evident in this intertwining of research and practice.

Conceptualizing students as inputs: alternative outputs

A further example that illustrates the way that the language of access has been shaped and in turn how it has shaped the evaluation of change in the system is in the research on the relationship between inputs and outputs. We have seen in earlier chapters how the formal designations of qualifications for entry accepted by government ministers and higher education regulating bodies have shifted over the last decade, in particular from 1987 with the inclusion of Access Certificates alongside two A levels as a recognized route into higher education. Some vocational qualifications such as BTEC National Certificates have had this formal recognition for even longer. Yet the data which would enable some assessment of the impact of the different labelling of these qualifications on admissions practices and degree performance have been inadequate (Molloy and Carroll, 1992). It is not my intention to provide a comprehensive review of such work here since this has been done by others (Gallacher and Wallis, 1993). Instead, I wish to chart the interconnections between such research and the concerns of the divergent positions in the discourse of access and institutional practices.

For example, one study by Johnes, (1992:10) examined 'The potential effect of wider access on higher education degree quality' by comparing A level scores on entry with degree results and concluded 'it is clear that any policy to induce an increase in student numbers by lowering entry standards can be expected to have a significant negative effect on degree results'. The only entry qualification investigated in this study was A levels and yet conclusions were developed that were generalized and applied to the concept of wider access. Such research confirms the views of the academic traditionalists: that A levels are good predictors of future academic success. The contribution of the work of Johnes and Taylor (1990:60) to this discourse position can be further seen in the way that they have questioned the reliability of data on which other studies, which have drawn alternative conclusions, were based. And more recently, Johnes (1992) has debunked the research findings that have been quoted by the movements to widen access, by commenting on their adequacy, completeness and generalizability. In this way the set of research findings which have argued that 'the only feasible measure is the average A level score of each university's entrants' (Johnes and Taylor, 1990:60), have contributed to the development of a discourse of derision around the legitimacy of those without a particular standard qualification entering higher education.

In contrast, studies that have explicitly conceptualized the student population by disaggregating their entry qualifications, into standard, non-standard and Access qualifications, have found that the relationship of a degree outcome to A level or other qualifications, was complex, and that the predictive value of A levels was not high (Brennan and McGeevor, 1985; Brennan, 1986; Bourner and Hamed, 1987b; Molloy and Carroll, 1992). Moreover, these studies have suggested that there is qualified support for the hypothesis that non-standard entry students perform at least as well as standard entrants and that there is a strong case for widening access to higher education for those mature students who do not possess conventional entry qualifications (Molloy and Carroll, 1992:41). Yet, interestingly even this last study, which was careful to distinguish analytically between qualifications and types of students, has conflated maturity (a non-traditional attribute of entrants) with non-standardness (an indicator of entry qualifications) when identifying the conclusions and recommendations for policy and practice. Not surprisingly then, such slippage in terminology is rife among other players in the discourse of access.

The work of those described above and that of others who have considered the performance of mature students and/or Access students in higher education (Davies and Yates, 1987; Fulton and Ellwood, 1989; Britton and Baxter, 1994), have acknowledged the limited nature of the populations that they have investigated and so their work has enabled the access movement and some policy-makers who identify with this position to argue for more research (HEFCE, 1996a). Moreover, many of these research studies are most notable for their close ties with policy funders, particularly organizations with an interest in quality or the provision of education and training for adults. Funders included the Department of Employment, the CNAA (which funded over 30 studies through its Access Development Fund Services), UDACE and FEU. It is interesting to speculate on the interconnections between such research and the competing voices in the discourse of access, given that all of these organizations have ceased to exist now and have been recast into other bodies.

Finally, a further concern is how research about student entry and performance is used to justify different strategies in relation to learning, about which we know very little. For example, Bargh *et al.* suggested that non-standard students are perceived in different ways depending on who they are being compared with, whether it is students with good or indifferent A levels. They argued that 'It is hardly surprising that they [non-standard students] are seen as potentially remedial and so a resources burden in the "old" universities and as well motivated and above average students in the "new" universities' (Bargh *et al.*, 1994:37). Thus the study of input-output measures has been used to provide a commentary on a differential experience of learning associated with standard and non-standard students and consequently the research material contributes to differential assessments of quality, and may encourage the development of a deficit model of the non-standard and, by implication, non-traditional learner.

In a more cautionary voice, Barnett (1992:21) described the inputs-outputs approach to measuring quality as the 'tail wagging the quality dog.' He argued that the quality of the student experience is a 'black box' that has not been studied because it is difficult to measure, and yet it may form part of the explanation for the pattern of association between the inputs and outputs, and so should be examined. However, funders have not commissioned a great deal of research on comparative student experiences, other than through quantitative measures (HEFCE, 1996a:41, 47). Perhaps this is because, as Dale (1989:35) suggested,

> Policy options are selected on the basis of solutions available, and often it seems questions are framed with available answers in mind. What appears as the available answers will result from the particular combination of bureaucracy/technology dominant in the state apparatus at the time.

The analyses that this research area have developed tend therefore to be descriptive and oversimplified accounts of relationships between variables and to have limited explanatory value, although they are often used within the discourse as if they had such powers. The divergent positions in the discourse use the research on inputs and outputs to rationalize and legitimate their practices, but rarely are the research propositions exhaustively tested.

Alternative students: the mature student as a species

Throughout the 1990s a frequently repeated statement was that mature students formed a majority of entrants to higher education (Benn and Fieldhouse, 1993; NIACE, 1993; HEFCE, 1996a) and yet as we have already shown, these statements are an artefact of aggregating different populations and may be misleading (see Tables 2 and 4 in Appendix 2).

The 'mature student' has become a key element in the discourse of access. The demographic downturn that led to the expectation of a sharp fall in the numbers of 18- and 19-year-olds who could enter higher education increased the salience of older recruits. The age of maturity though has been positioned at different points by different players in the discourse. The label 'mature' has also, as I have shown, been used interchangeably with non-standard or non-traditional in spite of the evidence that there is a sizeable proportion of non-standard students who are under 21 years (Webb *et al.*, 1994a; Table 4 in Appendix 2) and that the majority of entrants of 21 years and over to full-time degrees use a wide variety of routes, including standard qualifications (Table 4) and comprise individuals from a wide variety of backgrounds (Metcalf, 1993).

The focus of many of the studies on mature students has been to identify their 'special' characteristics, and frequently this has involved large-scale sampling and been undertaken through questionnaires or analysis of secondary sources (Percy, 1985; Smithers and Griffin, 1986; Woodley *et al.*, 1987; Redpath and Robus, 1989; Keen and Higgins, 1992; Roberts and Higgins, 1992). Such work has been possible because there has been external funding from a limited range of organizations with a policy and planning interest. For example, the funders included departments of government such as the Department of Employment, and the Department of Education and Science, and educational organizations and institutions such as the CVCP, CNAA, FEU, UCAS/HEIST and UDACE, as well as more disinterested funders such as Leverhulme. A small number of studies such as those by Pascall and Cox (1993) and Britton and Baxter (1994) were supported by the institutions in which the researchers worked and studied, so that they provided in-house research and planning material as well as having more general applicability, whilst others such as Edwards (1993) were developed from their Ph.D. theses. These differences in funding sources correlate significantly with the types of information the researchers had access to and the forms in which their findings were presented. The studies funded by policy-makers and planners were overwhelmingly quantitative and involved large-scale surveys, although a small number did include some interviews with students. In contrast, nearly all of the studies not associated with policy-makers used a range of methods and posed a wider range of research questions. The effect of these differences was that much of the publicly funded research was descriptive and contributed to the mapping of who was in higher education and what they felt about this, but it did little to further understanding of why certain students had been admitted, and perhaps others excluded, from higher education.

Moreover, by constructing the research around positivistic assumptions about how to conceptualize the 'mature' student, the complexity of the differences in educational experiences within this grouping was masked (Britton and Baxter, 1994; James, 1995), and not all the variables considered could be easily articulated through a mapping model. For example, Usher and Bryant (1989: 107–8) questioned the appropriateness of the survey method and the constraints of multiple categories to reveal the 'complexity, contingency and self-constituted nature of experience.' In addition, the notion of mature students as returners who previously 'missed out' has become a dominant motif in the discourse (Parry, 1995:107), and their construction as a species by researchers has been echoed in policy-makers' categorizations such as 'second chancers' (HEFCE, 1996a). Such labelling underplays and oversimplifies life histories and the resistance of students to this positioning. What is it about all students over 21 years of age which makes them so different from 18–20-year-olds? The use of this categorization reinforces stereotypical notions and a deficit model of students, although this may not be the intention of the authors. Frequently studies of part-time, Access or non-standard entry students have documented the students' concerns for study support and financial help and have noted a tendency towards non-completion (Bourner *et al.*, 1991; Tight, 1991; Metcalf, 1993). Consequently, the research may contribute to such a reading by the academic traditionalists and perhaps even the liberal meritocrats, and provide support for dividing practices between normal students in higher education and abnormal or problem students for whom special compensatory arrangements would need to be made. James (1995:454) argued that when research studies problematize the student individually and collectively, they do the following:

> They seem to promise an answer to the question 'in what ways will these students differ from those we know?' In doing so they conveniently reduce the complexity of the issues involved for institutions in responding to an increasingly diverse student body, whilst claiming to be practical, in the sense of providing the sort of information that could be used to inform practice.

Frequently, the mature students are positioned by such research as having to 'fit themselves into the system' (Tuckett, 1990:127) and the notion of the accessibility of institutions to a more diverse population becomes muted as some positions in the discourse attend more to the idea of access in terms of increasing numbers, encouraging equity through specific courses aimed at the deserving, rather than considering equity in the student experience.

In sum, in spite of the plethora of research studies on the mature student there are still many things we do not know because much of the work has concentrated on the taxonomy of the species, mature student. For example, there is a research silence around testing the relationship between specific institutional practices or funding strategies and the mature consumers' behaviour. We do not know the effects of loans and the removal of the mature students' allowance on intake and progression, and although there has been some evidence that vocational aims are important to mature students and to alternative entrants (Webb *et al.*, 1994a), there is little ongoing research exploring the employment experiences of such graduates or those who participate in lifelong learning using credit frameworks. Such a research vacuum reinforces complacency and established practices and enables policy-makers to draw their own conclusions about the effectiveness of the policies which they may have advocated.

Alternative students: conceptualizations of difference?

In the debate about what expansion of the system of higher education means, and whether the enlarged system is more inclusive, attention has focused on who the students are and what categories are used to assess social justice and equity. Student profile data are available through a range of sources, most notably UCAS and HESA, but as stated already these data measure different things and are collected from different constituencies. Nevertheless it is to these data that research studies have looked most frequently and the ways that researchers have used them illuminates the relationship between research, policy and practice. To explore this further, I will discuss the handling of three social characteristics, gender, 'race' and social class, in order to identify the ambiguities and the silences in these conceptualizations of difference among students. Other variables such as material circumstances and poverty, disability, locality and region of origin, have been less frequently studied (see, for example, Redpath and Robus, 1989; Metcalf, 1993; and HEFCE, 1996a for a summary of the paucity of work in this area). Finally, I will outline a fourth way of constructing difference around entry qualifications by considering data generated by the alternative entry project (Webb *et al.*, 1994a).

'Under-representation' is the concept most frequently used by researchers, policy-makers and practitioners when examining the nature of equity in higher education. There is a taken for granted element, stemming from the history of both educational research and political understandings around social disadvantage that gender, 'race' and social class are central categorizations. There are three particular difficulties stemming from current research which will be highlighted in this section. The first concerns the nature of research problems: what is meant by the labels gender, 'race' and class? Who counts them and why? The second is an explanatory problem: why are these categorizations so important? Are they being used as proxies for cultural or educational capital? How are they related to each other? The third is a linked policy problem: what consequences follow from particular research foci? Who is positioned as the problem? There is an expectation among some, for example, that by engaging in the 'political arithmetic' of participation figures, their research will be useful in shaping policy and creating a more equitable system (Hammersley, 1994:141). However, other researchers' concerns with the issue of under-representation may go further and they identify more explicitly with empowerment strategies for these under-represented groups (Bird *et al.*, 1992; Taylor, 1992, 1993; Edwards, 1993; McFadden, 1995), and they align themselves with notions of increasing accessibility rather than just access to higher education.

Gender

The ease with which data on gender are collected and their high completion levels should not let us ignore the fact that these data incorporate many assumptions that are not always examined in research studies. The problem for research is how to use gender, and this stems, in part, from lack of clarity about what the variable is measuring. From one point of view it seems obvious: it is measuring a bi-polar distribution that has a biological base in sex. Yet very often its use as an independent variable in research studies treats either these presumed sex differences, or the presumption that there are similarly distributed cultural differences of femininity and masculinity, as being equally causal.

An example of the way in which gender is selected as the cause of differences might be in discussions of why women and men are differently distributed in subjects studied at undergraduate level – women are overwhelmingly clustered in education and subjects allied to medicine, including nursing, and men predominate in engineering and technology (see Table 3 in Appendix 2). Our own study of 'Alternative Entry to Higher Education' (Webb *et al.*, 1994a) indicated that the alternative entrants also showed a very similar gender difference in distribution across subjects to that of all other entrants. The interesting question is, why this pattern? Is it because of gender differences or is it multi-factorial and linked to other distributional variations such as a segmented labour market? Such a discussion illustrates that gender may be relevant but how it causes differences may be more complex than first appears, and perhaps can only be answered by research which includes a focus on students' decision making.

A second concern is that gender may be subsumed into other categories and its significance underplayed, or it may not be considered with other variables and its significance overplayed. For example, discussion of variables such as social class, age, course level, entry qualifications, mode of study and types of institutions need to be considered alongside gender in order to assess the significance of the increase in student numbers (Table 3 in Appendix 2). In a review of higher education since the 1960s, Halsey (1988:278) concluded:

> Summing up the post Robbins period it may be said that within the framework of expansion, the main feature has not been the growth of full-time, male undergraduates reading science or technology in universities. The really spectacular growth has been women studying the arts and humanities or part-time students in public sector colleges and at the Open University.

However, without taking account of the social class of the student, the subjects they studied, and the part-time nature of much of their participation, the discussion of the increase in women studying in higher education may overstate the changes that have taken place. For example, whilst by 1995 for the first time, slightly more women than men entered undergraduate study, both part-time and full-time, there were some interesting differences in participation by age, mode of study and level of course (see Tables 1–3 in Appendix 2). Moreover, studies that have examined social class and gender (Heath *et al.*, 1992) have shown that 'social class effects were not either alleviated or accentuated by the gender of the respondent or vice versa' (Egerton and Halsey, 1993:186). In other words, such studies suggest the increase in participation by women has done little to ameliorate the social class inequality that persists in higher education (Blackburn and Jarman, 1993).

Yet the relationship between social class and gender is complex, not least because of how social class is constructed. This issue will need to be re-examined because if 'university degrees have become increasingly important measures of high ability, but ability is socially defined in a society structured by class and gender' (Blackburn and Jarman, 1993:203) then we may not be able to 'read off' that there has been an achievement of social justice simply because the same number of men and women from each social class are being admitted to higher education. However, this is the reading that could be construed from the articulations by some voices. In these readings, gender has become a category that no longer needs to be used as a measure of the exclusivity of the system. There is an assumption that equity has been achieved because there are now more women entrants. Others have argued that the working class and ethnic minorities are still not fully represented, and that Access courses have not done enough to change the profile of higher education because it is women, in the main, who are benefiting from the legitimation of these new routes, and they are white and middle class (Babbidge and Leyton, 1993; Benn and Burton, 1995:7, 10). Such generalizations do not adequately conceptualize the differences in life-chances among women and between women and men, and between working-class, minority ethnic group and disabled women, and the differential opportunities that 'graduateness' opens up for these entrants without cultural capital (Brown and Scase, 1994). It is qualitative research which allows for the exploration of such diversities (Thomas, 1990; Edwards, 1993). Yet as I argued earlier, such qualitative research has been marginalized in the discourse of access. This is because the discourse has focused largely on the aggregate numbers of men and women in the system and on the decline in under-representation rather than problematizing their experience of study, and the notion of what might be meant by an accessible system in relation to gender differences.

'Race' and ethnicity

Turning now to 'race' (the quotation marks are used to denote a categorical problem with the term), from one point of view it appears to be a term like sex that has a biological base, but classifications derived from such criteria have been discredited (Banton, 1970). By contrast, ethnicity has been defined as a more inclusive term that refers to a cultural group that has a shared past and a conscious sense of belonging (Bulmer, 1986). However, such an emphasis on developing subjectively meaningful criteria in relation to this classification has led to two difficulties for education research. The first is about which criteria of 'race' and ethnicity are meaningful and acceptable to all groups, and the second is that because of this difficulty, educational data were not collected nationally for much of the period during which higher education was expanding (1973–1990). In spite of these differences and difficulties, increasingly there is a consensus that 'race' and ethnicity should be classified according to people's own self-identity, and accordingly the agitation from activists and researchers has been about the development of a range of categories to which everyone can subscribe (Bulmer, 1986; Skellington *et al.*, 1992). These classifications, which have been developed in association with the Commission for Racial Equality, do not capture fully differences in self-identity, but they are widely used and have become the standard ways in which general population and education data are recorded. They have institutionalized particular 'dividing' practices.

In higher education, national data are currently collected through UCAS and through HESA, but this is a relatively recent activity that only became comprehensive in 1995, so the 1994/95 data contained a high non-response rate (see Table 6 in Appendix 2). Consequently, although there are data from 1990, when these have been the subject of research, they have measured different things in different parts of the system of higher education; and where data have been collected through the applications and admissions system, it has been on a voluntary basis and so has not been comprehensive. Assessment of the impact of expansion has been influenced by this past silence, and a further consequence of the paucity of national data was that research was small-scale, drawn from a limited number of institutions and based on the successful applicants only (Tomlinson, 1983; Lyon, 1988; Singh, 1990; Bird *et al.*, 1992). More recently, national data on 'race' and ethnicity have been the subject of high profile, publicly funded research and debate over their meaning. For example, in the early 1990s the CVCP sought an explanation for the apparent lower acceptance rates of minority ethnic group applicants to universities. This resulted in the Taylor reports (1992, 1993) which suggested that some factors of educational disadvantage such as A level point scores and school/college attended were operating to create a negative bias towards minority ethnic groups applying to universities.

Debates among researchers have centred around the extent to which equity in the system is measured by the comparability of the experiences of different ethnic groups in selection, or the levels of their representation. These opposing views are linked with a definitional problem that has been associated in part with the politics of race relations. For example, for some, 'race' and a bipolar distinction between black and white enables the notion of racism to be revealed both at the individual and the institutional level, and so the focus has been on student experiences of disadvantage and discrimination. For others, differences within and across all ethnic groups have been more salient in their accounts and the focus has been on levels of representation. Consequently, research on 'race' in higher education reveals a polarization between the studies that present an optimistic picture of the levels of representation of students from minority ethnic groups (Modood, 1993; Modood and Shiner, 1994) and those that identify discriminatory practices against such applicants (Taylor, 1992; Connolly, 1994). The differences stem in part from the ways that the applicants and entrants are categorized and compared with national populations, and illustrate how the legitimation of particular categories for measuring 'race' will either highlight other differences within ethnic groups such as class or gender or will underplay these.

Modood (1992), for example, has expressed concern about the use of the term 'black' to denote all non-white groupings, suggesting this prioritizes colour as a contributory variable over other factors such as class, employment, capital assets, skills, gender, religion and others, and assumes that all non-whites will be members of underprivileged groups. Consequently, in his analyses of admissions and acceptance rates, he has tended to disaggregate the experiences of different ethnic minority groups and has concluded that the only groups that are significantly under-represented are Bangladeshis, particularly women, and to a lesser extent Pakistanis in UCCA institutions (Modood, 1993:169, 171–2). The most controversial contribution Modood (1993) made to the debate though, was to suggest that some minority ethnic groups are doing better than their white working-class peers in entering higher education. He suggests that since

> ... some ethnic minorities are using higher education to alter their own class composition, [it] offers one, if small, counter example to the view that class inequalities in higher education remain unchanged, and that education has failed to operate as a force for 'class abatement'.
>
> (Modood, 1993:179)

The inference he has drawn from this analysis is that access to higher education is being widened for ethnic minorities, that there is no general ethnic under-representation and that those who are still the most likely to be under-represented are white and working class. The most appropriate access measure would therefore be to focus on the class disadvantage of particular under-represented ethnic groups rather than target access strategies at all ethnic minorities, thus questioning the idea prevalent within the access movement that ethnic minorities need special programmes to provide access to higher education (Modood, 1993:168).

In contrast, the aim of those who subscribe to the use of the term black is to encourage subjective identification by all those who experience racism, with a view to transforming the society based on racial inequality (Gilroy, 1987). For those who adopt this conceptualization of 'race', Access courses become on the one hand the remedial route by which ethnic minorities are legitimized and gain entry to higher education (Bird, Yee and Myler, 1992) and on the other hand, they have a more radical aim in which ' "blacks only" Access courses, and admissions quotas . . . (re)insert anti-racism into the "populist" Access agenda' (Leicester, 1993:224). Taylor (1992, 1993) and Connolly (1994) emphasized similarities in the experiences of disadvantage across sub-groupings of ethnic minorities, the practice of institutional racism alongside the continuing importance of class and gender. Not surprisingly, these conclusions have chimed with the broader approaches of many within the access movement that question the rationalizations surrounding current admissions practices by pointing to an apparent institutionalization of racism, and by idealizing special Access schemes and the role of higher education shops (Taylor, 1992:371–2; Leicester, 1993).

In sum, this discussion suggests that whilst many of these research studies have conceptualized 'race' in ways that may have included differences within ethnic groups, only some researchers have acknowledged consistently how these differences have intersected with other categories such as gender and class. This is because research categories have been aligned with the categories developed by policy-makers and practitioners for collecting and monitoring ethnicity data. The researchers have tended to focus on participation questions, and have by and large measured changes in the system only in terms of inputs, rather than in terms of the meanings and experiences of expansion for those who have been counted. One conclusion to draw from this is that when researchers do not problematize policy-makers' and practitioners' categories, their research practices will serve to reinforce the agendas of those who have had the power to construct the institutional and national data-collection frameworks. In addition, when contradictions arise in the findings of researchers using different conceptualizations of 'race', they may encourage different voices in the access discourse. On the one hand, the academic traditionalists and liberal meritocrats may find comfort in the evidence of a system that appears to be maintaining entry standards and recruiting those with academic potential from among deserving ethnic groups. They can see that the system is becoming more inclusive and representative of the whole population without the need to disturb the academic boundaries between those whose qualifications give them legitimate entry and those who do not possess the 'gold standard'. On the other hand though, the access movement may feel encouraged to continue to raise questions about equal opportunities because they perceive under-representation in higher education of particular social and ethnic groups as evidence of institutional differentiations in terms of 'race', gender and class. Access courses become then a remedial strategy to widen participation and a site of challenge to institutional dividing practices.

Social class

During the 1950s and 1960s issues around educational inequalities in general and under-representation in higher education in particular prioritized social class as a key variable. During the 1970s, 1980s and 1990s, references to the enduring relationships between social class and educational differentials were made (Ball, S.J., 1986:84) but in some cases, and certainly by the 1990s, they often have a ritualistic quality rather than being of central analytic importance. This decline in the salience of a social class discourse in many social policy arenas has many complex causes which it is not possible to develop here. In the study of higher education it has stemmed *partly* from two major research problems: the first is generic to attempts to classify social class, and the second is specific to the ways data are collected in the higher education system. As a consequence, policy-makers have noted that the data on the socio-economic profile of the higher education population have been 'poor, difficult to collect and full of caveats. There is no simple way to draw a conclusive picture on the subject' (HEFCE, 1996a:23). The response of different access voices is that they have used this conceptual complexity in diverse ways when assessing whether or not the system is equitable. These have included measuring the participation of the unemployed, those without A level qualifications, those with Access qualifications, the mature, and using the more generic terms non-standard and non-traditional; in so doing, very often the notion of class has been played down. Operational data designed to encapsulate social class membership pose problems across all social science research. In education, as in other areas, parental or own occupation is used as a proxy for access to cultural and/or educational capital or to represent some notion of individual or group identity. Both researchers and practitioners draw quite differing conclusions as to the contemporary salience of social class as a measure of equity and its relevance in informing policy initiatives.

Let us look at three interrelated issues: the technical/research problems in measuring social class participation in higher education; what can be said (is being said) about the extent of such participation; and the differing interpretations placed on research by policy-makers and practitioners.

It is not possible to rehearse here all the problems inherent in measuring social class participation; they are well known to researchers. Occupation is the most common proxy, used as an indicator of other things such as income, status and worth as shown by income differences, market and work situation which represent life-chance differences, and cultural and life-style differences. But whose occupation is counted? Most class data sets, including census data and most educational data such as that produced by UCAS, group individuals in households and allocate class on the basis of the head of household or highest earner. However, this model may not be a very satisfactory basis on which to construct class, because it is common to find household members working in different occupational categories, and these differences are often to do with gender, age or the stages people are at in their careers (Garnsey, 1978; Abbott and Sapsford, 1987). Leaving aside the apparent sexism in the categorization, the effect of designating the class position of women in this way has been under-explored in education research. Age also compounds the difficulties when educational data have been compared with other national data to determine levels of representation of different social groups in higher education, because the age at which people are classified according to their own occupational position has varied from 18 years to 30 years across these data sets. Chapter 3 (page 56) has highlighted the use by UCAS of categories based on the highest earner in the household and the ambiguities and inconsistencies involved in this use, particularly for the classification of mature students. Interestingly, within the access discourse, the lack of an occupation, or rather being unemployed, has become the proxy for identifying those who might benefit from measures to increase their individual educational opportunities and for defining who are the working class for whom educational change is required. For example, although Benn and Burton (1995:8–11) acknowledged that the national framework for Access programmes was set up as an alternative route for social classes IV and V among other groups, in their analysis of their survey of Access course directors, these categories disappeared and the term 'unemployed' was used. It is not clear whether this term was derived from the practitioners or imposed by the researchers, but in reporting the study in this way in a journal aimed at practitioners, the account is an interesting example of how constructions of who should benefit from access are normalized and legitimized. Such repositioning, though, has not rendered class completely invisible. In Garner and Imeson's (1996:106) survey of Access tutors' views on the impact of new financial benefits rules, several tutors argued that it would 'fundamentally change the class balance of successful [Access] entrants.' These tutors had targeted the unemployed as a way of reaching the working class, and the benefits changes were regarded as reversing the principles of Access because only the financially independent would be able to afford to study.

Given the particular problems involved in research into social class participation in higher education, can *any* generalizations be made concerning the increase or decrease in such participation? A review of some recent work in this field has shown that those studies that have attempted to measure the effect of social class on participation have produced remarkably similar findings, even though they have used a variety of data sources. The findings are that social class inequalities have not changed substantially in spite of the expansion in the higher education system (Blackburn and Jarman, 1993; Egerton and Halsey, 1993). However, the study by Egerton and Halsey was based on General Household Survey Data for the period 1985–1987, which was just before the large-scale expansion in higher education had taken place, and the work of Blackburn and Jarman was based on a narrow construction of higher education. Their focus was the then university sector and full-time degrees, but was presented as indicative of the whole of 'UK higher education over the period 1938–1990' (Blackburn and Jarman, 1993:197). My concern is that in conflating the experience of full-time students in the then university sector with the whole of higher education, misleading generalizations will become part of the taken-for-granted knowledge of policy makers. Blackburn and Jarman (1993) derived most of their findings from data collected by an ESRC-funded survey in 1986 and analysed by Marsh and Blackburn (1992). From this study they observed that social inequalities in participation were reduced during times of expansion in the system so long as this was accompanied by funding for students in the form of grants, but that there was an increase in social inequalities when only one of these factors was in operation. This theory would be interesting to test across the whole system of higher education, particularly since the 1990s has become a period of consolidation and changes in student funding have been continuous. It needs to be developed further and tested by taking account of all sectors and forms of higher education and considering all categories of participating students. For example, the argument about the persistence of social class differentiation was based on data from the Oxford Mobility Study and drawn only from men (Blackburn and Jarman, 1993:199). Given the difficulties already described about the categorization of the social class position of women, to have relied, if only in part, on such a narrow data focus may have led to the conclusions about the persistence of social inequalities being either underplayed or overplayed. Once again, contradictions and ambiguities in research findings may have contributed to the legitimation of diverse claims.

Finally, the issue for the discourse of access is understanding how to interpret research findings on social class in higher education and what measures would indicate an increase in social justice or equity. For example, if the participation in higher education of certain class groups does not match their proportions in the general population, the system is considered to be unfair since a large pool of ability has been left untapped (Blackburn and Jarman, 1993). Particular voices in the discourse of access such as the liberal meritocrats and the access movement have used such research findings to support their arguments that large parts of the higher education system are elitist and certain groups (that is the working class) have traditionally been excluded on grounds of their class. The consequences for policy and practice, however, are not straightforward. Even those advocating radical change draw upon distinctly differing traditions and interpretations, one of which, as Chapter 2 highlighted, links with notions of collective empowerment and community development. For example, Parry (1996:12–13), in identifying the shifting boundaries of movements for access, suggested that the ideas of some practitioners could be traced back to early movements for working-class and popular education, and their engagement with students was collective and critical. Garner and Imeson (1996:98) positioned themselves in a similar way and argued that 'Access education must be understood in relation to the inequalities of the economic and social structure within which it operates and serves' and that 'the demand for genuine equality of opportunity in education . . . cannot be met by tinkering but only through radical and fundamental change.'

There are others within the access movement for whom the process of creating educational opportunities is more individual and less obviously identified with education for a social purpose. For example, Benn and Burton

(1995) found that the vast majority of Access practitioners they surveyed felt that the prime purpose of Access courses was to give individuals increased opportunities; only a small minority sought to change the position of designated social groups. Marketeers and trainers tend to ignore social class in any direct way, though there are clearly hidden class agendas in the notion of consumers and in an emphasis upon skills training. Current research, apart from studies such as those by Brown and Scase (1994), has done little to expose these hidden agendas. Key players can therefore continue to assert 'common sense' assumptions about the contexts within which consumer choices are made, the egalitarianism of student loans or the unimportance or non-existence of student poverty for example, without being subject to a rigorous and researched challenge.

Alternative entry project

Appendix 1 summarizes the history and reseach methods used in the alternative entry project from which this book has stemmed. It was an ambitious attempt to compare national and cross-sectional data on students entering higher education with alternative qualifications between 1991 and 1993. Thirteen institutions provided us with access to all their alternative entrants (3925) from whom we received 1145 questionnaire replies. The data generated by this project were based upon a different dividing practice, focusing on entry routes to higher education and linking these to the types of conceptualizations prevalent within the access discourse: that is to the categories of age, gender, 'race', class and educational qualifications. However, the focus was not simply on providing a more comprehensive map of who was participating in the expanded higher education system of the early 1990s, but was also on unpacking the notion of difference in a more complex way. The project sought to examine the experiences and backgrounds of those entrants who were frequently conceptualized as 'other'. These were the entrants that I argued earlier were described in many policy documents and research reports as non-standard or non-traditional because they had entered without the recognized qualifications of two A levels or their equivalent. The project attempted to clarify these divisions and to consider how these interconnected with age and notions of maturity, and other dimensions of life-chances. Only a few of the findings can be discussed here.

There was an attempt to redress the balance in the ways that researchers had complied with the institutionalization of categories for narrowly conceptualizing entrants in the system as inputs measured typically in terms of age, gender and 'race' to the neglect of class. This was done through questionnaires and interviews that not only compared such categories with other national data but at the same time collected additional information so that different conceptualizations of educational experiences, constraints and opportunities could be explored. Information was sought about the educational and occupational background of both of the entrants' parents and partners, as well as themselves, in an attempt to explore by such proxy measures the cultural capital of these alternative students. Currently, there is little empirical evidence about the relationship between a woman's own occupation and her educational ambitions and performance as an adult, or a mother's occupation and the educational achievements of her children. The value of our project was that it enabled greater explication of the meaning of the data that showed that participation rates had increased for women, ethnic minority groups and to some extent those from working-class backgrounds. In what ways were they 'new' or 'different' students? Importantly, they were 'new' entrants to higher education in the sense that they were the first generation of their family to study at this level. Three-quarters of the sample in 'old' universities and colleges and more than 80 per cent of those in ex-polytechnics had parents who had not been educated in higher education and nearly half of those parents who had studied for a degree had entered after a break from school (Webb *et al.*, 1994a). This notion of 'newness' is fairly straightforward to research and it is surprising that it has rarely been included in studies. In addition, the study identified a significant minority (15 per cent in the 'old' universities and colleges and 19 per cent in the then polytechnics) of alternative entrants who were young, under 21 years, which raised a question about the assumption in the access discourse that different/abnormal students are always mature (Webb *et al.*, 1994a).

Moreover, the project showed that when the social class and gender data on entry are examined using the dividing practice of alternative entry, the complexity and diversity of participation is made more explicit. For example, alternative and Access entrants appeared to come from two contrasting types of social groupings; the two largest groupings were those who at the time the entrants left school had fathers who had professional occupations and those who had skilled manual occupations (Webb *et al.*, 1994a). The groups that were missing were from the skilled non-manual and unskilled manual categories. This contrasts strongly with the social class profile that aggregated analyses of all entrants produced. It also differs widely from the profile which emerges when the alternative and Access entrants were classified according to their own occupations prior to entry to higher education, because in the then polytechnic sample by far the largest group consisted of those who had skilled non-manual occupations, and in the 'old' universities and colleges the majority had either skilled non-manual occupations or intermediate and supervisory positions. This confirms the argument that assessment of the impact of expansion needs to consider how many of the categories used in input measures cross cut, and challenges the over-generalization that alternative entry students are largely working class.

Age, gender, 'race' and class were interconnected in different ways across the population of alternative entrants. There was some support for the view that those from the higher social classes have a greater propensity to enter higher education when they are under 21 years of age, with progressively more from the lower social classes entering later (Metcalf, 1993:6), but not

all older entrants who entered in alternative ways fitted this model. A conclusion to be drawn from this is that there is a need for more caution in
assessments of whether or not the system has become accessible, and for
questions to be posed about the 'truth' of data that purport to show that
gender and 'race' are no longer issues in selection processes because women
and ethnic minorities are present in higher education in proportions that
are representative of their numbers in the population at large (HEFCE,
1996a). It is the interconnections between gender, race and class which are
crucial. Separate data sets tell us very little, though they are useful to policy-
makers selectively claiming virtue.

Finally, a further question that this project raised is about the ways that
alternative and Access routes are being used by different students for different purposes. Only qualitative data and analysis could explore these
questions and yet very often such discussions have been absent from assessments of social equity in the discourse of access. These issues will be taken
up in Chapter 7 when some of the findings about student identity will be
explored to consider how alternative are the students' self-conceptions.

Concluding remarks

In this chapter, the discourse of research on access has been examined in
order to consider how students, particularly those defined as 'other', 'alternative', 'abnormal' or 'illegitimate', have been categorized and framed. The
review of the research on access showed how the concerns of policy-makers
and planners have helped to shape research questions and the conceptualizations of students by funding and supporting particular kinds of research.
This has tended to be quantitative. This act of producing 'facts' that appear
to have general applicability has enabled the subject of the discourse to be
spoken about with authority and planned for in ways that have legitimacy.
Yet ambiguities and contradictions in the research have been highlighted,
particularly in the case of the quantitative data on gender, 'race' and social
class. Disability has more recently been added as worthy of study. Conceptual muddles and inconsistencies have been identified around the notions
of increasing and widening access and in the use of non-standard and non-
traditional categorizations. Such weaknesses, though, have not undermined
the power of such data to be used to sustain the different voices of the
discourse of access. HEFCE, for example, selectively uses particular pieces of
research to make the case that the under-representation of women and ethnic
minorities has largely been solved. The recruitment of socio-economic groups
III–V is still a problem, but one where 'success in increasing participation
from these groups may not depend solely on the activity of the HE sector;
action is required at an earlier stage in the education process' (HEFCE,
1996a:26). We are given the impression that institutional activity has achieved
all that could be expected of it in the current policy of consolidation and
funding regimes. Non-traditional students are referred to throughout the

report as a resource burden requiring extra costs and changes to teaching and the curriculum. It is the nature of the higher education experience itself which is now defined as the problem, not access. Thus, as particular data become the institutionalized way of categorizing inputs and outputs to the system, they gain a significance as measures of the effectiveness of access strategies and indicators of the 'value added'. Consequently, whoever has the power to legitimate the use of particular categories to measure the meaning of expansion is likely to have influence over the allocation of resources as the notion that 'access related objectives should be given greater weight in [the Council's] approach to funding' (HEFCE, 1996a:42) gains sway among the funders.

Finally, in reviewing some of the data from the 'Alternative Entry to Higher Education' project I have shown that the project was unable to completely disengage from the forces identified in the discourses above. The question that arises from this is how we as authors of this book have handled this issue. We have also been engaged in discursive practices in the ways in which we have constructed categories and used data to support our case. What we have tried to do though is be explicit about this and show that our framework has been the agenda of access, and so the foci have been access to and the accessibility of undergraduate study. These concerns have informed the rationale for our conceptualizations of students and reconstructions of national data. In addition, in the project we found that by constructing difference around entry qualifications, and by exploring the interconnections between a range of conceptualizations of difference designed to reflect students' experiences as well as positionality in the discourse, there was some evidence that 'alternative' students were different. In the next chapters these differences will be examined further to consider the part played by the discursive practices within institutions in shaping the profile of the participants.

5

Institutional Rhetorics and Realities

Jenny Williams

Introduction

The first four chapters have focused largely upon national agendas in higher education, the last three detailing the way in which the discourse of access has been constructed by differing players, in differing contexts and for differing purposes. The discourses of politics, of educational policy formation, of research and national statistics interweave and recombine in many alternative ways to provide the wider context for access debates. This chapter shifts the focus. It looks at a narrower but equally complex set of discourses: those within higher education institutions. It focuses upon the ways in which key players at different levels within institutions reflect and reinterpret the wider discourse, both in their promulgation of formal policies and in their practices. To what extent do institutional forms of agenda control exist and how successful are these in determining the practices of those who organize and deliver the admissions process? What differing discourses of selectivity and equity manifest themselves within higher education institutions?

I cannot, on the basis of one study, provide detailed answers to these questions. I can provide only an illustrative account, drawing upon the limited published material available and our own survey in 13 institutions. Scott (1995) outlined 17 distinct sub-sectors within British higher education, with differing histories, academic traditions and organizational forms. To take examples from all these sub-sectors would not have been possible. Instead I look particularly at some English institutions on either side of the old binary divide, asking how different their positions are within the discourse of access. Are the old university/polytechnic divisions deep and lasting and if so, in what ways? Is the move to a mass system taking place only within certain types of institution? The chapter begins by focusing upon the public discourse of mission statements and the precursors of these in charters and equal opportunities statements. It then turns to a discussion of the range of institutional discourses which affect admissions practices, such as those of strategic planning, student numbers, marketing, internal and external monitoring, quality and accountability and the management of admissions. It ends with a limited analysis of data from the 13 institutions studied and a more detailed look at one institution. The focus here is official documents, the discursive practices of institutional management as exemplified in their language and policies. Chapter 6 will spotlight practice at the level of departments and admissions tutors.

Institutional missions

The most succinct and public representation of an institutional discourse can be found in the mission statements published by higher education institutions. These have emerged in the last decade as a distillation of an institutional rationale. They 'should demonstrate a clear idea of the purposes and distinctive characteristics of the institution' (HEFCE, 1993). The aims, outlined by Peeke (1994), are to establish a sense of purpose, facilitate decision making and communication with outsiders, aid evaluation and monitoring and clarify marketing strategies. The origins of 'missions' lie within the world of large corporate business, and Peeke's outline of the ways they are to be understood illustrates the influence of both market rhetoric and business management on university practices. They symbolize, in their form rather than their content, a system which is supposed to be a consumer-led rather than producer-led service, which implies both a differentiation of the product on offer and the linking of this to a market segment. Later in the chapter I shall try to unpack who that consumer is and the implications for an understanding of access. Once the product is differentiated, then forms of accountability, particularly those which require evaluating 'fitness for purpose', become possible. For example, Peter Williams, Director of HEQC Quality Assurance group, in the introduction to *Learning from Audit* (HEQC, 1994:viii) stated that one of the basic principles of the national framework for audit is to 'take as a starting point an institution's own aims and objectives, rather than a "gold" standard against which to measure compliance.'

Prior to the emergence of mission statements, higher education institutions encapsulated key elements of their purposes and ethos in relation to access and equity within the discursive practices of equal opportunities statements and policies. Williams *et al.* (1989:11) provided a summary of responses collected in 1987 from 92 per cent of universities and polytechnics, responses elicited within this earlier equal opportunities framework. What this survey showed was a clear binary polarization of both understanding and acceptance of this discourse as relevant to higher education. Twenty-four of the 26 polytechnics replying to the survey stated that they had an equal opportunities policy, some however stemming from the position of staff as local authority employees. All those statements forwarded to the research team included designations of groups for whom 'equal opportunities' was seen to be particularly relevant in the sense that they experienced both direct and indirect discrimination. Here is an illustrative example of part of such a policy:

> The polytechnic affirms its commitment to the equal treatment of all human beings regardless of their sex, age, race, ethnic or national origins, colour, marital status, sexual orientation, family responsibility, physical and sensory disability, political or religious beliefs and activities, unless those activities are contrary to the policies of the polytechnic.

Twenty-three out of the 42 universities replying denied both the existence of any such equivalent policy, but more importantly the relevance of such a statement to them as institutions. (ibid:12):

> Discrimination on the grounds of race, sex, religion or social origins is quite incompatible with the spirit of university life.

> Equality of opportunity is inherent in the concept of a university [*sic*].

> This formal policy [the university charter] has not been developed . . . although it still represents the university's formal position. Acceptance on a course of study in the university is solely by academic performance in qualifying examinations. The university does not seek to make allowance for poor qualifications on the basis of the applicants background.

The differences in discursive practices between the two sectors in 1987 were stark, even in response to research conducted under the auspices of the Commission for Racial Equality. The tone of the replies from many old universities was a mixture of indignation and incomprehension. The traditionalist academic discourse of merit as measured in a specific, 'qualifying' examination was seen as unproblematic and demonstrated a commitment to equity. The majority of the then polytechnics subscribed to a liberal meritocratic version of equity, a widening of the notion of 'merit' and an acceptance that the race was not an equal one. There were elements in a few statements of a more radical approach, one which echoed the position of the access movement, in particular the clear acceptance of the effects of structural inequalities:

> Nationally there is clear evidence of inequality in life chances, including inequality of opportunity in education on the basis of colour, sex, ethnic origin, age, social class and physical disability. Such inequalities are, in part, the consequence of direct and indirect discrimination within many institutions, including educational institutions.

To what extent has the polarization of the 1980s been softened with the ending of the binary divide? Virtually all universities now have equal opportunities policies (HEQC, 1994). HEFCE itself has published an EO statement for use in quality assessment (1996b), but do mission statements continue to reflect the pre-1992 divide and if so, how? They are accessible public statements, usually short and are provided, together with a history and structure of each institution, by HEFCE (1994), in a summary publication which lists

148 institutions in England. From this 148 I have omitted 46 specialist colleges or postgraduate institutions and concentrated this analysis of mission statements on 36 new universities, 43 old universities and 23 colleges of higher education. The language of mission statements could be studied in many different ways and with insights gained from many differing academic traditions. For example, a detailed linguistic study 'Missioning Democracy' is being undertaken by Connell and Galinski (1996). Smith *et al.* (1995) looked at the history and function of statements and undertook an analysis of their content in terms of status and market position, intentions and management style. The focus in this chapter is more limited. It has two main aims: the first is to examine certain icon words outlined in Chapter 2; the second is to question whether such uses relate to the binary or tripartite divisions within higher education. Initially, therefore, the inclusion of particular words or phrases within mission statements was counted.

Sixteen of the 36 new universities used the words 'access', 'accessibility' or 'wider access' in their mission statements, whereas only three of the 43 old universities did so. Warwick University claimed to be distinctive because of its ability both to be rated in the top group in the research assessment exercise and to be giving high priority to improving access. In contrast, 24 of the 43 old universities prioritized excellence in both teaching and research, whereas only four new universities did so. This was the sharpest divide, as those old universities which did not the use the word 'excellence' used instead words like 'scholarship', 'advancement of knowledge' and even 'wisdom'. Only four new universities dared to use such words. Thus there still seems to be a polarization of access and excellence which was noted in Chapter 2. Only very rarely were the selective consequences of 'excellence' spelled out, notably by Durham University in its aim to recruit 'top quality students and staff.' Brighton was the only new university attempting to combine 'excellence' with 'accessibility', but unusually added, 'to all who can benefit' as a rider. Most new universities used no such qualifiers. Eight colleges of higher education included an access statement but the distinctiveness of this sector can be found much more in its professional or vocational aims and in its presentation of student-centredness:

> The college is a learning community in which all staff and students are involved and can learn from each other.
>
> (La Sainte College of HE)

> Nene College accepts its responsibilities to develop students' capabilities and to empower them to achieve their fullest potential as individuals and members of society.
>
> (Nene College of HE)

Many such colleges are religious foundations and so included explicit reference to a particular denominational focus and/or spiritual values. In other aspects of mission statement language there was less difference between old and new universities. More old universities (18) acknowledged their national and international status and more new universities (19) prioritized their contribution to their local and regional hinterland. But both included industrial and commercial elements in their mission and economic and professional services in terms of students' vocational skills:

> The objects of the university shall be to advance learning and knowledge by teaching and research, particularly in science and technology, and in close association with industry and commerce . . . the application of knowledge to useful ends.
>
> (University of Bath)

> The university's mission is to serve the needs of industry, commerce, the professions and the country as a national and international institution.
>
> (University of Huddersfield)

The differing emphasis contained within these two quotations is important. The first suggests that the core purpose of the university can be of use to industry; the second that industry will determine the core purposes.

Who is positioned as the prime consumer of education or university services is a particularly interesting question but one which is complex, as many mission statements deliberately include a range of targets, with no clear prioritization. However, reading them one gets some sense of the differing audiences, the differing 'market positions' they are speaking to. The majority of old universities are speaking to an international and national academic community, to current and potential teachers and researchers. The relevance of their work to other audiences is very important but it is a by-product, not its rationale. The majority of new university missions are speaking to a range of audiences within their locality: to traditional 18-year-old A level candidates; to older students whose families have no or little tradition of higher education; and to employers needing particular sorts of trained labour. Colleges of higher education also speak to students, but with a greater emphasis upon both their spiritual learning and/or vocational needs. Of course, institutions are also speaking to each other and positioning themselves within alternative hierarchies which particular phrases represent. The binary and tripartite divisions were still visible in 1994 but in a more complex way than in my 1987 study. The sharpest contrast was in the inclusion of 'excellence' or 'access' as signifiers of an equity position.

Other interpretations of the words and phrases outlined here have been used as part of the discourses of derision referred to in Chapter 2. Earwaker (1991), for example, ridiculed polytechnic mission statements in the *THES*:

> Anyone who still hankers for traditional values of independent scholarship, academic community, or education as intrinsically worthwhile will find their worst fears confirmed. . . . The barbarians have taken over with the advent of incorporation.

He distinguished what he called 'hurrah words': international, technology, market-oriented, cost-effective for example, from 'boo words' such as academic community, scholarship, learning, and student welfare. The dominance of the hurrah words was explained in terms of political expediency overcoming academic integrity! Though mission statements, as was suggested by Peeke (1994), are linked with marketing strategies and represent an extension of business practice to education, the language of the marketeers was, in spite of Earwaker's assertions, hardly represented. The term 'consumer' was used only once, and South Bank University was unique in referring to its students as its 'clients and its products'. 'Enterprise' was mentioned only twice. Services were provided, but much less so than teaching and learning and research. Nor was the earlier language of equal opportunities very visible, the phrase being used only three times and 'equality' once. 'Mass' higher education occurred three times, all in the new university sector. Smith *et al.* (1993) also noted this tendency. They looked in their study of mission statements for the terms 'mass', 'comprehensive' and 'lifelong learning' and found them very rarely. It is to other internal discourses that we have to turn to trace further connections with national discourse positions. Scott (1995) raised a crucial point, concerning who writes mission statements. He suggested they are executive statements, emanating from top management, and so reflect changing patterns of authority within higher education, in particular the development of non-academic forms of authority. The increasing dominance of strategic and executive management, which is bureaucratic and hierarchical, Scott did not see as a permanent trend, but one which, while it lasts, will influence the public discourse and discursive practices of institutions. The way mission statements have been written was the subject of Peeke's (1994) study. He provided case studies illustrating their differing nature and form depending upon who participated in their construction. Rarely was participation extensive; in the majority of cases they were the public face of the directorate.

Mission statements are reinterpreted, prioritized and translated into resourced policies in strategic plans. But strategic plans, produced almost exclusively by top management, are designed largely for an internal audience, or for a different external audience concerned with finance, audit and assessment of 'fitness for purpose'. Unfortunately in this study I was unable to scrutinize strategic plans and have to rely on other researchers to provide insights into their relationship to access and equity. Smith *et al.* (1993:321) studied 118 mission statements and 76 strategic plans in order 'to assess the extent to which an ethos of access has penetrated the official statements of purpose and planning in a broad range of institutions.' The numbers making a commitment to 'wider' access in strategic plans were very high, with 87 per cent of universities and 100 per cent of ex-polytechnics doing so. Those groups targeted comprised mature students, part-time students and those with non-traditional qualifications, with over half of the older universities naming such groups. By far the most popular strategy for achieving these aims was to increase the numbers of courses on offer, but with the older universities outstripping the other sectors in plans for modularization. The authors of this survey, even when including strategic plans within their analysis, and finding much rhetorical commitment to widening access, suggested that much less will be delivered in practice. They undertook their study at the point of greatest government encouragement for expansion, and it was this, they suspected, which determined the language of planning:

> Such commitments, however, have to be set in the context of government induced expansionary policies. Indeed, attempts to widen access to a broader constituency of students may be seen as a rational strategy given the need to increase recruitment generally.

> (ibid:124–5)

HEFCE (1996b:27) highlighted a contrast between mission statements and strategic plans, suggesting that the access radicalism of mission statements was often not carried through into the prioritization and resources embodied in strategic plans. Only 18 per cent of institutions had identified specific targets for the recruitment of non-traditional students. What else therefore influences institutional admissions policies, internal planning and actual practices? How does the institutionalization of access objectives work in differing institutions?

Contextual discourses

This section attempts to answer the above questions. What are the alternative national and institutional discourses which frame admissions policy and practice? We can only understand the discursive practices of admissions tutors (the subject of the next chapter) if we understand the complex and often contradictory internal and external discourses which they are expected to reconcile. They are positioned by these discourses in ways which affect quite crucially their mechanisms of selection and the legitimation of these to their peers and external agencies.

Numbers and marketing

Clearly a very powerful discourse which affects the institutional operation of admissions is that emanating from the detailed control by government over student numbers. The changing nature of these numbers, from contraction in the early 1980s through expansion in the early 1990s to consolidation in the mid-1990s via MASN (maximum aggregate student numbers) has meant that there is a crucial institutional discourse around meeting targets, around the financial penalties of under- or over-recruiting. There is a 'selectors' discourse, exemplified by Pickering and Gardner (1992) and discussed in Chapter 6, consequent upon this control over numbers which is quite different from the demographic discourse of the mid- to late 1980s, when a dramatic decline in the numbers of 18-year-olds led to some fears for institutional survival. Mature students and Access students in particular were then often seen as 'saviours'. Hollinshead and Griffiths (1990) for example, produced a report for CDP, PCAS and CNAA on mature student marketing and admissions. Though mature students comprised 25 per cent of full-time first-year entrants to degree courses in polytechnics at the time, their numbers had only risen by 1 per cent between 1984 and 1989. The authors therefore argued that special marketing strategies were needed to attract such entrants, that central institutional policies should be developed to deliver an expansion, and staff should be trained to implement these policies. Thus internal institutional access discourse will vary depending upon the retrenchment/expansion/consolidation funding policies of governments, the demographic context within which these operate and the extent of the selective nature of admissions in particular institutions (Ainley, 1994).

Particular institutional policies, highlighted in publicity material, illustrate the ways in which attempts to signal market position are also strategies for controlling both the number and types of entrants, and ways of holding on to a particular market share (Stowell, 1992; Fairclough, 1993). Four particular strategies may be highlighted. The first, partly illustrated in the discussion on mission statements, emphasizes elite academic status and reflects the academic traditionalist discourse at the national level. Research ratings will be used as part of this strategy. Admissions tutors will wish to increase their share of good A level candidates (Fulton and Ellwood, 1989) and will operate largely within the logic of points score = quality and selectivity = the best. Pickering and Gardner (1992:232) put it succinctly: 'The task for selectors is not to challenge elitism, but to identify the elite as efficiently and fairly as they can.'

A second institutional strategy can perhaps be labelled a technical/structural approach, with an emphasis upon CATS, APEL, GNVQ, modularity, etc. Publicity will emphasize different ways into the institution or pathways through degree study. Admissions tutors will be expected to be familiar with the language of credits, of prior learning, of learning outcomes. The language of selectivity, of differentiation and normalization will be quite different; the ways of assessing 'ability to benefit' legitimated in different ways. Outreach is a third approach, where Access consortia, Year 0/foundation courses, franchising or compacts with feeder institutions will be of prime importance. These initiatives clearly represent ways of guaranteeing a local or particular market. The taking of further education colleges into university control, beginning to occur in 1996, develops this local market control even further. SCUE/Open College/PCAS (1992:21) suggested, with very little supporting evidence, that compacts, which are based on a special relationship between an institution and a school or college, 'will improve the flow of under-represented groups into higher education.' Stowell (1992) saw them as a form of positive action. The language of admissions tutors, their understanding of access and equity, will again be different as a consequence of an outreach strategy. If they are expected to engage with such activities, to be part of the process which delineates and validates what preparation for higher education means, then the language of threshhold competencies, of generic and specific subject skills, will be part of their vocabulary. The discursive practices which are integral to both the technical and outreach strategies can and do claim legitimacy from several of the access positions outlined in Chapter 2. They may be justified by liberal meritocratic or market rhetoric.

Finally, there may be a strategy of 'accessibility', of looking at the nature of the institution and the ways it responds to the needs of a wide range of potential applicants. In particular, advice, guidance and counselling will be prioritized, possibly together with child care provision and almost certainly the range of curriculum combinations/subjects on offer, provided by part-time routes, sub-degrees or in part by open learning alternatives where possible. What may well happen is that aspects of this 'accessibility' become professionalized within particular services and fail to permeate the whole institution. Stowell (1992) for example, argued that special initiatives often leave traditional admissions practices untouched. HEFCE (1996b) located the 'problem' of widening access firmly within institutional initiatives, describing many of the strategies highlighted here as examples of either specific or indirect action. Institutional strategies to guarantee the recruitment of externally imposed student numbers, to expand or contract intakes, become manifest through marketing priorities. These priorities encapsulate typifications of potential students, of what and where key markets are, and the discourse of admission will, at least in part, reflect these strategies.

The management of access/admissions

We have already seen that differing perceptions of institutional goals emerge from studies of mission statements and strategic plans. Few institutions have formal admissions policies with clearly delineated implementation strategies. Peinovich (1996) provided an interesting study of what 'openness' to mature learners might mean in theory and the muddle evidenced in institutional practices. Three contrasting ideal-type management forms can be usefully highlighted here, though the range of actual forms is clearly far greater than this. The first model is that of a decentralized system historically common in the older universities, where admission decisions are an integral part of academic control over a subject area. Only a relevant subject academic can assess the potential of applicants to flourish within a particular subject environment. Any attempt to remove this control is fought hard, though the intrusion of UCAS and MASN and the huge increase in numbers applying have eroded it considerably. Academic decisions on particular candidates may well be taken only at the margins, only the 'non-standard' students interviewed (see Chapter 6) and the rest, the anonymous majority, given point scores to achieve. 'The result is that in most places institutional policy is still in an important sense the sum of the policies of separate departments' (Fulton and Ellwood, 1989:22). In such a decentralized system the discursive practices of institutional managers form the peripheral noise of admissions rather than its central thrust.

The second model is a move to a centralization of admissions, which appears to have its origin in three quite different rationales: the bureaucracy necessary to comply with the UCAS system, the perceived failure of a decentralized system to deliver an access mission, plus the complexity of admissions decision-making in a large modular system. Robertson (1994:250) illustrated the rationale for such a system, necessitating the removal of discretion from admissions tutors in order that 'the admissions process can become the process of inclusion rather than exclusion.' Few institutions have moved to a completely centralized system, the struggle for power and costs involved being the main reasons. The discursive practices of this struggle around academic values, academic integrity, and collegiate responsibility resonate with a national discourse and with subject-specific discourses. Only a very few institutional managers appear to wish to fight such a battle head-on.

The third and probably most common model of access management is that of the 'strategic by-pass': a separate individual or unit is given cross-institutional responsibility for initiatives to recruit mature and/or non-traditional students. Thompson and Parry (1992) undertook a very detailed study of the majority of universities and polytechnics, showing 74 per cent of institutions had one or more members of staff with such a responsibility, and 82 per cent were members of some kind of access consortium. At one level, therefore, an access mission has been institutionalized, but often ghettoized in particular corners. However, these large percentages hide very distinct patterns. Historically, in the older universities, continuing education departments were the providers of adult, part-time, usually non-accredited courses. Both Duke (1994) and Tight (1991) have stressed the neglected history of this type of part-time provision. But by and large continuing education left the 'normal' admissions processes for undergraduates intact. Access units on the other hand were designed to impact on 'normal' admissions. They ranged from one person to the Liverpool John Moores version with 45 staff at one time. Thompson and Parry (1992) provided a very useful model of the varieties of ways in which such strategic by-pass initiatives were integrated within institutions. Through such processes of management control over admissions, differing discourses enter, compete and become dominant or peripheral within higher education institutions. They legitimate or undermine differing elements within contrasting discourse positions. Different forms of institutionalization rely on different forms of compliance and legitimation processes (Marshall, 1990).

Quality monitoring

Internal institutional structures, of necessity, have had to respond to external monitoring, particularly the new forms instituted by HEQC and HEFC. In what ways are institutions accountable for their access/admissions delivery? At one level their forms of selectivity are available for public scrutiny.

Applications and admissions data are collected nationally via UCAS and HESA and published. Particular ways of categorizing students have emerged which are clearly responses to notions of under-representation and social justice (see Chapter 4). The Commission for Racial Equality did undertake a formal investigation into the admissions practice of one higher education institution (CRE, 1988), but such forms of public scrutiny are rare. Institutional audits undertaken by HEQC are another form of external assessment, this time of quality and 'fitness for purpose'. The discourse of quality has come to permeate higher education, in disparate ways, illustrated in such phrases as academic quality or total quality management. What is interesting for our discussion here is that in *Learning from Audit* (HEQC, 1994), a snapshot of quality assurance in 69 institutions audited to that point, Chapter 9 is headed 'Admissions, diversity, promotional materials and equal opportunities.' It contains the statement that admissions had not been prioritized in audit work, and simply gives a list of access initiatives undertaken in some institutions. The chapter also goes on to say, 'the audit reports advised universities that had recently increased the numbers of non-traditional [*sic*] students to ensure that they had the capacity to monitor the quality of experience of these new groups of students' (HEQC, 1994:45). From both these statements it appears that quality monitoring around admissions has been less than rigorous. This may change shortly with guidelines published by HEQC (1996) concerning admissions policy and practice.

Is monitoring used internally in a more rigorous and systematic way? Data collected by UCAS or for HESA or for the Continuous Student Record can be disaggregated for internal purposes. Are they used as part of the public face, the mission of the institution? In policy formation? For funding mechanisms? For department/subject accountability? We did not have the resources to provide detailed answers to these questions. Published accounts suggest that internal monitoring is extremely limited. Allen (1992:38), talking just about polytechnics but with very detailed data on their access activities, was struck by how little was internally monitored: 'It is perhaps too often simply assumed that approaches such as access courses, modularity and CATS widen participation.' Fulton and Ellwood (1989) supported this interpretation, going as far as to suggest that internal financial measures such as rewarding departments that recruited the non-traditionally qualified, would both necessitate using monitoring and reward the virtuous. Stowell (1992:78) phrased her admonitions in the form of good practice alternatives: 'Clear and systematically applied admissions criteria, training of admissions tutors and the monitoring of applications and offers are essential prerequisites to the implementation of a target managed approach to widen access.' Because the internal use of monitoring is limited, and because external quality audits have not prioritized admissions, the discourse of access within institutions can replicate many of the assumptions and contradictions highlighted earlier in this book, but in a localized form – that entry qualifications are clearly and unambiguously related to degree output, for example. Normalization processes and compliance can rest on the silences of the national discourse.

The admissions process: the legitimation of selection

Chapter 6 will provide a detailed account from our empirical study of the gatekeeping role of admissions tutors. In this section I wish simply to illustrate the ways in which institutional discourses impinge upon the admissions process. As we have seen, this is not an easy process to describe as there are many positions within this discourse which will be manifest within one institution. Management and subject lecturers may disagree on the meanings of merit or equity. The imposition of, or resistance to, certain meanings may be part of a wider struggle over changing forms of management. Subject staff may frame their meanings within a wider subject discourse with which they identify, rather than in response to the institution within which they temporarily reside. However, most studies of the admissions process suggest that it is framed by an academic elitist tradition, or at the most there are two approaches, a traditional elitist and an equal opportunity approach. Clarke (1995), in making this distinction, suggested the crucial difference is in an understanding of equity. It is represented either by A levels as a neutral and fair predictor of future success or the identification of a wide range of criteria capable of demonstrating ability to benefit. Smith *et al.* (1995) suggested the distinction is a product of a sponsored or an open mobility system, thus linking the admissions process with wider institutional frameworks. Stowell (1992) included political ideologies within her typology, contrasting a liberal view of formal equality with a substantive, radical view which judges on the basis of outcomes, identifying processes of structural and indirect discrimination.

These binary typologies are often linked to the pre-1992 binary divide, exemplified in the study of Home Counties and Inner City universities by Ainley (1994) and in HEFCE (1996b). Thus the argument appears to be that the selection process is framed by an institutional ethos which stems from a historical position in the structuring of higher education. But the shift from a more to a less elitist system, towards a mass system of higher education has, as Chapter 2 demonstrated, altered the nature of the discourse around selectivity. What appears to be the case is that a range of alternative discourse positions have permeated institutions in particular ways, have been appropriated (normalized) by managers, but have had a limited effect upon other staff members. As was outlined earlier in this chapter, mission statements emanate from corporate managements; they are very rarely the product of widespread collective discussion; they are not owned by the majority of staff and do not clearly represent their views. Nor perhaps are they designed to. The relationship between institutional planning and the implementation of access strategies and targets is limited and sporadic. There is therefore in most institutions space for other discourse positions, for admissions tutors to use language and develop practices at odds with or different from those of their managers.

> Different academic disciplines develop different criteria for evaluating the capabilities or intelligence of the students who apply to them. These same criteria are then applied by staff in reaching their judgements of student performance. In other words, the staff are agents in constructing – through the processes of selection and assessment – the structural positions of their institutions in the newly defined hierarchy of competing universities and colleges. Not only staff but students also collude as agents in consolidating institutional identities which are socially distinctive.
>
> (Ainley, 1994:120)

Comparative data – thirteen institutions

The introductory paragraph to this chapter asked whether institutional forms of agenda control concerning access existed, what forms they took and how successful they were in determining the practices of different actors. So far I have tried to tease out the complexity of these agendas. A review of other studies has suggested a lack of coherence, at a minimum a differentiation between management, marketing and admissions discourse. A recurring theme was a differentiation across the pre-1992 binary divide, a strong suggestion that there was a patterning of discourses which was different in each sector, with the implication that recruitment outcomes would therefore be similarly distinct. This section provides a very limited test of these assumptions stemming from our empirical study of 13 institutions. We collected data on the entry routes of first-year full-time undergraduates and so were able to compare public rhetoric, in mission statements for example, with practice. We were not able to undertake a detailed examination of the range of institutional discourses in the 13 differing settings. We were however able to look at sectoral divisions, mission, locale, academic structures and modes of course delivery.

We collected data on entrants with two or more A levels or their vocational equivalents, recognized Access certificates and those with 'alternative' qualifications (see Preface). Among the seven 'new universities', alternative entrants comprised between 4.9 per cent and 24.6 per cent, and Access entrants between 1.6 per cent and 7.6 per cent of all first-year full-time degree entrants. Among the three 'old' universities, the proportion of Access entrants varied from 0.9 per cent to 3.5 per cent and the latter figure represented a higher proportion than in two of the 'new' universities. Similarly the proportion of alternative entrants varied from 0.9 per cent to 6.1 per cent and the latter was higher than in one of the 'new' universities. Among the three colleges of higher education, one in particular recruited a lower proportion of Access entrants than any of the 'new' universities and a higher proportion of alternative entrants than six of the seven 'new' universities. Thus it is clear that comparing sectors does not adequately explain patterns of recruitment from different qualification routes. Indeed, generalization to sectoral level disguises an interesting variation between institutions. (See Appendix 1, Tables 1 and 2, for further summary data.)

Unfortunately there were no easy and obvious answers as to why the 13 institutions differed so significantly in their student intakes. There was no discernible relationship with size or location. The presence of a flourishing Open College or AVA locally was not directly linked to the proportion of Access students recruited. The mission statements of the 13 were scrutinized carefully. Five of the seven new universities included words such as access, accessibility or open, highlighted earlier in this chapter as indicating a particular mission stance. But the institution with the highest percentages of alternative and Access students did not include any such commitment in its mission statement. All of the old universities used the language of excellence and scholarship, but the one which also made claim to fostering access had the lowest percentage of alternative and Access students of all 13 institutions. Two of the colleges of higher education made reference to scholarship and excellence in academic provision, two to openness and improving access. One did not mention access at all and yet had the highest number of Access entrants of the three. Thus mission gives us only partial and often misleading clues to practice.

Were there any more useful predictors? The development of modular programmes and facilitators such as CATS or APEL systems did not appear to be as important as the discourse of management, highlighted earlier, suggested. This is a very difficult area to unpack. Justificatory discursive practices concerning innovations may not be aimed at delivering widespread institutional change. Or there may be resistance and negation in practice. One possible explanation highlights the differing ways in which the discursive practices of 'ability to benefit' and 'threshold competencies', for example, interact with the discourses of academic disciplines. Some disciplines or awards define relevant entry competencies far more widely than others. Entry to teacher training for example, with the requirement to ascertain suitability for a teaching career, is assessing a very different range of factors than is mathematics. Education programmes tend to recruit significant numbers of Access students and some institutions have no such provision. So the subject profile may affect the institutional profile. However, in some subjects offered by all institutions, widely differing proportions of alternative and Access students were recruited. In engineering and technology for example, the proportions varied from 2 to 40 per cent, with all three older universities recruiting *higher* proportions than five of the new universities. In science the proportions ranged from 2 per cent of the intake to 20 per cent, again with considerable overlap between the old and the new sectors.

Three particular processes stood out as deserving further scrutiny, providing possible ways of understanding the above data. The first stems from the practice of monitoring highlighted in Chapter 3. Very variable care was taken over the collection of data within institutions, even when these data

were for outside agencies such as CSR or the FESR. An error rate of between 8 and 20 per cent was uncovered in this project among the 'new'
universities, and in one 'old' university the definition of non-standard students initially included those with two or three A levels but without maths
or English at O level, and one institution aggregated all BTEC qualifications together, whatever their level. There were also differences in the way
institutions treated intermediate awards. For example, some registered
students for a Diploma in Higher Education in the first instance and
then transferred them to a degree programme at the end of two years if
they continued; they were thus excluded from the count of entrants to
first degrees. Other institutions registered them for a first degree with an
opt-out after two years with a DipHE; they were thus included in the count
of entrants to first degrees. Similar kinds of problems arose with the way
in which entrants to Foundation Year/Year 0 were treated relative to the
entrants to Year 1 of the same degree programme. Thus the management
of access manifests itself in institutional data. The low priority given to
accurate monitoring in resource allocation is important in understanding
discursive practices around access. To be able to claim virtue seems to be
more important than an ability to demonstrate it!

The second key factor appeared to be the extent of autonomy exercised
by subject/course/award admissions tutors. The complexities of management
control through centralized systems or strategic by-pass initiatives have been
discussed earlier. Our data clearly showed the extent of subject variability
in who was recruited. How was this related to the level of demand for a subject? Low demand subjects did not necessarily recruit more alternative and
Access students. Detailed analysis of the 'new' university data, using PCAS
ratios of applicants to admissions as a base-line, showed that among low
demand subjects, the alternative entrants sample was higher than the national
average in maths, IT and computing, but significantly lower in engineering
and technology and built environment. Among the high demand subjects
the position is again mixed: the proportion of alternative entrants is lower
than average in business and management but higher than average in science,
art and design and education. Such data do not demonstrate any simplistic
relationship between demand and the admission of alternative entrants.
Thus discursive practices highlighting the link between competitiveness and
selectivity bear only an indirect relationship to practice at this aggregate level.

The third factor linked with institutional variability connects with the
discursive practices of both management and disciplines. What become
institutionalized are labelling processes which associate particular sorts of
students with particular sorts of courses in certain institutions. Thus the
majority of sub-degree mandatory award study, whether Diploma in Higher
Education (DipHE), Higher National Diploma (HND) or Higher National
Certificate (HNC) and part-time degree study takes place in the 'new'
universities, being part of the history of polytechnic provision. The range
of alternative pathways on offer, in terms of mode or level, impacts on first
degree recruitment, either providing initial entrants or siphoning them off

into a 'more appropriate' pathway. Data in one institution were collected on all non-two A level entrants on four pathways: full-time degrees, part-time degrees, full-time sub-degrees and part-time sub-degrees. This is summarized in Table 3 in Appendix 1. The importance of the sub-degree study pathway is clear from these comparative figures: 47 per cent of full-time sub-degree entrants came via an alternative or Access route. Yet studies of this pathway have been extremely limited (Smithers, 1990, is an exception). The numbers of students moving from sub-degree to degree study is likely to be far larger than those entering via Access courses. Yet the research discourse, and to a large extent the political discourse of access ignores them. Similarly part-time non-certificated continuing education, historically provided largely by the older universities, is rarely included in the discourse of access. Its impact as a route into full-time study therefore is hidden; it is largely uncounted and unacknowledged. Thus forms of differentiation, historically institutionalized in particular sectors, may or may not be counted by particular institutions within their access mission.

Institutional case study

Because of the complexity of processes outlined in the previous section, it was decided that an in-depth study in one institution would allow for an exploration of the interlinkings between aspects of institutional power, varieties of discourse positions and a range of discursive practices. Quantitative data were collected from the chosen institution in 1992. Interviews and documentary analysis continued until the end of 1995. It is presented as a test case for the contextual analysis just outlined. How do the discursive practices of mission, numbers, marketing, the management of admissions, monitoring and quality interweave to frame a particular admissions system?

The institution produced two mission statements in the 1990s. The first prioritized the extension of open access and equal opportunities. It included a vision statement with the aim to become 'the best mass higher education institution in Europe'. The second, which involved more internal consultation, removed this particular vision and the term 'mass higher education' but still included both equal opportunities and access as key priorities, drawing upon a high equal opportunities profile, with a policy and unit initially established in 1986. The current equal opportunities statement, part of which is reproduced below, spells out both a radical 'access mission' philosophy and the institutional understanding of accessibility and equity.

> The University is committed to working towards the creation of additional educational and employment opportunities for groups currently under-represented among students and staff and to ensuring that access to these opportunities is not obstructed by conditions or requirements that cannot be justified. The widening of access to the institution will be encouraged by policies and practices which foster accessibility to:

- information;
- guidance;
- funding and financial support;
- admissions procedures;
- credit for existing skills and knowledge;
- relevant knowledge and curricula;
- buildings;
- a variety of courses and modes of study;
- differing learning processes;
- a supportive environment;
- a variety of certification and accreditation mechanisms;
- a range of vocational and occupational outcomes.

The access mission is overt and widely publicized, for example the 1994 Annual Review, a glossy public document detailing the strengths of the institution, began by highlighting 'structural' and 'targeting' measures to enhance open access and equal opportunities:

> Assisted by further developments in the innovative Modular Degree Scheme, the University's track record for extending access to higher education to 'non-traditional' students remains impressive. It has improved the opportunities for study for more people by opening between 9am and 9pm and delivering study in the workplace through credit accumulation and transfer. The university was ranked second out of 97 institutions for 'adding value' by the Times 1994 Guide to Universities. The University redoubled its efforts to recruit more ethnic minority students by launching a two-stage marketing strategy to recruit more Afro-Caribbean students across the board and to target specific courses where ethnic minority recruitment is traditionally low.

At the level of public rhetoric and policy statements therefore, the access mission is clearly visible. How does it manifest itself in the discourse of managers, strategic planning and the allocation of resources?

In the context of government encouragement to expand student intakes, but a lowering of the unit of resource, increasing access becomes part of remaining financially viable; in the context of consolidation, of financial punishment for over- and under-recruiting, maintaining access takes on a more desperate resonance. 'Maintaining a market share', 'ring-fencing a local area', 'subjects in penalty', 'refocusing upon traditional 18-year-old students', become part of the language of managers negotiating numbers for their academic schools. Full-time student targets have become more precise and expansion linked primarily to part-time or full-cost students. As the expansionary markets change so does the language of access. The delivery of part-time, in-house company training schemes becomes very clearly included in the notion of widening access. Part-time vocational qualifications are defined as 'added value' for those previously excluded by full-time jobs from this process. Who is prioritized within the numbers game therefore alters the meaning given to 'access'.

Linked with the discourse of numbers is clearly that of publicity and marketing. Earlier in this chapter four differing marketing strategies were outlined. This institution uses three of the four. The focus upon 'accessibility' was spelled out in the documents quoted earlier. The technical/structural approach is evident in a range of sub-degree study, a very large modular scheme with over 6000 modules in 90 subject areas and specialist CATS, APL and APEL staff employed within a continuing education unit. Thus marketing will focus upon both routes into and pathways through advanced study. But it is the outreach approach which is strongest and most clearly developed. A town centre higher education shop was established in 1988 and has continued to expand in terms of staff and services. During 1994/5 between 8000 and 9000 individuals were counselled by staff, with over 20,000 calling in or phoning to obtain leaflets or forms. Other elements of the outreach strategy include providing a 'home' and support from 1987 for the local and now regional Open College network which comprises 21 colleges and three higher education institutions, in the employment of school/college liaison staff and new outreach venues in towns in the region.

It is a marketing strategy, however, which now frames both the access discourse within the institution and the discursive practices which justify the above allocation of resources and the prioritization of activities. This is exemplified by the role of the Counselling and Guidance Service, which runs the higher education shop, the personal and financial counselling system for existing students and the Equal Opportunities Unit, and administers the access fund. Its head, who is responsible to the Pro Vice Chancellor for Marketing and Development, holds a pivotal role spanning both access and marketing remits. He produces numerous reports, in which the drive both to maintain the traditional access mission and adjust to new consolidation targets is clear:

> Access policy must be safeguarded. If the policy is adversely affected as part of short term strategic response to the need to reduce numbers, we run the risk of damaging long term credibility among a number of vital client groups. Within the local area we top the league for the proportion of students who can be defined as mature. We enjoy a national reputation for excellence in access. Future well being will depend as much upon the diversity of student intake as on absolute numbers.
>
> (Planning Review, 1994/5)

A whole range of action strategies are suggested in the review to prevent a reduction in numbers falling exclusively on the non-traditional applicant market. For example:

> Within reduced targets explore the notion of positive discrimination in favour of 'local' applicants who are more likely to accept offers
>
> continue to develop initiatives aimed at ring fencing the local catchment area

provide centralised evening counselling service for part time enquirers
...
(Planning Review, 1994/5)

Though the language of markets has permeated such institutional documents, it is not that of 'the marketeers' in its entirety. The contradictions
highlighted in Chapter 2 are manifest. The market, local this time, needs
to be 'managed', to be protected. The legitimation for targets is numbers,
not a political or moral ideology. There is also an acceptance that many
consumers cannot afford the product on offer and are having their choices
limited by new funding systems. Thus a combination of a historical access
mission, provided within a liberal/meritocratic institutional framework,
framed by the market position of a new university, has produced a particular set of discursive practices which clearly merit much further analysis than
could be given here. The complexities of the position can only be illustrated, for example in the emergence of compacts. A member of the Education Counselling and Guidance Service is responsible for developing
compacts with local schools and colleges. In 1992 there were 24, generating
around 100 applicants. By 1995 there were 78–80 institutions involved, generating over 900 applicants. All applicants' forms from compact institutions
are clearly marked centrally and such applicants have to be given a standard offer by an admissions tutor, adding up to the equivalent of six A level
points if they have achieved a negotiated set of compact goals. Compacts
illustrate the way in which institutional power is discursively constructed.
They constrain admissions practice right across the institution in that they
centrally instruct all admissions tutors to make certain kinds of offers and
they are directly and clearly linked with marketing strategies which focus
on the local area. They enable the university to gain access to students in
particular schools and colleges and, through guaranteeing an offer, to per-
suade some students to choose the local institution. There is a real sense of
threat to territory involved as 15 other higher education institutions have
compact arrangements in the regional area.

As recruitment becomes more difficult for a wide variety of reasons
(not least more aggressive action by competitors) the generation of
healthy numbers of first choice applications from other local compact
feeder institutions should be welcomed even in currently over-subscribed
subject areas.
(Counselling and Guidance Service Performance Review, 1993/4:2)

The above account appears to point to a centralized admissions management. In practice things are rarely so straightforward. No member of the
directorate has a clear and unambiguous responsibility for admissions. Heads
of schools negotiate target numbers for full-time recruitment but no quotas
or targets for particular groups of students are imposed. Internal monitoring, which is well advanced for planning purposes, is not used systematically to enforce subject accountability in practice. It appears to be an activity

more geared to outside audiences, to marketing priorities and to supporting a public image. This is succinctly illustrated by the management response to the new HESA codings on entry qualifications. These disaggregate
many more qualifications which are coded separately and clearly labelled as
standard. An internal discussion paper looking at these new codings commented that the proportion of mature non-standard students 'will appear
to drop dramatically from 37% to around 6% when what is in fact being
illustrated is our success in recognising a broad range of entry qualifications
and preparatory routes as standard, which is in itself a measure of our
access performance' (internal memo, Access Working Party, 1995). Quite
specifically the memo highlights the need to look at the range of audiences for whom internal monitoring data are prepared and the political messages they embody. Under the new codings it is more difficult to distinguish
the institution from its more traditional rivals. The answer put forward was
to group the HESA codes in particular ways, giving them particular labels
appropriate to different external audiences. As was noted earlier, many
institutions present their access reality within a marketing/public relations
framework, not often being so open and explicit as in the above memo.

The admissions process is centrally controlled only in particular ways.
The UCAS process is centrally organized, for example. The very large
modular scheme requires control over the A level points scores required for
each subject, which are negotiated annually with subject staff. There are
central instructions on what happens to offers for joint subject applications
with big discrepancies on required points (i.e., whether to offer the top
score or an average), on the points equivalences for qualifications such as
ONC/OND and an acceptable threshold pass for Access students. Direction concerning compact applicants has already been outlined. These guidelines are outlined in an Admissions Handbook and reinforced at a yearly
training meeting (which is not compulsory). In many ways, therefore, the
selective function of admissions tutors is limited. The particular version of
quality which has been adopted within the institution limits the processing
of admissions even more directly. The adoption of a BS 5750/ISO 9000
system necessitates following detailed generic procedures and work instructions. Different levels of institutional power and the bureaucratization of
admissions seem to be dominant in terms of both decisions and processes.
In practice it is less so. A division between admininstrative and academic
activities is perhaps sharpened, but variations in the points score for offers,
the involvement in outreach activities, ways of safeguarding (or not) places
for mature unqualified students, the numbers of applicants interviewed,
the ways of assessing potential or ability to benefit, are all subject to admissions tutor/subject team discretion. Subject traditions remain. Those subjects recruiting few alternative entrants in 1991, in our original study, still
recruited few in 1995. There is less institutional space for academic traditionalists but they remain. The majority of admissions staff could probably
be labelled 'pragmatic liberal meritocrats', by virtue of the institution's market position as much as by conviction. A new Admissions Guide, published

early in 1996, contains an introduction by the Vice Chancellor, in which he acknowledges the relationship between mission and practice, between formal policies and their implementation. It positions admissions staff quite specifically as deliverers of the institution's access mission, expecting conformity with an institutional culture and practices:

> In these days of finely balanced recruitment targets and financial penalties it is vitally important that the University's admissions procedures are operated as efficiently and effectively as possible. It is however equally important that the policy underlying those procedures and systems reflects and facilitates the achievement of the University's mission in the areas of access and equal opportunities. In particular admissions practice should be based upon a shared set of corporate values around opportunity and choice for a range of student constituencies. The admissions operation must give real substance to the Institution's commitment to meeting the needs of the individual. It should recognise the increasingly wide variety of qualifications and experiences which equip people with the skills and competences needed for them to benefit from the University's learning programmes. Every member of staff involved in the admissions process is in effect a custodian of the Institution's mission and values.
>
> (Introduction to the Admissions Guide, 1996)

The following chapter looks in more detail at admissions practice and the legitimation of that practice. This institutional case study has established some of the parameters within which admissions staff operate and outlined some of the tensions, which at times become very public. The newspaper quotations given at the beginning of Chapter 2 ridiculed an aspect of its outreach strategy, the development of Foundation or Year 0 courses, which provide a route into the institution in particular subjects for applicants without two A levels. Such language of derision affects all levels of staff within an institution. It had to be responded to publicly. The academic legitimacy of alternative routes and qualifications, the poor relationship between A level grades and degree results, the importance of a value-added framework and comparisons of student output not input, were ways used to claim academic integrity in the face of such onslaughts. In spite of such defences, admissions staff often felt themselves personally tainted by the attacks, attacks which position them as guardians of one particular form of selectivity, and not one the institution in its public or internal documents has chosen to embrace.

6

Gatekeeping: Inclusionary and Exclusionary Discourses and Practices

Anne Thompson

The language of access, like that of quality, operates with a variety of vocabularies. These disclose not only competing philosophical and ideological positions, but they reflect the plurality and specificity of alternative access arrangements for non-traditional students.

(Parry, 1986:43)

Introduction

Underpinning the practice of admission to higher education are assumptions about legitimacy and entitlement. Who legitimately has access to higher education? Who is higher education for? The answers to these questions rest in turn upon further questions. What is higher education for? Is higher education now homogenous, post the binary divide, or will a new stratification (Scott, 1995) mean a newly differentiated higher education for differentiated students? Chapter 2 has examined the debate about expansion of access at national level and Chapter 5 at institutional level; this chapter will focus on the policy and practice of admission and examine how the discursive practice of admission makes the discourse of access concrete.

Qualitative data from our interviews with selected admissions tutors will be used, supported by evidence from earlier and more recent research by others, to examine the discursive practice within a national context, in particular in the early 1990s at the moment when the shift from a policy of expansion and 'widening' of access to higher education became one of 'consolidation'. I will be arguing that the process of admission of students to full-time first degrees, and the individual student's ability to enter, are determined by the way in which applicants are constructed – collectively and individually – as subjects in the national, institutional and departmental discourse, underpinned by philosophies of equity and selectivity, and by the discursive practices of admissions tutors which operate to include or exclude. This inclusionary or exclusionary practice rests, I will argue, most notably on a process of differentiation or dividing practice (see Chapter 1) which constructs applicants as 'standard' or 'non-standard' and 'traditional' or 'non-traditional'. As noted in Chapter 4, there is a lack of clarity about these terms (including among those researching the applicants) and they have been used interchangeably and conflated – I will return to this point later.

Admissions tutors are clearly key actors in the set of practices which culminate in the entry (or otherwise) of an applicant to a higher education institution. They determine the outcome of an application, since they determine whether or not a conditional or unconditional offer is made and on what basis. They also control the applicant's experience of the application process in ways which may determine whether she or he accepts such an offer (see Chapter 7). Chapter 2 has presented five ideal types of discourse. The discourse of admissions tutors as described in this chapter does not fit neatly into these categories. Academic traditionalists with, increasingly, more than a dash of marketeer, liberal meritocrat and the access movement are discernible, with the utilitarian trainer evident in some more obviously vocational courses. However, in the majority of cases, our analysis indicates that the discourse and discursive practice of admissions tutors do not articulate the component elements of the discourse in a manner which corresponds consistently to the typology. Admissions tutors' practice is carried out within an institutional and a national policy context which imposes parameters and guidelines on their discretion and may lay down specific directives, and there is a complex interplay between national, institutional, departmental and individual levels within a discourse. Consequently, elements of the discourse, for example, 'mature entrant', have different and floating meanings. Admissions tutors, unsurprisingly, display contradictory or multi-positional practice.

The discourse of admission

The 1963 Robbins 'principle', somewhat ambiguously, and the 1985 Green Paper reformulation, more explicitly, signalled support for the 'alternative entry' of candidates without traditional academic qualifications. By the late 1980s (see Chapter 1), both expansion of higher education and 'widening access' were embedded in a discourse of access to higher education espoused by the access movement. However, this discourse, underpinned as it was by a philosophy of 'social justice' or 'equity', has continually been challenged by the academic traditionalists in discourses of derision. The introduction of consolidation in 1993, specifically, maximum aggregate student numbers (MASNs) and, more recently, the terms of reference of the Dearing Inquiry into higher education, have sent a different official signal.

Thus, while the late 1980s and early 1990s saw an expansion of the intake of 'non-traditional' and 'non-standard' entrants to higher education, and in 1995 Scott and Smith (1995:14) were able to conclude that the presence of 'non-standard' (they conflate the terms non-traditional and non-standard) students 'is now more widely accepted as legitimate in higher education', this claim to legitimacy has been and is contested; increasingly so, I would argue, in the current educational climate.

Policy does not make practice

In the late 1980s, access had become 'one of the central policy concerns for higher education' (Fulton and Ellwood, 1989:7) particularly in the then polytechnic sector. However, access policy was, and is, more rarely translated into an admissions policy and associated practice; the practice of admission is commonly driven by administrative convenience. Fulton and Ellwood found a minority of their sample of 25 higher education institutions could refer them, in 1988, to a formal admissions policy statement. This implementation gap continued; in 1992, after summarizing the responses to the PCFC, Allen (1992:41) noted that despite the fact that a commitment to widening participation was reflected in 'most institutional strategic plans and aims', there was a need to achieve 'a closer fit between policy objectives and policy outcomes' and to set and monitor targets: a need endorsed by those committed to widening participation (e.g., Bird, Yee *et al.*, 1992; Stowell, 1992). Thompson and Parry (1992:66) examined formal arrangements for coordination of access for mature and non-traditional students and found 'more systematic as well as widespread attempts by institutions to facilitate and coordinate access for adults' but drew attention to their recency, diversity, contingency and, in many cases, informality and fragility. Peinovich (1996), in research conducted in 1994/5 in 20 English universities (chosen to represent Oxbridge, London Colleges, redbrick, green-site and 'new') found that in at least a third of the institutions she visited a high institutional priority was given to access issues in the form of policy, mission or plan, but in only a few cases were policies and programmes designed to facilitate the entry and success of mature learners woven into their fabric.

Institutional admission policies, as reported by the 28 admissions tutors in our sample of new universities were rarely formal or extensive; they tended to take the form of generalized commitments to equal opportunities, or to offering equal treatment to mature students or guaranteed interviews for Access applicants. Exceptionally were underpinning philosophies of equity explicitly operationalized. Similarly, Bargh *et al.* (1994) found 'soft' generalized commitments to equal opportunities rather than 'hard' policies, particularly in old universities. Any attempt to embed an institution-wide policy on admissions, to institutionalize it is, it would appear, likely to be countered by, on the one hand, the ethos of departmental (indeed, individual admissions tutor) autonomy (Fulton and Ellwood, 1989; Kelly, 1990; Thompson and Parry, 1992; Bargh *et al.*, 1994) and, on the other, by a perception of admissions as an administrative rather than a policy issue.

Universities, notes Robertson (1994:247) 'have always been loosely coupled organisations.' Where we did find evidence of institutional policy, underpinned by a philosophy, there was also evidence of its subversion by department, course team, or individual admissions tutor. These local noncompliant practices might be conscious resistance, or based on simple ignorance of institutional policy, or both, as illustrated in the following comments by three admissions tutors:

> Well, the problem I've got at the moment is that politically, and I don't agree with politics too much anyway, I've got to interview all the Access students. I mean is that true everywhere? . . . But there is no, well there may be some guidelines, I don't know them.

> You asked me on the phone about institutional policies and I said there weren't any. I think I said that and that was not correct. I thought about it afterwards, there are. But the institution doesn't sort of emblazon them in big letters in front of my window, it's very easy not to be aware of them. What they do as an institution is have a group of people who set policies for the institution about how many mature entries, how many women, how many of racial minority students and so on, and when the annual returns are produced by each course they get these and they look at the intake to see whether you are in line with institutional targets or not, and they don't really do anything if you are not in line . . .

> . . . we've recently got an equal opportunities unit set up. And they did set up a target for ethnic groups. I can't remember what it was off the top of my head, but we had an idea that it might have been the wrong number. I can't remember what happened about it . . .

While we found evidence of institutional policy and target-setting being subverted at departmental level, it was also at departmental level that we found, in a small number of cases, a real commitment to targeting and its practice. However, with these (three) exceptions, there was little evidence of a conscious decision to formulate departmental policy, illustrated by the response of an admissions tutor in our sample: 'I don't think we are that sophisticated really, I mean that would need a kind of philosophical sort of understanding of things. . . .' Similarly, Fulton and Ellwood (1989:6) found not only were departmental practices 'rarely overridden by central policy statements' but the concept of a central admissions policy was alien:

> The concept of 'policy' in relation to admissions was as foreign in departments as it is in many institutions. Indeed, at the most practical level ATs simply did not think of their work in these terms. Their main

task was a complex administrative one . . . The central aim of ATs is to fill but never overshoot the target allocation.

(Fulton and Ellwood, 1989:22)

With the capping of higher education expansion and the introduction of the period of consolidation and MASNs in the early 1990s, this aspect of the admissions tutor's role became even more crucial.

As entry to higher education has increased, there has been a trend toward centralization and routinization of the admission process. Robertson (1994:250) has argued that, in order to extend participation in higher education, the process of 'enrolment management' should be centralized, made routine, and become a process delivered by trained administrative staff working to a policy which welcomes mature students, Access students and students bearing GNVQs and NVQs in a 'process of inclusion'. However, evidence from our research and that of Peinovich suggests that this has not operated in the interests of the alternative or the mature applicant. Instead, I will be arguing, the attraction of A level point scores as a selection tool is enhanced, and the 'non-standardness' or 'otherness' of the non school-leaver, non-A level applicant reinforced.

The discursive practice of admission

The discursive practice of admissions tutors, we argue, comprises ways of conceptualizing and speaking about students, and patterns of behaviour which together produce the outcome of admission (or rejection). This may reflect expressed national, institutional or departmental policy, or it may recognize but resist it, or it may be constructed in apparent ignorance of expressed policy. Despite the centrality of the admission or 'gatekeeping' role, we found (as had Fulton and Ellwood) admissions constructed as a largely administrative process, a chore; the process of acquiring the role somewhat ad hoc and its status correspondingly low and training virtually unheard of.

> Admissions has a very low status as a job . . . we've just had some promotions come up and one of the criteria was not admissions and it was made clear that admissions would not be a criteria for promotion.

> I was asked to do it and at the time I wasn't sure whether it was a high status job or a low status job because I was new in the department. I now realise it is perceived as low status.

> . . . the two younger members of the staff really had to get on with their research and development careers rather than do the admissions work.

In conducting interviews with admissions tutors we wished to establish how they saw the role – how they constructed it or had it constructed for them.

Did they perceive it essentially as *selecting* the best applicants? Or as *recruiting* those able to benefit? Were they *reactive* or *proactive*? What was the process of admission? Did they treat all categories of applicant in the same way? Specifically, what did they consider a 'non-standard', a 'non-traditional' and a 'mature' student to be and what were the consequences of this labelling in terms of their practice?

After 1987, the recognition of three 'routes' into higher education formally expanded the category 'standard' entrant. Thus it is our view that 'non-standard' is accurately a descriptor of those applicants who are not formally qualified and who therefore need to demonstrate 'ability to benefit' in some other way, and 'non-traditional' a descriptor of groups (defined most commonly by age, class, gender, ethnicity and/or disability) not traditionally participating in higher education. If this definition is accepted, it can be assumed that non-standard students require special procedures of admission, while those who are non-traditional but qualified by virtue of one of the three recognized routes do not. However (while it is acknowledged that the categories overlap and that the applicants' non-traditional characteristics may have operated as a factor influencing the fact that they did not acquire the standard qualifications), we find that in the discourse of access, in the construction of students in the institutional data (see Chapter 3), and in the discursive practices of admission, these categories are often conflated; most notably by the equation of mature with non-standard. Thus the perception and classification of an applicant by our sample of admissions tutors was apparently not determined simply by their possession or otherwise of recognized qualifications, but by a combination of the nature of the qualifications, the point at which they were obtained and the personal history and social characteristics of the applicant, in particular her or his age. In 1992/3 the majority of admissions tutors in our sample deemed only A levels to be standard, with a small minority including BTEC or Access as standard. Bargh, Scott and Smith (Bargh *et al.*, 1994; Scott and Smith, 1995) found similar patterns in 1994 and 1995 with respect both to the conflation of non-standard and non-traditional and a continued exclusion of BTECs and GNVQs from the category of standard qualifications, particularly in old universities.

The gold standard?

Only the A level, for which the prefix 'GCE' has been happily dropped by all but the cognescenti, is a common currency, thanks largely to the 45 years it has had to establish itself. This long life, and its innate quality, have earned the A level its designation as the so-called 'gold standard'.

(Dearing, 1996a:11)

As admissions tutors described the process of admission to us, the salience of A levels was evident. It was also evident that, despite the suggestion in

1985 that the test of ability to benefit should be 'applied as stringently to those with formal qualifications as those without...' (DES, 1985b:10), A levels (grades) are taken, as a matter of 'common sense', to be evidence of ability to benefit and no further investigation is required for the (traditional) school leaver who presents them. In the discourse of access, as for Dearing (1996a:11), the longevity of A levels and their 'innate quality' (despite discrepancies between the 'standards' of subjects) are self-evident – their quality 'speaks for itself'.

Underpinning the 'access mission' was the premise that wider access could only be achieved by both expansion of the more recently recognized routes and national qualifications and recognition of the ability to benefit of non-standard (i.e., without recognized qualifications) applicants. However, research since 1987 suggests that perceptions, policy and practice have been slow to change. Indeed, there is a striking congruence between the evidence from our interviews and those conducted by one of the authors in 1985/6 (Davies, 1986). All admissions tutors wish to be fair but conceptions of 'fairness' reflect ideological (Clark, 1995) and discursive positions. Fairness may be equated with giving students the opportunity to show how they are capable of benefiting from higher education based on demonstration of skills, competencies and experience, or with the use of apparently objective measures based on qualifications and grading. Applicants to higher education may be positioned as individuals who can demonstrate ability to benefit in a variety of ways or, more mechanistically, as bearers of evidence, of recognized currency, in the form of standard qualifications where 'standard' is narrowly defined. In a competitive market, the latter approach appears to dominate and A levels operate as the preferred currency. Despite questions raised about the predictive quality of A levels (notably Bourner and Hamed, 1987b) and the recent emphasis on competencies and core skills, A levels continue to be used as a ' "quick fix" about ability' (Brown, 1992:3) and A level point scores are taken, in the regime of truth of admissions, to be a simple, efficient, effective and fair selection tool – or at least 'objective' and intelligible: 'what else can we do? At least this way everyone understands it and most people accept it so in that sense it's fair' (an admissions tutor; Davies, 1986:51).

The decision to use, or not to use, resource-intensive selection procedures (scrutinizing personal statements and references, examining the nature of non-A level qualifications, interviewing) is a political choice reflecting commitments to particular client groups, beliefs about who and what higher education is for, and/or pragmatic concerns about funding and quality audit. Point scores, on the other hand, provide a simple tool for selection and for regulating admission and hitting targets, currently MASNs. Certainly, as Tuckett (1990:115) noted, 'using point scores to ration scarce places is tidier and neater than developing systems to evaluate the fitness of mature student applicants.' Non-graded qualifications (and no qualifications) present selectors with particular 'procedural difficulties' (Pickering and Gardner, 1992:230).

If the assumption that point scores accurately reflect ability is accepted, then they offer a 'conveniently workable model of selection' (Babbidge and Leyton, 1993:213) and a 'selectors' strategy' (Pickering and Gardner, 1992:222). Despite the advent of ungraded credits and competency-based qualifications and calls for recognition of this in entry procedure, the admissions process is viewed primarily as a logistical exercise, illustrated with a fishy analogy by Pickering and Gardner (1992:223):

> When it comes to how selectors decide on an admission policy, the earlier metaphor of selector-as-navigator may be refined to that of selector-as-trawler. A yearly tide of applications begins to run in October, reaching a peak flow around early December and then tailing off until by late March few new applications are to be expected. On this tide are borne shoals of candidates and through it selectors drag the net of their admission policy. A net with a fine mesh will retain many candidates of all sizes, where 'fine mesh' translates as 'a low offer' and 'size' as 'likelihood of performing well'. A high offer is more like a coarse mesh catching fewer, but larger, candidates. Undershooting is to end up with a meagre catch, having trawled too diffidently. Overshooting is having trawled too vigorously and being stuck with a catch that is too big to handle properly. Since the aim is not so much to catch as many candidates as possible, but rather to fill a certain volume of places with the 'largest' candidates, there also needs to be ways to return any surplus catch to the tide and also to have a reserve from which to make up any unfilled places caused by a thin trawl or by candidates who, although drawn up in the net, refuse to remain on board.

Critically unpacking this reasoning and the language in which it is expressed, Babbidge and Leyton (1993:213) noted that 'nowhere in the argument justifying the A level grading system is there explicit reference to the matching of student outcomes in terms of competences to degree course requirements in terms of types or levels of skills required.'

A levels are assumed to be a measure of both individual ability and potential and the 'quality' of the department and institution to which A level students progress (Fulton and Ellwood, 1989; Parry and Wake, 1990; Gallagher *et al.*, 1993). Thus selection is legitimized or rationalized. The use of point scores for selection is discursively constructed as fair, accurate, efficient and administratively simple. The recent work by UCAS on a more complex 'tariff' is designed to recognize the 'breadth' of achievement and 'enable selectors fairly and consistently to assess applicants' suitability' (Dearing, 1996b:83), This is premised on the assumption that a numerical score can summarize a two-dimensional representation of the 'width of a programme' and the 'quality of performance'. Thus the selection process is further legitimized and rationalized through such technologies of power, described in headlines in the *TES* as 'academic profile at the touch of a button' (Young, 1996).

A catalyst for change?

The presence of significant numbers of mature students or other non-traditional students in higher education is frequently cited as evidence of a shift from an elite to a mass system. For the access movement, mature students provide a stimulus, a catalyst for positive change, not only in entry mechanisms, but in teaching and learning styles:

> They're [mature students] really wanted, not for recruitment reasons, but because they actually help the process of education . . . they're wanted – that's the important point. It isn't just because of the kind of mission statement or a political commitment to equal opportunities or whatever. They are recognised as an asset.
>
> (Bargh *et al.*, 1994:60)

However, while the access movement assert that ability to benefit should be the criterion for entry and that an appropriately structured curriculum and learning experience will lead to a 'quality output' equivalent to that of the traditional student but with an enhanced value-added', the academic traditionalist model assumes that a standard input, followed by a standard learning experience, will produce the expected output. For the academic traditionalist, any curricular adjustments necessary to support or acculturate the non-standard student are deemed 'remedial'. This construction of non-standard students as a potential resource burden, if imprecisely established and largely anecdotal, has increasing financial implications in a climate which emphasizes efficiency and unit costs. While in the period of expansion and the imperative to widen access, non-traditional/non-standard students were attractive to marketeers (and resource models which 'weighted' mature or non-traditional students were proposed; Kelly, 1990), now, the threat such students pose to quality as identified in the discourse of the academic traditionalists is complemented and compounded by their perceived expense as expressed in the discourse of the market.

This perceived threat to quality has been reinforced both by the monitoring and audit of higher education and by the developing research culture. On the one hand, if students deemed to be non-standard are perceived as 'less able' or 'problem students', or suffering from a 'skills deficit' (Evans and Crivello, 1995:136), output quality is threatened; on the other, or in addition, if they absorb time and divert resources to their selection, counselling and 'remedial' on-course support, performance in the research assessment exercise is threatened (Kelly, 1990; Bargh *et al.*, 1994; Scott and Smith, 1995). This concern, once the province of the old universities, becomes more pertinent as the newly unified higher education system is being restratified on the basis of performance of individual institutions and teaching and research are polarized. The assumption that A level point scores mean quality – input and output – is entrenched within the discourse: 'The reason for setting the input threshold [in terms of point scores] is to make sure that we can maintain the quality of the course' (an admissions tutor quoted by Scott and Smith, 1995:49). A head of department in Bargh *et al.*'s sample noted of a new degree course:

> We wanted to go and start this course, and show that we are competing with Keele or Essex or one of the others. So we took a clear but tough decision that it would primarily be A level driven and we would take only a few students through various Access and non-standard routes. We have had to demonstrate quite specific criteria because we felt that was the only way to establish a quality programme.
>
> (Bargh *et al.*, 1994:38)

As monitoring and audit in higher education focus on quality, Scott and Smith (1995:47) found concern with output quality manifested in pressure within departments for 'grade inflation' to increase input quality, even in institutions where open access was embedded in the mission and operational procedures. Essentially this discursive practice of selection is formulated within the quality paradigm of the academic traditionalists. However, talk of point scores as a rationing device in the competition for places and the assumption that a request for high grades indicates to potential students that a course is high quality (and thus attracts high scoring applicants, which it is assumed will lead to good degrees) is the language of the market.

A dividing practice

Because A level point scores are seen as both a measure of and a predictor of ability and quality, they are assumed to operate as a fair and just selection mechanism, or at least an objective and simple one. Qualifications whose legitimacy may be less established and whose status is lower for admissions tutors (and some policy-makers, parents and applicants) have less currency in terms of institutional or departmental competition and, where they are ungraded, are less usable in an administrative context in which adjusting the required grades can be used as a mechanism for controlling admission. However, an emphasis on the mechanics of selection obscures, I would suggest, underpinning assumptions about who should legitimately be admitted to higher education. In our sample it was clear that routine processing of applications and conditional offers based on points scores was premised not just on the currency of the qualifications but on the characteristics of those possessing them; on a dividing practice, an 'othering' process.

Our evidence and that of Scott and Smith (1995) suggests that applicants who are mature (who may of course have other non-traditional characteristics) are assumed to be and are treated as, non-standard and thus are problematized; the interview is used to establish their credentials. Whilst the admission of the standard (i.e., school-leaver), standardly qualified (i.e., A level), applicant is a matter of logistics, of hitting targets; the decision to be made about the non-standard applicant is more fluid: 'it's difficult to generalise with these non-standard students because they are non-standard' (a head of department quoted in Scott and Smith, 1995:42).

> The Gordian solution of trying to avoid interviewing school-leaver applicants may also reflect the hard won experience that such interviews are not always very revealing, one school leaver being far more like another than one mature student is like another . . . Putting it somewhat simply, mature candidates, coming as they do from a wide variety of backgrounds are more likely than school leaver applicants to vary in ways that interviews reveal best.
>
> (Pickering and Gardner, 1992:225)

Gallagher *et al.* (1993:20) concluded after a survey of the literature on mature students that 'most mature applicants are interviewed before being offered a place', as did Bargh *et al.* (1994:30) who also found 'their interviews are more detailed.' In our sample, in most cases only a minority of all applicants was interviewed and this group was frequently restricted to those considered non-standard. Almost without exception, our sample of admissions tutors reported that mature students who were being considered for a place were interviewed.

> . . . assuming they are doing A levels he [the administrator] just offers them conditional places upon getting 16 points. So he does that, I never see those applications . . . but in terms of accepting mature students or overseas students or Access students, then that's my responsibility.

> If they are school leavers, it is a fairly quick decision, I decide which A levels I am going to ask them to get. Mature students I take a bit more time over, see what they have to offer, consider their cases. Depending upon the qualifications and what they are doing now, I might call them in for interview . . . People I tend to call for interview are older people . . .

While mature applicants were usually constructed as non-standard regardless of qualifications, younger students were apparently constructed as standard regardless of lack of qualification. Nineteen per cent of our institutional sample of Access and alternative entrants (N = 2643) was under 21. However, the presence of this significant category of non-standard entrants was not recognized in the discourse of admission. Logically, since they can, in the main, be assumed to lack alternative evidence of capacity to benefit, the unqualified recent school leaver should cause particular concern within the discourse of quality, yet there is a resounding silence.

Constructing the mature student

Increasingly higher education is presented as being part of a flexible continuum of education for 'lifelong' or 'lifetime' learning, with a seamless interface between school/further education and higher, into which people can move at will and within which they can move horizontally as well as vertically. The fact that since 1988 mature students have formed a majority of entrants in higher education is oft-quoted. However, mature students have not, I would suggest, been normalized. Lifetime/lifelong learning is part time, it is vocational, it is professional or it is for 'returners'; full-time first degrees are not 'for' adults:

> Adult learners frequently have different needs and expectations to those of young people. They may therefore find it hard to settle in colleges or universities where initial education is generally regarded as the core business (despite the fact that adults often outnumber younger students).
>
> (DfEE, 1995:30)

At its most overt, the way in which applicants were constructed by our sample of admissions tutors determined the entrance procedures to which they were subject and consequently their chances of entering higher education. We have seen in Chapter 2 the way in which concepts are discursively constructed by polarity. Mature is not a positive contrast to immature, or even young. Rather it is a synonym for non-standard. The 'otherness' (see Stuart, 1995; Stuart and Thomson, 1995) of such applicants was sometimes made clear in the use of terms in our interviews like 'untypical', 'difficult cases', 'odd'. Mature students were equated with overseas applicants ('there is a process which goes through centrally in which they note things about whether they're mature applicants, whether they're foreign applicants . . .') those with 'unusual qualifications'. This perception of mature students as not traditional students is shared by many of the students themselves (see Shah, 1994; Wakeford, 1994). Indeed, Wakeford found that some, mainly 'younger mature' students, distanced themselves from the label of 'mature student', preferring to be seen as a 'proper' student, avoiding the 'shaming' label (Stuart, 1995:200).

If non-standard students have to demonstrate their ability to benefit, on what then is that decision based? Not, it would appear, on clear or systematic criteria according to one of our sample of students: 'It was hard to judge what the criteria for accepting people was . . . I think the system is a lottery.' Rather, in the words of Peinovich (1996:73), it is on ' "gut feelings" . . . about how well they are prepared to succeed.' Shah (1994:257), writing of her own experience of becoming 'a mature student' argued, 'as subjects we are constructed kaleidoscopically within "networks of power". . . .' The mature or alternative applicant is also an actor in the process of admission, but not, generally speaking, one with power. The way the admissions tutor positions the alternative applicant by and within the interview process is likely to negate the possibility of the applicant positioning the tutor and limits their ability to project a particular view of themselves. While Pickering and Gardner (1992:225, 227) argued that 'mature applicants are on a more equal power footing with their interviewers,' they also acknowledged the 'power imbalance in such interviews.' Interestingly, the experience reported by the mature students in our sample diverges from the process as described by the admissions tutors. Although it should be noted that there was no attempt methodologically to directly match the admissions tutors interviewed with the responses of the students (and that these responses are of course from those who successfully negotiated the admission process), it would appear to be significant that many of the students reported obtaining a place without an interview and the majority of those who were interviewed described their interviews as 'informal'. This very frequent perception ran from such extremes as:

. . . arranged to meet me for an interview and a chat in the pub. I asked how would I recognise him, he said he would be the one holding up the bar

to the more representative:

. . . if anything it was easier [than expected]. I expected the interview to be a far more traumatic experience, found it very informal

and:

Found it easier than expected. You hear all these horror stories about interviews. I was quite surprised it was quite easy.

Students expressed surprise, indeed concern, at the nature of, or lack of, interview and assessment, clearly associating what they perceived as a lack of rigour in their selection with a drive for expansion:

Although I entered without the usual qualifications, I would not have minded taking an exam to get in. I got the impression that the polytechnic was trying to pull in numbers rather than looking at the capabilities of certain students.

I had a very cursory interview. There were a lot of places for mature students at the time, so was immediately offered a place. It seemed to be instant entry, simply on a quirk. . . . The interview was very informal. I felt very much a pawn in a game, because the chap that interviewed me was very angry and he was quoting to me that the government had issued directives, saying that the polytechnic must take so many more students, but the resources and the funding and everything that goes with tackling those extra students wasn't available. He said this is just to get people off the dole queues and rearrange the statistics, because we were coming up to a General Election.

This disparity between the description of the purpose of interview by admission tutors and students may be attributable to differential perceptions of the process of admission but may also be explained by the fact that, although we did ask the tutors to describe the process in place at the time of the entry of the student cohort, the students were admitted during expansion, but admissions tutors interviews took place after consolidation had been introduced. Discursively however, I would argue, there is no con-tradiction. The concern on the part of the students (explored further in Chapter 7) reflects, as does the decision to interview, an assumption that higher education is not 'for' the non-standard applicant. They did not perceive it as their right and had expected more difficulty in gaining entry – the fact that they had passed the gatekeeper without apparent difficulty then led them to feel their success was arbitrary. In the discourse of access to higher education the non-standard entrant may be denied legitimacy; the corollary of this is that if they are included this may lead to the course/ institution being labelled as not 'proper higher education' and for the entrant to feel either that they are there on sufferance or that the admis-sion process was not sufficiently rigorous.

The 1987 White Paper (DES, 1987:10–11) referred to the importance of measuring and supporting the commitment of Access students as one of the ways of avoiding 'risk to quality and wastage of talent.' There was a need for higher education to select students 'responsibly, taking advantage of the predictive value of their performance at access level and weighing the evid-ence of their commitment to learn,' and of 'supporting their motivation.' Motivation was cited time and again as the key to acceptance of mature students by our sample of admissions tutors (as it was by Pickering and Gardner, 1992, and by the samples of Davies, 1986; Bargh *et al.*, 1994 and Peinovich, 1996). It appeared to operate generically as some form of sub-stitute for qualifications (although of course many were qualified), for 'standardness':

> From the point of view of the current selection for this year, then for the non-standard applicants I'm most concerned about their motiva-tion and their ability to achieve to a reasonable standard . . . as far as younger applicants are concerned, then the offer system is so standard that I am not really exerting much discretion . . .

Standard students are presumed to be prepared to perform adequately, non-standard are not, but motivation will compensate, indeed may lead them to perform particularly well:

> I think if they've [mature students] got a lot of motivation and are prepared to apply themselves to a course of study, they can often do very well and certainly our experience on other courses is that they end up with firsts just because their motivation is so high and they're very disciplined.

Some admissions tutors noted that the younger students lacked motivation ('you can't expect younger students to know what they want') and for that reason preferred mature students: 'I would rather go to mature students that take on more 18-year-olds with fewer qualifications because of the higher commitment mature students bring.'

Bargh *et al.* (1994) found that though motivation and commitment were cited as attributes of non-standard students by staff in both old and new universities, in the old this tended to be rather negatively constructed, with the students being described as 'plodders', while in the new it was much more positively viewed: 'they were recognised as a legitimate, and even high [*sic*] desirable, presence in the institution' (Bargh *et al.*, 1994:59). While the non-standard students were just that in the old universities, in the new they might be idealized.

Supply and demand clearly affect the practice of admissions. Their impact on the chances of entry of non-standard applicants is, however, complex. We found no consistency in practice across the institutions and departments surveyed. Where demand is high, a principled commitment to access may be maintained, or rules of competition may be applied and in such a competition the non-standard applicant will start, at best, with a disadvantage and may be disqualified. An admissions tutor for a popular course in our sample had done a 'selling job, a nice PR job on it' when the degree started out, but no longer did so as 'we just couldn't cope with the applications.' He perceived a tension between popularity and competition and equal opportunities, as 'some polys are asking for 24 points at A level, now ditch the rest, and others are saying, no, we've got to look at equal opportunities, we've got to increase participation rates for other groups. . . .' For this tutor a principled commitment to clients other than the high point-scoring A level student involved a commitment of time and energy, since:

> I could fill the course without any difficulty at all . . . in fact we needn't look at the application forms the admissions office get, we could just say 'I want 60 students and that means 1 in 5 come. You can accept 300 out of the 4000 applications, the rest you can just bin' and I know I'll get 60 excellent students.

However, research suggests that for many tutors there is little doubt who are the valued applicants when demand exceeds supply:

> We don't *need* to take on any non-standard students. We can take on many more times the number of students that we actually do take on with the two As and a B, or an A and two Bs . . . We won't take non-standard students for any altruistic motive . . . There is no policy as such.
>
> (Bargh *et al.*, 1994:46, emphasis added)

From our sample:

> We're dealing with say, 50–60 students and they're dealing with 600, so it's a vast difference. And I think they do have many more school leavers because Business Studies is much more sexy than Librarianship.

When numbers are capped:

> We're not necessarily going to cut access and other such entry totally, but we don't want to cut the good A level entrants out . . .

In one institution high demand from local Access students was leading to a move away from a guaranteed interview to 'judging' the applicants, and 'we are going to have to bring some sort of grading . . . we are going to have to be more selective. . . .' Under consolidation, ability to benefit could not be the criterion:

> We are trying to give access to all, to as many people, well to everybody that wants to come to higher education, but I'm sorry, it's going to come to the day when you've got to be at least, where there will have to be a certain amount of selectivity.

From another tutor:

> I was getting the next year so many more Access people that in order to, I didn't want to turn away the good A level people who are the potential researchers we are really looking for, so I was saying, right, if someone applies, they've got to be doing a Science Access, that's the first thing, and second, the course leader has got to be prepared to talk my language.

His 'language' was the language of grading.

Where demand is low, however, non-standard applicants may be seen as a recruitment pool. One tutor for a less popular course in our sample said she would take 'odd' applicants, those whom she assumed traditional universities would turn down and who were therefore more likely to come to her department; indeed, she was explicitly looking for students other institutions didn't want. Another said:

> My experience is, that if we selected just the best students we wouldn't have any students. So yes, obviously you select the best students, but you don't expect them necessarily to come, some of them do, but one has to make up numbers and my attitude is that if somebody wants to come on the course, it is my job to try to ensure that they will have a reasonably good chance of success on the course. The advantage that mature students have is that they know why they want to do the course and, knowing why they want to do the course they are prepared to work at it.

The comments above may suggest why some of the mature entrants felt that their selection had been less than rigorous. Perceptions that they were 'bums on seats' for some institutions were evident from some of our sample of alternative entrants, and negative evaluations of the expansion or massification of higher education with accompanying concerns about 'quality' are common (see Chapter 2). Dawson (1994:155, 159) in discussion groups with members of the public in Sheffield in 1992, found that most participants had noticed an increase in student numbers in the preceding years, but only those who worked in education viewed the increase in a positive light and perceived it in terms of increasing access; others 'believed the government and higher education are encouraging people for the wrong reasons and that more are entering higher education when they are not capable of succeeding.' Interestingly, only participants who themselves fell into the categories who traditionally enter higher education ('the white middle class able bodied groups') believed that access for 'non-traditional' students was improving. The perception of non-traditional groups of higher education was that it was 'for' the middle class, males, the young and the 'clever' (not to say, boring: 'boff heads' and 'clever clogs').

Tuckett (1990:116), extrapolating from Smithers and Robinson's (1989) observation that the institutions with the most liberal admissions policies tended to be the ones experiencing least demand, stated: 'From that it is a short step to conclude that the recruitment-centred debate about access sees mature students as an optional extra, useful to fill under-subscribed courses, but not central to the needs of the system.' Offers to non-standard students are perceived as 'firmer' because they may be unconditional or, in the case of Access, where they are conditional it is perceived that there is a high likelihood that the conditions will be met. This may benefit non-standard students at a time when institutions are attempting to meet very precise targets and take-up of offers is low. However, evidence from our interviews showed that, even when they did perform well, the mature students continued to be undervalued and unconsciously or deliberately their numbers capped. This is, we suggest, a product of the multi-positionality of admissions tutors, located as they are differentially within the discourse. At the time of our interviews there was a particularly strong dissonance between the discourse of access and accessibility and of equal opportunities for non-traditional students (which had been compatible with the expansionist period during which the students had entered higher education) and that of cost-effectiveness and strictly controlled MASNs that accompanied consolidation. This dissonance was encapsulated in an institution studied by Bargh *et al.* (1994:44) where the Rector explained that a quota for non-standard students had been identified to 'protect' traditional applicants from a projected rise (to 40 per cent) in non-standard applicants:

> We had an extremely difficult debate. The group who had a very strong commitment to social justice was arguing that there should be no limit. Equally there were strong arguments in the opposite direction . . . And, in the end, we settled for a guide ratio of 25 per cent. There is a feeling that represents a reasonable balance between protecting the traditional entry and making a reasonable contribution to non-traditional entrants, particularly locally.
>
> (Bargh *et al.*, 1994:44)

And:

> Departments recognise that offering a place to a mature student will *take it away from* a school leaver but also acknowledge the enrichment that gifted mature students bring to the university.
>
> (Kelly, 1990:13, emphasis added)

Even some admissions tutors in our sample, whose language indicated that they shared the idealized view of the mature and Access students, felt their numbers must be, or would be limited:

> I sometimes fantasise that we will one day just recruit mature students to the 200 places that we've got. We won't, we wouldn't be allowed to. . . . What we've always said is, 'Let's have as many matures *as we feel we can admit*. . . [emphasis added].

> . . . and in general, because the mature students are for the most part better, yes, I'll say the word, better students, we take as many of them *as we can* [emphasis added].

In the discourse of access, mature students are not constructed as traditional higher education students, not there by right, and they need to make adjustments, to conform if they enter university, or alternatively, the university will need to adjust to them – possibly at the expense of standards and certainly with expense. A lack of standard qualifications is perceived by admissions tutors as a risk in the 'numbers game' of entry; the assumed unpredictability of the performance of students so lacking is a threat to output performance indicators; and the expectation that they are more likely to need personal and/or academic support suggests a potential cost and a diversion of resources from research and teaching. Mature students pose a risk of the most fundamental kind: '. . . if we took more than 20 per cent of students as mature entry we wouldn't be a university' (an admissions tutor, Davies, 1986:57).

Even when tutors report that they wish to, and do, encourage the entry of mature students, it is necessary to examine what is actually meant by this. At one institution, for instance, the admissions tutor for social science reported:

> the institution is encouraged to get a number of more mature students, but that doesn't really affect us because we take a high proportion of mature students anyway, in fact, the majority of the institution's mature students are on the social science courses.

However, this tutor estimated that 20 per cent of the intake to this programme was mature (mainly female), which would clearly be considered very low at another institution where departmental targets led to concern when the mature intake dropped below 65 per cent. Similarly, another tutor who talked extremely sympathetically about mature students with regard to entry and was very positive about their performance on the degree, noted with regard to his offers for the next intake: 'I think this is the first year we have probably got two [Access/mature students], which is a lot you know . . .' (out of a target of 40 for the course and 110 offers). These risks are highlighted, while those of young 'standard' students (e.g., support through the maturation process, the need for accommodation) are taken for granted.

Until recently, mature students have tended to be perceived and presented

as a relatively homogenous group of 'returners' who missed out on qualifications (see Parry, 1995). The implications of constructing mature students
as returners are variable, dependent on the position of the actor classifying
the applicant. For example, the need for them to return may be perceived
as evidence of the deficiencies of the education system in an unequal society
(the equity model of the access movement), or of the fact that the individual failed to, or was not capable of, taking advantage of their opportunities (the deficit model of the academic traditionalists). The nature of this
construction will impact both upon the practice of the admissions tutor
and on the identity of learners who have internalized the label (Stuart and
Thomson, 1995). More recently, in some research and policy documents,
the heterogeneity of this group has been stressed and different classifications or ideal types advanced to describe their characteristics and their route
into higher education (e.g., Gallagher *et al.*, 1993; NIACE, 1993, Britton and
Baxter, 1994; Webb *et al.*, 1994c). The mature student may have made a
choice not to enter higher education and may well have the academic skills
and indeed, the academic qualifications, to enter and to respond to the
demands of a conventional degree programme (perhaps to out-perform
the traditional entrant). Their presence in the system has then required little
conceptual or curricular adjustment from higher education. Britton and
Baxter (1994:220), in a survey of mature entrants to one university, noted
that while mature students were assumed to be without traditional qualifications and to be 'educational failures', only three out of their sample of 59
had entered higher education without recognized formal qualifications.
Bargh, Scott and Smith (Bargh *et al.*, 1994; Scott and Smith, 1995; Smith *et
al.*, 1995) used Turner's 1960 model of upward mobility via 'sponsorship' or
'open' competition to propose that many non-standard entrants have been
admitted by the (elite) gatekeepers because they are deemed to have the
qualities which will allow them to be absorbed into higher education without challenging the status quo. It is only the students who have entered via
the open model (those from social and ethnic groups who have sustained
discrimination which has made them unable to acquire standard entry
requirements, skills and knowledge) who will require the university to act
to compensate for these structural inequalities both in their admissions
practice and their curriculum. Their entry, Smith *et al.* argued, signals a shift
from an elite to a mass system.

Despite varying constructions of the mature entrant as abnormal, a process of normalization of the non-standard student could be seen to be
taking place in some departments and institutions. The more familiar a
tutor was with a particular group, the more they perceived them as standard
or traditional:

There is the institutional view, which you take on board obviously,
that someone without the relevant points and A levels is deemed to
be non-traditional, but I think that this university now has got quite
a long history of taking students with other experiences and other

qualifications that it's difficult to tell what's traditional and non-traditional any more.

A non-traditional student? It's very difficult because we have always had a reasonably fair intake of mature students and so they are not non-traditional to us.

Access courses as an entry route

Access courses have operated as a condensation point within the debate over access and standards in higher education: their supporters proposing that they offer a more suitable and appropriate route for adults; their detractors viewing them, at best, as an easy option.

The discourse about Access courses which culminated in the letter of invitation from the then DES to the CNAA to set up a national scheme for the recognition of Access courses has been examined elsewhere (Davies and Parry, 1993; Diamond and Kearney, 1994; Parry, 1996). The reasons cited by the DES included enabling Access courses to achieve a wider acceptability and currency across higher education as a whole and to act as a safeguard against the risk of erosion of standards (CNAA, 1992) and it has been suggested that the framework rested on 'features and assumptions associated with an elite rather than a mass phase of higher education' and represented 'an act of accommodation and normalisation.' The guidelines for recognition were intended (Parry, 1996: 22, 23) to 'reassure admissions tutors about the suitability, sufficiency and identity of those Access programmes accepted for recognition.' However, several years after the framework had been established, it was clear from our interviews that most admissions tutors did not deem Access to be a standard qualification (although this must be read in the light of the fact that, in most cases, they did not consider BTEC or GNVQ to be 'standard' either), nor did the majority ascertain whether Access courses were 'kitemarked'.

Some admissions tutors welcomed Access courses as a selection mechanism (as predicted by Kelly, 1990:8), equating it with A levels: '. . . with the mature applicants you have to look at a wide variety of factors, but in recent years a lot of it has been sorted out by the use of Access courses and that's solved the problem really quite dramatically.'

Bargh *et al.* (1994:32) similarly found some admissions tutors felt that Access courses acted as an 'effective sieve'. Other tutors, however, complained that grading or ranking was not utilized. Babbidge and Leyton (1993:215) found ungraded courses were viewed as a threat to university automony: 'satisfactory completion . . . seemed to place the process of selection with the Access provider in the adult and further education sector rather than the university.' The 'grade inflation' identified for A levels is paralleled in Access. In the 'bottleneck' produced by expansion followed by consolidation, argues Clark (1995:137) 'a solution to the "Access courses problem" is sought in grading.' Bargh *et al.* (1994:56) found demands for grading and some confusion: 'Different validating bodies kite-mark at different points. What are admissions tutors to make of it?' In 1995, Scott and Smith found evidence of 'grade inflation' generally and an 85 per cent pass in all subjects requested of a local Access course:

> The only grounds that they [the tutors] were given for making that kind of an offer [were] we can fill our places with three A levels so why should we make an offer less than 85 per cent?
>
> (A member of the Access movement, quoted in
Scott and Smith, 1995:52)

Concluding remarks

I have argued here that the discourse of admissions and the discursive practice of admissions tutors construct and position the applicant. Central to this process is the definition of an applicant as traditional and standard or non-traditional and non-standard. This discursive activity is located within a particular historical formation and conducted within a context of institutional and national policy and conflicting expectations and demands. Selectors, argued Pickering and Gardner (1992:222) must 'steer a course through troubled waters,' coping with 'fluctuating demands' and 'changeable political winds.' The political wind of change which blew to widen access has been replaced by the chillier wind of consolidation and, as Scott and Smith (1995:66) point out, 'consolidation, *symbolically* if not statistically, [has drawn] attention to the wider question of what makes a "good" student other than by grade' (emphasis added). As we have seen, the discourse of derision which has acompanied massification has, in the words of Scott and Smith (1995:67), 'made it possible for non-standard entry to be identified as a "problem", often serving as a proxy for other ills.'

Despite the increase in the variety of routes and qualifications (including national qualifications) which emphasize skills and competencies, admissions tutors appear to be more rather than less likely to operate a mechanistic selection method. In these circumstances, I would argue, A levels remain the gold standard. In so far as the currency offered by non-standard and non-traditional applicants is subjected to scrutiny to establish its exchange value, this will, I suggest, strengthen their discursive construction as non-standard. I cannot but agree with Peinovich who concluded (1996:73):

> On the horizon there appears to me to lurk a two tiered admissions process, one for traditional students and one for non-traditional, mature learners. Many institutions have already arrived at this point, whether they are conscious of it or not.

The more the 'standard' or normal is routinized in terms of the admissions process, the more the discretion and power of the gatekeeper is enhanced with regard to the 'non-standard'. The autonomy of the admissions tutor is increased; their discursive practice determinant. The majority of applicants are selected mechanistically but those who do not have the accepted currency to present are scrutinized on an individual basis:

> ... and there's a girl in divisional office [name], who I work very closely with and for some years she followed rules I gave her for dealing with what I would call standard applications and anything which fell outside the rules was non-standard and came to me and I made a personal decision.

7

Student Voices: Alternative Routes, Alternative Identities

Pat Green and Sue Webb

Introduction

> Who one is is always an open question with a shifting answer depend-
> ing on the positions made available within one's own and others' dis-
> cursive practices and within these practices, the stories through which
> we make sense of our own and others' lives.
>
> (Davies and Harre, 1990:46)

The concern in this chapter is with the stories or narrative accounts through
which some students who have formed, and been formed, as the subject of
the discourse of access, have made sense of their admittance to higher
education. They have achieved this within an economic and political context which has increasingly polarized expansion or consolidation, grants or
loans, binary or unitary structures, and have been positioned by national
discourses and institutional and admissions practices. This chapter will
examine the ways in which this group have defined and redefined themselves from the time that they completed their period of compulsory full-
time schooling until the point at which they entered higher education. We
will argue that the construction of these self-narratives is a continuous and
incomplete activity that is affected by the contexts in which the stories are
being told. Through these stories a link between the past and the present
is made and they become the mechanism through which the students attempt to provide plausible accounts of their positions, as successful entrants
to higher education. Therefore, this account of student identities will consider the extent to which students have accepted or redefined positions
made available to them by a range of discursive practices.

The students we focus on are alternative and Access entrants who formed
part of the 'Alternative Entry to Higher Education' project. We interviewed 92
students from seven institutions (see Table 1 in Appendix 1). We have chosen
to draw on this study because these students successfully negotiated entry
to higher education without the use of the two main officially recognized

qualifications routes, and as a consequence they have been frequently positioned as non-standard and non-traditional in the discourse of access to higher education. The processes of power/knowledge construction within discourse analysis might suggest also that, as subjects, students have little or no access to power, or control, over the discursive practices being currently played out and so they have had to accept the positions made available to them. However, we have seen that the discourse of access is divergent and that the discursive practices of the key players such as admissions tutors have been variable, and so it is likely that the ambiguities in the positioning of students will be used by different students in different ways to reposition themselves.

By focusing on students' accounts of the alternative routes taken to higher education and their identities at significant points in the period of transition, this chapter will attempt to uncover the processes by which students can, and do, construct elements of the discourse. It will examine questions such as, how do they perceive themselves within the discourse of access? How does this sit with an 'authoritative allocation of values'? (S.J. Ball, 1990a:3) Do they feel legitimated, 'normalized' by a process which has allowed them access to higher education? This account charts the journey of these students and the various ways in which notions of self-identity are re-affirmed or re-shaped while undergoing the transition to higher education as alternative or Access students. Students were asked to be retrospectively reflective about identities at particular points in their histories and there may be different ways of interpreting and understanding the stories they tell. On the one hand, they can be read as accounts of the past and in some senses attempts to re-present the past in the light of the present in order to rationalize the transition from who they were when they left school to who they are currently as students in higher education. On the other hand, what they choose to tell may be contingent upon who they are talking with and so should be read as attempts to define their present identity.

> ... people's accounts are always contingent: upon available time and discourses (the regimes of truth which govern the way one's thinking can go), upon the relationships within which the accounts are produced and upon context. ...
>
> (Hollway, 1989:39)

Accounts then, are a product of the sense-making and stock-taking processes by which students construct their current identities.

Identity becomes known to others through discursive practice. It does not seem fruitful to conceptualize identity as a static and unchanging notion particularly in contexts where unequal social relationships are open to challenge (Bush and Simmons, 1981; Webb, 1991; Bhavani and Phoenix, 1994) since people will seek to present different or multiple identities as alliances shift and positions are questioned. Similarly, Hall (1990), when writing about cultural identity, has alerted us to the shifting processes within identity construction:

Identity is not as transparent or unproblematic as we think. Perhaps instead of thinking of identity as an already accomplished fact . . . we should think, instead, of identity as a 'production', which is never complete, always in process . . .

(Hall, 1990:220)

In this chapter, this production of identity is examined in narrative accounts through which we highlight three important stages in the formation and transformation of identity. First, identity at the point of leaving school; second, the experiences and changes in perception in that identity which mark out higher education as a possibility; and finally the transition to an identity as a student in higher education. In this way, we map out important transitions that form the 'continual production' of identity (Wakeford, 1994:242) and illustrate the complexity underpinning 'a sense of reawakening to learning' (Johnson, 1994:3). It is our intention through this mapping to link student identities to the discourse of access, and the discursive practices and positions of key actors, with particular reference to the five ideal types explored in Chapter 2.

Educational identity on leaving school

There were three main ways in which alternative entrants described themselves and accounted for their learning at the point at which they left school. These categories suggested both positive and negative attitudes towards school, but either way, they discouraged progression to higher education at that time. For all three groups it was not simply a matter of 'failing' at the age of 16, and therefore not being able to proceed further. The majority of the alternative entrants (50 of the 92 interviewed) saw themselves as never having had the choice and the opportunity to 'succeed' or 'fail' in the first place; for these entrants access to higher education was denied at the point at which they completed their full-time compulsory schooling. It is this group which experienced most the 'disjunction' that Weil (1993) described between earlier statutory school experiences and their later engagement with higher education, and echoes that of other studies (Johnson, 1994; Adams, 1996). Our interviewees typically described themselves in the following way: 'we weren't expected to become scholars', so we characterized this group as those for whom access was denied.

A second group (29 out of the 92 interviewed) felt that they could have got further educationally if they had had more confidence in themselves. They said: 'I could have done better', so we typified this group as those who had untapped potential. The third grouping was somewhat smaller, only ten of the interviewees, who saw higher education as an option for them which they actively decided not to pursue at the age of 18. These entrants claimed that they 'didn't like [school] at all' and yet frequently they had achieved some academic success. They were exercising a resistance to higher education that suggests an opposition to the power of education, which for them suggested freedom at the time (Willis, 1977; McFadden, 1995). Because these ten retrospectively recognized this process, we labelled this group as those with wasted potential.

Three further entrants in the interview sample had experiences and identities which set them apart from these three main groupings, forming a fourth type of young entrants, including some under 21 years who had always intended to progress to higher education, but entered through alternative routes because they had acquired formal qualifications in unorthodox ways. They identified themselves as legitimate students in higher education and questioned the positioning of themselves as abnormal simply because they had qualifications that were considered non-standard by the discursive practices of admissions tutors. While we will not be discussing this group further in the detailed analysis which follows, it is nevertheless an interesting one because in the overall alternative entry population from which the interview sample was drawn, 19.5 per cent of entrants were under 21 years and in many cases they had one A level at a low grade or they had qualifications from overseas that were not recognized by the admissions tutors and so they were categorized as non-standard in the institutional and national data records. In the questionnaire survey a number of these entrants expressed concern that they had not been treated as normal entrants by admissions tutors. One female entrant with Italian qualifications commented, 'I was very angry, I have qualifications that are as good as A levels but they wouldn't accept me at first.' Clearly the academic gold standard of A levels was being used in these cases to position these entrants as abnormal and it suggests that admissions tutors were initially operating in part within the position of academic traditionalism and were displaying a discourse of derision with regard to unorthodox access. However, this position was not sustained, since these entrants had been accepted.

Access denied: 'We weren't expected to become scholars'

The majority of alternative entrants interviewed suggested that higher education was excluded from the range of possibilities available to them at the time of leaving school; comments such as 'schooling was to prepare us for work'; 'higher education was not for me'; 'we were considered factory fodder' were prevalent in the formation of the educational identities of this group. Their positioning at school-leaving age left them in no doubt that higher education was for someone else. Most of the students in this group were going through their school years when higher education was still for a small minority.

> I was an Easter leaver – I didn't even do the leaving exam. . . . It seemed that schooling was preparing us for work and that was the be all and

end all . . . Felt a failure because I'd failed the 11 plus. Went into [secondary modern school] thinking it was sub-standard. I don't think I ever knew about degrees or the education system. I knew of FE colleges. I might have known about universities, but they weren't for girls like me. They were for really high class people.

(Lucy, 43, secondary modern school, no qualifications)

It was an inner city comprehensive, and not that academic. Most of my friends did the same as me, left at 16 . . . I didn't enjoy schooling . . . The background I came from, an inner city, you weren't expected to become scholars.

(Christopher, 29, secondary modern school, four CSEs)

This perception of lack of expectation stemmed from processes both within the school and outside, at home and in the wider community. Their structural locations, already discussed in Chapter 4, had a clear impact on educational identity, leaving this group in no doubt that higher education was not for them. They had absorbed academic traditionalist notions concerning the pre-eminence of A levels and who was likely to achieve these. Awareness of who could enter higher education and, more importantly, who could not, demonstrated the agenda control of this position. They were positioned as 'other' and they continued to construct themselves in this way:

certain individuals and groups are thus constructed as 'other' to the educational norm and, perhaps inevitably, many people internalise this definition, articulating their negative learning experiences and identities through phrases such as 'education is for other people'.

(Stuart and Thomson, 1995:1)

The students articulated an identity framed by class, gender and ability. For example, a personal identity in terms of class is revealed by a 60-year-old male student whose earliest ambition had been to teach:

You were expected to play your part . . . I came from an ordinary working class family. It would have been a bit above our station . . . (I don't believe this now). As long I got a safe job, that was all they wanted. . . . I actually wanted to teach, but the chances were nil. You followed what your father laid down.

(Matthew, 60, grammar school, five of six subjects needed for a school certificate)

Whilst the interviewees in this group may have regarded higher education as something for other people, they were not without expectations about their own futures and for many of them, both women and men, the future meant jobs. We should remember that the majority of entrants who expressed these ideas had completed their schooling when the job market was relatively buoyant. The next student describes the process as one that fitted her and her kind for a particular type of paid work, that is, 'factory fodder':

I wasn't considered one of the more intelligent; most of the children in the school were considered as 'factory fodder', but there were five of us girls for whom the emphasis was that we were considered office potential . . . That was quite a compliment really. I actually wanted to do drama, science, biology, but it was a case of 'your results haven't been as high as they have in Art and English, commerce and typing, and that this is more suitable for a girl like you – office work.'

(Jane, 34, Church of England school, five CSEs)

The expectations of paid work held by this group who 'weren't scholars', was gendered. For Matthew, it was the need for a safe job, whilst for Jane different levels of intelligence were part of the sources of divisions between those for whom higher education was the norm, and those who were factory fodder or had office potential. While in hindsight she herself recognized the way she had been pushed towards a particular kind of educational outcome, nevertheless she suggested that she did not see it as a gendered process at the time:

It was very directed, but at 16 you don't realize that. It's very leading, you tend to follow compliments like that . . . Within my group I don't think it was a gendered issue as such – they just saw five girls responsible, working hard, unusual for this group [who usually went into semi-skilled or unskilled manual labour], we'd got potential to do that.

It is clear that the gendering process had implications for the formation of these identities. This process affected the status and value the interviewees attached to both education and work as compared to romance and marriage.

[When leaving school] I'd got a boyfriend then – I'm married to him now – so I was very much a romantic. I was thinking of getting married and having a family – that really was the most important thing then. . . . I hadn't got the confidence to do that [go into higher education].

(Vicky, 37, secondary modern school, four O levels)

Among our interviewees it was female students who were the most likely to articulate an explicit gendered position, not only in the way they described their educational experiences, but also in how they remembered their being framed by experiences within their family of origin:

I can remember my mother saying 'it's not worth keeping girls on at school, they marry at 20 and have children.'

(Lucy, 43, secondary modern school, no qualifications)

The barrier was my mother. Her attitude to education was completely different to my father's. She thought I should be aiming for a semi, a husband and a couple of kids.

(Tessa, 36, secondary modern, no qualifications)

Only one male student articulated his choices in terms of romance versus education, and chose to cohabit at the age of 16:

I suppose my relationship was of paramount importance over academic interests . . . the relationship became a lot more important than the academic and I left home and got myself a job . . . I'd left home and then left school so I wouldn't have wanted to carry on at school, and sort of being in this relationship at the same time it wouldn't have been allowed . . .

(Charles, 37, secondary modern school, five O levels)

These extracts demonstrate the extent to which students were positioned as subjects within the discourses of class and gender reinforced through the assumptions and expectations of family members, and so accepted that higher education was not for them. Indeed some even suggested that although educational success may have been seen by themselves and their parents as the route to upward social mobility, their horizons were limited and did not include access to higher education:

My father . . . thought it was a good idea to get into work . . . I was told not to go into a shop or factory – that was out; it was 'go into an office'. Obviously you can work your way up in the Civil Service, but it wasn't what I wanted to do . . . Therefore because I'd got some O levels, I'd got enough to enter the Civil Service at the lowest rung.

(Vicky, 37, secondary modern school, four O levels)

For those female entrants who were from ethnic minority groups, 'race' combined with gender had implications for their experience of education and the formation of their educational identity. At its most extreme this involved a denial of access to even full-time schooling.

When I was in my third year of secondary school I actually left school and went to Pakistan . . . When I went to Pakistan I didn't have any form of education because it was optional, it isn't like here, it isn't compulsory. . . . I was 13 when I went and when I came back I was 16. If I'd stayed in Pakistan I'd probably have been married by now with a couple of kids.

(Surita, 22, comprehensive school, no qualifications)

More typically though, girls from ethnic minority backgrounds were simply discouraged by their parents from continuing with their education beyond the school-leaving age:

My parents weren't keen on me doing any further education, felt it was not suitable . . . I was good at most subjects but there wasn't a demand for me to do anything in particular . . . My parents weren't interested in me going on with my studies.

(Satron, 27, comprehensive school, seven CSEs)

These students were articulating their belief that at the time of leaving school higher education was not an available option, but they were doing so with an understanding of the structural factors which explained why this was so. The categories of class, 'race' and gender identified in Chapter 4 as variables that could structure opportunities for access to higher education, were here made manifest in the narratives of the interviewees. These alternative entrants showed as much of an awareness of the structural inequalities that impeded their transition to becoming higher education students, as a belief in personal lack of ability. Thus their educational identities coincided with the ways the access movement identified students who could benefit from access policies and Access courses; in other words these entrants positioned themselves as people who had not been expected to enter higher education because they were working class, or women, or from ethnic minority groups. In the language of the discourse of access these entrants were from non-traditional backgrounds, and they were the types of people for whom the access movement has initiated more open forms of selection. They regarded their failure to gain educational qualifications at school as a consequence of structural inequalities, rather than any individual failings. In a similar way, the access movement has questioned the rigidity of boundaries between the 'normal' students who entered higher education at the age of 18 on the basis of qualifications such as A levels, and 'abnormal' students who failed to obtain these qualifications at school.

Although the majority of alternative entrants suggested that they had been denied access to higher education when they were at school, the next set of entrants that we will discuss considered themselves as having the potential to go further educationally, although they did not do so immediately upon leaving school. These alternative entrants divided into two groups. The larger of these (29 out of the 92 interviewed) identified themselves as having 'untapped' potential while the smaller group (ten interviewees) suggested that they had 'wasted' potential.

Untapped potential: 'I could have done better'

This group comprised those students who articulated both a lack of confidence and a belief in their ability to go on with their education at that time. Many of these held such views in spite of their acknowledged educational failure at leaving school. They talked of 'untapped potential', or of 'education being unfinished'.

> I did nine O levels but didn't pass any of the qualifications . . . Felt very embarrassed about failing, so left. Most of my friends got their O levels. For years I was really thinking 'I could do that'. But I've always regretted it . . . I went through a stage of feeling very inferior.
> (Charlotte, 33, comprehensive school, no qualifications)

Lacking confidence did not always result in failure or modest qualifications. Some clearly demonstrated academic potential by gaining O levels, but their diffidence contributed to their identification with having untapped potential.

I liked school until I did badly at O level stage. I feel that it was my own fault that I didn't get all my O levels. I also didn't get enough positive reinforcement from teachers . . . Didn't think school was that interested.

(Eleanor, 26, comprehensive school, four O levels)

Lack of confidence has frequently been invoked to account for the lack of educational success of women and the discourse of access has incorporated these ideas so that the notion of confidence-building has informed the organization of many courses for women returners (McGivney, 1993). Within our sample of interviewees, there was some support for this positioning of student returners as women who lack confidence, because the overwhelming majority (22 out of 29) who described themselves in this way were women. However, a small number of men regarded themselves as having left school with their potential for further study untapped because they also lacked confidence at the time, as the following shows:

Through all of this I kept feeling that I could do better than I was doing . . . It had always been at the back of my mind though, probably even whilst I was at school, but it's just that I didn't have the belief that I could actually do it.

(Ron, 37, boys' Catholic school, no qualifications)

These narratives suggest that entrants' identities coalesced with the discursive positioning of students associated with a liberal meritocratic position; they had talent and merit which could and should be given the opportunity to be developed. Such groups are identified as the 'deserving returners' who, at some point, need some additional support to equip themselves for higher education. Our examples demonstrate that a large minority of alternative entrants, and in particular women, did regard education as 'unfinished business' and so they may have been candidates for recruitment policies targeted at the 'deserving returners'. In the light of these gender differences in identification, it is interesting to note that some research studies have concluded that the recent expansion of higher education was based on 'tapping a female "pool of ability"' (Blackburn and Jarman, 1993:211). The frequency with which alternative entrants recounted the ways in which their working-classness had led to access to higher education being denied to them or that their class position was associated with a lack of confidence to go further in spite of their initial display of academic potential, would seem to suggest that many recognized the class basis of this untapped potential (see Blackburn and Jarman, 1993).

Wasted potential: 'Didn't like it at all'

The third and minority group of alternative entrants (ten interviewees) experienced some academic success while at school, but for various reasons this was not followed through with entry to higher education at 18. All of these entrants were in schools such as grammar and comprehensive where qualifications that would enable them to move into higher education could be gained. The routes to higher education were available, but these students decided not to use them. The bases of their rejections were various and this group was divided equally by gender. They displayed a range of understandings of class differences in relation to education, and resistances to gender, religious and class pressures. The students describe themselves as knowingly rejecting the assumptions and expectations of others, of parents and teachers at school. They did not regard themselves as academically incompetent but rather were aware of the multiple positions available to them at school associated with gender, class, 'race', religion and youth cultures. The following extract illustrates the way that one female entrant recognized that normal A level students did not behave as she did and so she turned down that route to higher education and chose to train for a job that fitted with her 'dyed pink hair' identity:

> Most people with eight O levels were encouraged to go to Sixth Form College. I was in the stage of dyeing my hair pink and it really wouldn't have gone down well . . . I was very much an exception. . . . They [the school] were horrified because I was probably one of the top of the top set and for me not to carry on with the school's reputation, and instead to go and do hairdressing. . . . They didn't like it at all.
>
> (Jenny, 27, grammar school, eight O levels)

Similarly the following male student left grammar school with qualifications but switched direction and enrolled on a vocational course:

> I left at 18, most, about 95 per cent, stayed on. The expectations were high . . . I left at 18 and at the last minute decided to go into catering, so did a two-year full-time OND.
>
> (Tony, 39, grammar school, seven O levels, one A level)

For some the pressures from parents and school were too much and they were quite glad to drift for a while and not accept the positioning of others:

> There was a pressure to go on to higher education – it was a built-in expectation of college. My parents were disappointed that I didn't follow through to higher education. I did get a place locally . . . but I did not take it . . . Quite glad to leave and get away from all this for a while.
>
> (Alex, 23, comprehensive school, three O levels, college,
> six O levels, one A level)

These entrants rejected the A level qualification route to higher education in spite of demonstrating a potential to achieve, and they rejected any further validation of their academic ability. In fact, they repositioned themselves as 'other' in relation to higher education, though for them this positioning did not mean an identification with failure nor with a lack of what it takes to benefit from higher education. Instead, they rejected a particular educational experience and they valorized their otherness. This discussion of the range of identities entrants presented about themselves at the point at which they left school suggests that alternative entrants were much more heterogeneous than the discursive practices of admissions tutors would imply. For example, they were neither all non-traditional, as measured by characteristics such as age, gender, 'race' and class, nor were they all similarly qualified for entry in ways outside of the standard A level or equivalent academic routes. The majority (50 out of 92) of those who entered as mature students (over 21 years) did hold some perceptions of themselves which matched with the discursive practices of the admissions tutors, in that they saw themselves as people who had missed out educationally when they were young. They were the 'second chancers', the late developers. However, two further groups (29 and 10 respectively) which in total were nearly as large as the first, saw themselves as having potential that was untapped or that they had wasted, and the fourth and smallest group of entrants (three out of 92) had always intended to study in higher education but they were accepted often following initial rejection, with qualifications other than two A levels, even though they were under 21 years of age.

In the next section we will concentrate on the first three groups of alternative entrants since these were all mature students and could be characterized as educational returners. The focus is on the shifting identities of these students and the extent to which they have internalized the accounts of their transition from school to higher education provided by different positions in the discourse of access.

Shifting identities

For all of these students, despite the personal and structural barriers explored above, subsequent experiences made access to higher education possible. Through a variety of circumstances, the educational identity formed on leaving school underwent a transition. This signalled a shift in expectations. But there was no clearly discernible linear movement between their leaving school with a particular identity position and the events that triggered the shift, or a simple causal explanation of such a shifting identity. It was not possible, therefore, to map exclusive categories for this section, or indeed the section which follows. For example, across all identity positions described in the previous section, issues concerning work were most frequently cited as a trigger for change. Similarly, many students used further education courses as a route to higher education, although family responsibilities impinged upon the timing and the nature of courses and subsequent entry to degree study. Therefore triggers are multi-faceted and impacted one upon another.

What we can say, however, is that those who identified with the notion of 'access denied' at school were more likely to spend longer in further education accumulating a wider range of vocational and academic qualifications than those who saw themselves as having untapped or wasted potential. These last two groups used further education in a more focused way as a short preparation for higher education entry. Some further patterns were discernible. The majority of entrants who considered that they had been denied access to higher education at school or who had shown untapped potential, were women, and these two groups were similarly more likely than those who felt they had wasted potential to cite changes in their family responsibilities as a reason for their shift in identity. There were three main areas which provided triggers for change; perhaps unsurprisingly, these were drawn from work, education, and family/relationships.

Work: 'I knew I had to do something else'

Paid work, or the lack of it, was an extremely important trigger for those in our study, and mentioned by the majority of entrants in each of the three initial identity types we have described. However, there were three different ways in which paid work contributed to shifting identities. The first two concerned those who had work but did not want it, either because they were disillusioned with it, or because their very success made them ambitious for change. The third concerned those not in paid work, and included here were those who were unemployed or had been made redundant, and those who had change forced upon them on medical grounds. A further small minority in our study revealed that success in unpaid, voluntary work also acted as a trigger for change.

For some, progression in work and gaining promotion led to an increase in confidence, confirming abilities and opening up further possibilities. This very success led to dissatisfaction creeping in once a job no longer challenged.

> Needed a career for the future.... I did a long term analysis ... and training, teaching and imparting of information came out very high and very strong. My decision was to get out, and the business was sold eventually.
>
> (Tony, 39, grammar school, seven O levels, one A level)

A recounting of the importance of some aspects of work experiences was provided by a majority of the entrants regardless of their identity positions when they left school. However, the way stories were told about work, whether positive or negative aspects were emphasized, varied in relation to these identity types.

The following illustrates the interconnections between success at work and confidence-building which leads to new expectations:

> As I went through the police force ... I came to realize it wasn't the career option for the rest of my life. I knew there was another challenge, a more academic challenge to meet ... it was when I started taking those police exams I really started to get interested in study and

academic qualifications and I realized that I did have the ability to pass these and go on to something like a degree.

(Charles, 37, secondary modern school, five O levels)

These students, who applied to higher education direct from employment, and others who have used further education as a speedy and specific mechanism for higher education entry, have been identified elsewhere as 'fast track' students (Webb *et al.*, 1994a). There we argued that this 'fast track' to higher education entry was the mechanism most commonly used by those who showed early academic success, here categorized as having 'wasted potential'. Having once defined themselves as 'other' in relation to higher education entry at 18, this group more than any other, then redefined themselves as potential higher education students by drawing on their recognition that they had wasted their potential when they left school and entered work. They were able to enter higher education relatively speedily and often without needing to return to further education because they had already acquired some of the appropriate qualifications or cultural capital (Bourdieu, 1977) at an earlier age. In contrast, the 'slow track' – a gradual accumulation of qualifications as an adult – seems to have been the pattern followed far more frequently by the women who were in our categories of 'access denied' or 'education is an unfinished business'. Dissatisfaction with work frequently triggered a return to education and this in turn facilitated a growing sense of confidence and raised expectations that perhaps higher education was a possible goal.

I started to think about doing a degree course when I realized that the job I was doing wasn't the job I wanted to do. I took the A levels to get out of nursing . . . My confidence increased . . . Found I was confident enough to see about doing a degree.

(Keisha, 25, comprehensive school, four O levels, five CSEs)

Nevertheless, the majority of entrants who cited work-related reasons for their shift in identity were dissatisfied with the 'soul-destroying' work itself. They redefined what they wanted to do and this involved a consideration of education as a route to improved life-chances. Frequently, it was women who expressed such dissatisfaction with paid work that was typically an extension of their caring and servicing roles in the home or simply a means of paying the bills.

I found it very difficult to settle at secretarial work because I didn't enjoy the work, so moved from job to job. . . . If, when you are 70 you can only look back and think . . . well, what did I do with my life? Well, I had a clean home and used a lot of Tipp-Ex. I thought, it's not much to look back on.

(Sarah, 35, grammar school, six O levels, one CSE)

After being at home for some years with the children, I was nearly going batty. Husband couldn't get a job, so I got one [care assistant in a residential home for the elderly] ... I enjoyed the job, but after a while realized it was just an extension of my life in the home; it was boring, repetitious, thankless ... I decided to go on to college.

(Jane, 34, Church of England school, five CSEs)

For some though, the work option had been removed by unemployment or ill health, and it was this change in circumstances that began the shift in their identity, forcing entrants to reconsider what they could do with their lives and in some cases draw on their previously untapped potential.

I started to think about applying for a degree after having to give up my job due to health reasons. I did not want brain ossification [*sic*]. A friend of mine, who also suffers from multiple sclerosis, prompted me to do a degree, she was doing a degree herself.

(Bernard, 47, grammar school, five O levels)

Others, who had left school with the view that higher education was something for other people, did not immediately consider this option when redundancy or ill health terminated paid employment. Rather, the processes associated with sudden job loss involved and sometimes required an engagement with educational and training organizations because of the way that the welfare system was organized. In returning, albeit not necessarily voluntarily, to further education, these entrants began to redefine their educational identity and consider higher education as something for them.

My father worked at the Brewery, and got a job for me, and I saw my future as working there for the rest of my life. ... I had an accident in 1985, so left. ... I was sitting in the house for four years, fed up and depressed. Took a Rehab course, then other courses. The tutor on the City and Guilds computing course said I could go on to a degree. They really influenced my life – it was a gift from God, being told I could do this.

(Ken, 29, comprehensive school, no qualifications)

Education: 'An unfinished business'

A significant shift in educational identity for many who left school viewing higher education as something for others, has been the contact with courses, often non-vocational, taken as part-time study or evening classes in further education. This was the second most cited reason and was found in all identity types, although the way that further education was used, what courses were taken and over what length of time varied by gender and in relation to family responsibilities. As the previous section has shown, distinctions could be drawn between those who 'fast tracked' to higher education and those who followed a 'slow track'. The former group were on the whole men, although there was a small number of women, and if they returned to further education they did so in a focused way often prompted by work-related factors. The latter group typically comprised women who recalled a general keenness to learn, often because access had been denied or because they felt an untapped potential. For example, Vicky's feeling was that her education was an unfinished business to which she had to return:

> Always felt my schooling was unfinished. I've always done some course or other, could never just sit at home and not do anything.
> (Vicky, 37, secondary modern school, four O levels)

The experience of returning to further education helped to shape ambitions and provided the confidence as well as the qualifications to enable alternative entry to be attempted.

> I have attended evening classes ever since the children were tiny. Gaining confidence in my academic ability. I wanted to go on to something else, but wasn't quite sure what.
> (Gillian, 42, high school, three O levels)

For some in this 'slow track', the opportunity to apply for higher education was often serendipitous. Their return to study in further education was unfocused and they acquired many and various qualifications.

> I always carried a chip on my shoulder that I wasn't allowed to go further with my education . . . I have been studying since my daughter was a year old . . . Maths, and other studies, various courses . . . It was sheer chance that I got involved with the Access course, it really was.
> (Gaynor, 38, comprehensive school, no qualifications)

Others, though, had a greater awareness of educational progression routes and worked their way slowly through these.

> I wanted to move on and do more after working as a care assistant. . . . Decided that I was as clever as anybody else and the rest was up to me. Did the GCSEs first . . . Once I'd done the GCSEs felt that this wasn't going to be enough, too easy . . . It was a progression, kept on changing my sights . . . once I achieved one thing, realized I could go on to something else. Doing one course led me to believe I could achieve on the next.
> (Jane, 34, Church of England school, five CSEs)

For these students, the move towards degree-level study can be seen as a long, gradual shift. Perhaps it is not surprising that by far the majority of these were women, attempting to straddle what Edwards (1993) and Acker (1980) before her have called the 'greedy institutions' of family and education. A few men such as Duncan, who gained some GCSEs and then went on an Access course, followed a similar slow route:

> I started thinking there's more future than this . . . I said I fancy doing some education, going to night classes . . . I was getting like grade As and Bs all the time . . . and when someone actually turns around and

says you can do this, you think this person is mad because all your life you've been told 'no, you cannot do this'. I come from a mining family background and that's all you'll ever be . . . [my tutor] said 'you should go and do a degree in English because you're good at this.' I said 'Me? Do a degree? You're joking.' But she put the seed in my mind.

(Duncan, 27, comprehensive school, no qualifications)

Family: 'My function in the family changed'

Often a changing identity was linked to changing family circumstances, such as divorce, or children growing up or moving away, though these affected people in different ways. These changes were found to be trigger factors most often for women, but not always, and they were invariably associated with the identity positions of 'access denied' or 'untapped potential' and not with those who left school viewing themselves as having 'wasted potential'. Vicky's dissatisfaction began in her mid-20s after a move because of her husband's job, and she began to conceive of higher education entry as a possibility but she felt that she had to delay this until her child was settled:

I didn't really see a way of following it through because my youngest child is only nine so I waited until he was well settled into school. Timing had to be right for family. I would have done it much earlier otherwise.

(Vicky, 37, secondary modern school, four O levels)

In contrast, Charlotte, who had left school without any qualifications, saw the birth of her child as the stimulus to return to education:

Up until I had G. it was very much you just did your job to get your money at the end of the week . . . I viewed having G. as quite a positive thing. It was a chance to break the mould and do something else.

(Charlotte, 33, left comprehensive school with no qualifications)

Both of these perceptions mirror closely the motivations for women returning to study explored by Leonard (1994:167). Divorce was the trigger that further encouraged Lucy to continue with her education:

My marriage split up while I was on the MSC scheme . . . I did the English O level while I was still married. I really enjoyed it. So went back to college every year then . . . from then everything just happened for me . . . It was smashing, I really enjoyed it.

(Lucy, 43, comprehensive school, no qualifications)

Identity in higher education

A shift in identity offered the possibility of higher education study. What were initial perceptions of higher education? In this section we examine the concluding parts of student narratives considering to what extent identities were affected by the positions made available to them through divergent practices within the discourses of widening access and the massification of higher education. The themes which emerged were contradictory, suggesting that alternative entrants were multi-positioned. On the one hand there was evidence that they had accepted the discourse associated with an elite system of higher education, using the language of the academic traditionalists to recognize dividing practices between institutions and between students and accepting the definition of themselves as abnormal and illegitimate entrants to some parts of the system. Their perceptions of difference related both to their qualifications and to their social characterisitics.

On the other hand, not all of our interviewees expressed these views. Some questioned the dividing practices of admissions tutors around age and qualifications and frequently used the language of equity associated with the access movement. They often sought to justify their applications as entrants qualified through alternative means, other than the gold standard of two A levels, by a process of story-telling that articulated deficiencies in the education system. Furthermore, some entrants identified with both the deficit model of the academic traditionalists and the equity model of the access movement. They considered themselves to have failed to gain the gold standard and therefore did not wish to compete with those who had, who were most typically to be found in old universities. However, they regarded such failure as structural rather than individual and so they saw themselves well qualified though in alternative ways, and able to benefit from higher education study. It is to a description of the ambiguity of this multi-positioning that we now turn.

Alternative routes to where? 'Universities are posher'

It has to be remembered that, at the time of these students' entry, the binary divide between universities and polytechnics still existed, although it was about to be ended by the Further and Higher Education Act of 1992. Frequently our student interviewees positioned themselves as entrants who were 'other' in relation to the 'old' universities and many chose to apply only to the polytechnic sector or 'new' universities. It was clear that higher education institutions were viewed hierarchically:

> I did not apply to any universities – out of fear of the status of universities. I did not have high grades.
>
> (Nicholas, 22, Greek high school, school-leaving certificate)

> The idea of going to university I found too daunting. The university seemed posher than the polytechnic; where you would have to be really clever. I thought the polytechnic would be less traditional and more accessible.
>
> (Carol, 30, grammar school, two O levels, 'some' CSEs)

What students meant by accessibility was interesting because although the questionnaire sample indicated that nearly three-quarters (70 per cent) entered a local institution and that they did so because this fitted more conveniently with their other responsibilities for families and with their housing commitments, nevertheless in six out of the seven locations of the study, entrants had a choice of types of higher education institutions but still tended to choose the polytechnic sector. Accessibility was constructed in part through the practices of admissions tutors:

> The woman at the university was a bit patronizing. She talked down to me rather than on the same level. She told me what she expected of me before she knew what I had done . . . and I thought, well, do I really want to come here? The interviewer at the polytechnic was really nice and I felt more comfortable. The university actually made me an offer!
>
> (Jade, 25, comprehensive school, four O levels, six CSEs)

Some Access entrants suggested that in the old universities A levels were considered the normal route and Access courses or other qualifications abnormal, whereas in the new, Access entrants were more normalized and in some cases idealized (see also Chapter 6 for a discussion of this). Consequently, many of them chose not to apply to institutions which did not consider them normal and legitimate entrants.

> I think it depends on the stigma of the university, of what they think of A level students and what they think of Access students. I mean, you would not get into [old] university with Access . . .
>
> (Duncan, 27, comprehensive school, no qualifications)

> I was offered a place at [old] university, but didn't accept it. I went to an open day there and got the impression that it wasn't really what I wanted . . . It was too highbrow for me, it didn't feel right . . . My Access programme was snubbed, and they said they would have to go on my O level, and that maths couldn't be my own subject . . . Then I went to the polytechnic, and had a very informal interview . . . I remember this interview being very relaxed and felt much happier there.
>
> (Charlotte, 33, comprehensive school, no qualifications)

Some may have been steered by further education tutors or other informal networks to restrict their ambitions in similar ways to those described by Mirza (1992) in her account of how teachers discouraged black girls from applying for higher education courses that were associated with 'socially elite' occupations. Therefore the discursive practices which made positions available to the alternative entrants were not solely located in higher education.

> I was told by my tutors not to be too ambitious and not to apply for some courses.
>
> (Toshicca, 24, Nigerian high school, no qualifications)

The determination of some students, however, led to a more positive perception of self, which enabled them to overcome the difficulties they met

during attempts to get into higher education. They demonstrated a repositioning of themselves within the discourse of access and an alignment with
the equity position of the access movement. For example, to Surita, all
qualification routes were equally valid:

> I'm not going to listen to anybody else, I thought. I now see GCSEs, A
> levels, Access course, any other method as just a stepping stone to get
> onto your degree. At the end it's the degree what you want, it's not
> really what helped. A levels OK, but it's up to you the route you want
> to take, but at the end of it everyone's going to be there doing the
> same thing . . . What does it matter what route you take as long as the
> polytechnic can see you've got the abilities?
>
> (Surita, 22, comprehensive school, no qualifications)

Alternative students or alternative admissions? 'Thought of as different'

In Chapter 6, admissions tutors were frequently shown to divide students by
age rather than qualifications and to problematize non-traditional students
as non-standard on the basis of their maturity. The majority of students in
our study accepted the discursive positioning of themselves as abnormal
entrants by admissions tutors, but they responded in a number of interesting ways. For example, some expressed surprise that the admissions process
was not more testing:

> I realize that their main aim is bums on seats, they'll have 'em so long
> as they can show the relevant paperwork, and whether or not they'll
> make good teachers.
>
> (Ken, 29, comprehensive school, no qualifications)

Some suggested that they did not know on what basis they had been accepted
since they clearly could not have been judged on the basis of the gold standard. The lack of transparency of acceptance criteria led some entrants to
question the legitimacy of their own entry:

> I think it was a little bit amiss not to be interviewed. . . . I often wonder
> how it was actually sorted out.
>
> (Vicky, 37, secondary modern school, four O levels)

These students experienced their entry to higher education as being
'snapped up' by institutions who were seeking to increase their market
share. It would suggest an inverted market-place where the institutions were
'shopping' for the available stock of potential students, rather than the
students being the consumers. As suggested in Chapter 2, this particular
market has, of course, not been able to operate freely. These students experienced entry to higher education while the sector was still in the process of
expansion. Alternatively, several students felt their entry was legitimated by

an admissions process that divided them from other entrants because they were mature and warranted different treatment.

> I found everybody very positive about the whole process of applying. This was partly because places such as [institution] want students, particularly mature students, so they are trying to 'sell' the course.
>
> (Peter, 42, grammar school, seven O levels, one A level)

These students felt legitimated because their prior experiences were valorized and their alternative ways of qualifying for entry were considered normal for mature students.

> I felt that it was a very good interview and they were very interested in my work experience as a mature student.
>
> (Debbie, 38, secondary modern, no qualifications)

Others though saw that such special treatment could label them as a problem, and so resisted practices of idealization, and instead sought to deny differences between themselves and younger entrants.

> I don't want to be labelled as a mature student, and thought of as different. I don't want to be seen as that granny in the corner.
>
> (Louise, 43, grammar school, five O levels)

These comments suggest that a number of the alternative entrants had come into contact with institutions and admissions tutors operating with models of access that normalized and legitimated their entry. Despite this, some expressed surprise that there were institutional mechanisms in place to accept them.

> They had 280 people applied and there were only 30 places. I felt very quite [*sic*] shocked and privileged...I feel honoured to be on the course.
>
> (Gaynor, 38, comprehensive school, no qualifications)

Alternative purposes: 'Doing it for myself'

Arguments for the expansion of higher education have been associated not only with what in the divergent discourse on access we have called the positions of the liberal meritocrats and the access movement, but also with the positions of the marketeers and utilitarian trainers. In particular the latter views have been predicated on an assumption that there is a link between higher education and economic need. Comments from alternative entrants would suggest that many of them also acknowledged a link between higher education and the economy, although they presented this in individual terms. Certainly, the notion of a return on an investment was sometimes part of an alternative entrants' decisions to enter higher education. They talked of their own personal and financial investment in their own education as a means to the acquisition of a more rewarding job or career.

> The degree is a means to an end. I want to go into teaching.
>   (Tony, 39, grammar school, seven O levels, one A level)

> Hopefully I will have a degree at the end of the course. It will give me better career opportunities. I want to do a further degree in housing/welfare. I want to work in this area.
>   (Abigail, 25, comprehensive school, three O levels)

This connection, made between the need for a rewarding job or career because of their age, was a logical outcome of narratives that had highlighted paid work or the lack of it and their levels of satisfaction with their experiences of work, as significant triggers in their redefinition of themselves as entrants to higher education.

For some, financial independence as a consequence of successful degree study added to this career dimension and it was linked in important ways to both gender and ethnicity.

> I've talked to them [parents] and it's better in the longer run if I can support myself financially. There's a whole lot more advantages if I do go away and educate myself rather than, you know, staying as a machinist for the rest of my life, you know, it's not going to really get me anywhere.
>   (Surita, after refusing an arranged marriage)

> I don't have great ambitions. I entered [higher education] because I realized that I would have to support myself [following divorce]. I thought it would enhance my career opportunities. More chance of getting a decent job, so I could pay for a decent pension.
>   (Susan, 46, grammar school, four O levels)

Others expressed a desire to give something back to the community and society, and very often this view was associated with those who had suggested that access had been denied to them when they were young. Their accounts suggested that they identified with the equity model of access and in recognizing how deficiencies in the education system had affected them, they were motivated to work in ways that continued to challenge such practices.

> My training as a nurse, work experience in the community, experience as a black working-class woman in society, directed my interest towards questions around race and community. I felt a degree in Sociology would . . . lead into social work . . . I definitely want to work in the caring profession, maybe an area related to therapy and counselling . . . I have a particular interest in issues of race, gender and the third world.
>   (Gabriele, 32, comprehensive school, three O levels and one CSE)

The two categories of 'instrumental' and 'personal' motivation revealed in our study were similar to those found by Leonard (1994) in her study of mature women students. For some, maturity enhanced the instrumental motive.

> For mature students it's important to have a job at the end, therefore it's important to choose a course that you will be able to apply later.

Needs to be rewarded as well, to see a career afterwards. Seems a bit futile to just do the degree just to improve your mind.

(Vicky, 37, secondary modern school, four O levels)

However, whatever the possible material benefits, the majority of alternative students regarded the notion of degree study as a reward in itself, an achievement which showed that they 'could do it' after all. For many of these, it reconnected them with an earlier belief in their own potential.

I had to prove it to myself, not my parents, or anybody else, that I could do it. I'm doing it for me now, not anybody else. And as my friend says, 'you probably won't do anything with it, but it's a great thing that you've got it.'

(Charlotte, 33, comprehensive school, no qualifications)

I put on the application form that I wanted to learn for learning's sake.

(Matthew, 60, grammar school, five of six subjects needed for a school certificate)

Concluding remarks

The analysis of alternative entrants' identities has shown just how varied have been the ways that they have accounted for their positioning on leaving school and their subsequent redefinitions of themselves so that they were able successfully to negotiate entry to higher education. The ways that students have told their stories have also been illuminating. In highlighting particular experiences, the students have told us something about how they see themselves now, where they think they have come from and how they feel they were enabled to enter higher education in alternative ways. They have presented identities which have been fluid, incorporating perceptions from the past within an awareness of their new positions. Within these, a range has been noted, and these entrants' identities have reflected many of the divergent positions that exist in the discourse of access and in the arguments about what a mass system should be like and who it is for.

Their identities have also reflected many of the silences in the discourse. What they chose not to talk about was significant. For example, in their acknowledgement of differences between themselves as alternative entrants and other students, they used the categories with which they have become familiarized through the discursive practices of admissions tutors and those of institutions which have required them to complete forms in particular ways to produce monitoring and research data. Such practices have legitimized the divisions between students using the categories of age, gender, 'race' and class as well as types of qualifications. In some cases the students in some of these categories have been idealized in the attempts to widen entry, for example mature women, or ethnic minority groups.

The students, though, did not simply accept the positioning made available by any one set of practices in the discourse of access, and very often these practices themselves were contradictory and influenced by a variety of ideas about what higher education is and who it is for. The small minority of interviewees who entered higher education directly following their compulsory schooling and in some cases after continued study in school or college, did not accept that alternative entry should define them as abnormal entrants. They had always expected to progress to higher education, and they considered themselves legitimate entrants, even though the discursive practices of admissions tutors and institutions designated them otherwise because they did not possess two A levels or their equivalents. In a different way, the students who entered as adult returners accounted for their entry to higher education in terms which suggested that they accepted on the one hand the positioning of themselves as both abnormal and illegitimate entrants, and yet on the other hand they also associated their entry with notions of the rights of adults to lifelong learning. They felt that some people like them had been denied access to higher education because there were deficiencies in the education system. The following example encapsulates this multi-positioning because it illustrates an acceptance of both the deficit model of who should benefit from higher education, and the equity model of access:

> Friends are right behind me [doing the degree]. One friend in particular that I went to school with, she thinks that I'm doing it for all of us. 'If you're doing it, then we all could have done.' She really feels good that I'm doing it. If anything, she was probably cleverer than I was . . . oh, it makes you think, if we'd worked when we were younger.' But we didn't even know it existed then. So it does really belong to all of us . . . it's a terrible shame, to feel that you have all that potential for it to be wasted by not trying.
>
> (Lucy, 43, secondary modern school, no qualifications)

In conclusion, the multi-positioning exhibited in this student's identity may be a reflection of the ambiguities that have surrounded increasing access. This narrative and many others incorporate old identities that developed from experiences of education differentiated by level and institution, among other things, and they carry with them the notions of difference associated with elite systems. Nevertheless the processes by which these students re-entered education and gained admittance to higher education on the basis of alternative qualifications and experiences, resulted in shifting identities and the formation of new identities in which the old ones may not be completely abandoned. Looking again closely at what Lucy has to say, her linguistic choices reveal the tension between the old and new identities that the transition to higher education brings. On the one hand, she presents a stakeholder or equity view of education that might be associated with mass systems when she says, 'it does really belong to all of us.' On the other hand, she associates herself with a deficit model, in which higher education should be confined only to those who are the deserving, when she suggests that potential would be wasted 'by not trying.'

8

Conclusions

The focus of this book has been upon the discourse of access and equity, particularly during a shift towards a mass system of higher education. Maclure (1994) argued that the usefulness of a discourse approach lies in its ability to deconstruct a range of policy texts and identify the meanings in them, to highlight the power of acts of naming and categorization, and to understand the technology of power exercised in discursive practices such as examinations or selection interviews. We would add a fourth strength: it provides the conceptual tools which enable differing and alternative versions of 'the truth' to be highlighted, contrasted and explored, particularly when there appears on the surface to be a consensus emerging over the way forward in higher education, and a similar vocabulary used in many social policy arenas. The language of marketization, consumer choice, provider management, accountability and quality control both reflects and produces changes in funding, power and provision in a range of social services. In education we need to add vocationalism, economic growth, competitiveness, training, lifetime learning, enterprise and standards. The terms of reference of the Dearing Inquiry into higher education (1996a) contain all of this latter group of 'condensation symbols'. The support provided by opposition front benches, the majority of MPs and press education correspondents initially suggests a remarkable consensus concerning the immediate future of higher education. As we have argued throughout this book, this is not the case. There are deep divisions and conflicts, sometimes overt, but often hidden by similar vocabularies. The typology of discourse positions, though oversimplified, is a way of highlighting these divisions and tracing through their consequences in different contexts.

We have tried to provide more than a descriptive account of these conflicts by using a discourse approach in two particular ways. In Chapter 1 we suggested it was useful to draw upon structuralist and post-structuralist understandings and to combine the two where possible. This is a difficult task in view of their quite different theorizations of power, particularly the power of the state. The debate between Hatcher and Troyna (1994) and

S.J. Ball (1994c) exemplifies the incompatibilities. Hatcher and Troyna argued that both Foucault's and Ball's use of a discourse model rests upon an inadequate and sometimes contradictory view of the state and its power. 'Foucault's conception of power, by denying altogether the state as the privileged site of power serves to . . . undermine the explanatory status of the state in Ball's analysis' (1994:161). Ball's reply claimed that he does not deny the power of the state, but is 'unhappy with the totalitarian vision of the state and the disempowerment of the "ordinary" social actors which that involves' (1994c:172). This debate has taken place in the context of research into recent changes in compulsory education. Higher education is in a different position vis-à-vis state power. It is formally autonomous and independent (by Royal Charters and the 1992 Higher Education Act) in a way that schools are not. One of its prime functions is the production and delineation of knowledge, not just its dissemination. Its curriculum therefore cannot be as easily and directly controlled. Because such control is more likely to be indirect, then an explication of discourses and discursive practices becomes more important to an understanding of the operation of power. The legitimacy of government interventions has to be continuously asserted.

So one task has been to illustrate the power of government and the complex ways in which this power operates. Thus changing forms of funding, both of institutions and students, the differential allocation of resources for particular purposes, appointments to and the delegation of powers to intermediary quangos (in particular the funding councils), control over the granting of university status, removal of power from other bodies such as local authorities, the establishment of a particular form of student loan system, control over numbers of full-time students admitted to individual institutions in individual subjects – all exemplify the crucial control over higher education exercised by central government. Other writers (Salter and Tapper, 1994; Scott, 1995 for example), have provided greater detail. What we have done is to illustrate the legitimating discourses underpinning this power. But these discourses are not unitary, straightforward and uncontested. There are battles within government, between ministers and ministries for example, concerning the future form and funding of higher education. The appointment of the Dearing Inquiry in 1996 was a way of deflecting, postponing and possibly reconciling these conflicts. What has interested us and what we have documented are both the broad forms of the debate and its discursive specificities.

Our second focus, clearly presented as the chapters have moved from macro to micro arenas, has been the way power is constituted at different levels within the higher education system. A discourse approach allows us to do this without falling back into a pluralistic model in which all forms of power are equally important and not systematically connected. Central government, for example, crucially determines numbers of full-time entrants via funding mechanisms with drastic financial penalties for non-compliance. But which individuals are admitted, constituted by what academic and social justifications, is determined by a range of other players, drawing upon distinctly different discourse positions. Hartley (1995:411) suggested that central government defines strategic ends but deliberately devolves to higher education professionals the ownership of the tactics whereby centrally defined targets are achieved.

We have tried to illustrate the complexity of the discursive processes involved in the making of judgements about merit, in the construction of new and competing institutional hierarchies. Not just academic disciplines, but academics as researchers, as gatherers of intelligence about the system are involved. The framing of research questions reinforces particular discourses and silences others. The failure to take account of sub-degree and part-time routes in the educational press and academic journals results in a very particular framing of a policy of 'widening' access, and monitoring practices. The UCAS process, formalizing full-time admissions within a set of discursive practices, is a clear example of the operation of technologies of power. It prioritizes A level routes through its timing, credit tariffs and administrative systems; it constrains the admissions operations of all institutions and the decision-making processes of admissions tutors, and this dominance remains accepted and largely unchallenged because it is so woven into the fabric of everyday admissions practice.

There is rarely an unproblematic articulation between policy and practice, or between practices at different levels. For example, the Dearing Review (1996a) of 16–19 qualifications suggested a categorization of qualifications into A levels, applied A levels and vocational qualifications, with a numerical score allocated to particular achievements indicating equivalences across the three types of courses, so providing the possibility of higher education entry for a wider range of students. We will leave others to debate this spurious egalitarianism of numbers and the interplay of different discourse positions in its construction. Our point here is that even if these proposals are followed by government and examining bodies, there are no present mechanisms whereby they can be imposed as criteria for selection in higher education institutions (although the potential to do so exists within the funding formulas). Some may decide they are an acceptable, laudable model for them to follow. Indeed the institutional case study has shown some have already anticipated many of the proposals. But within most institutions, admission tutor discretion, resistance or ignorance limits the implementation of national or institutional policies. The strength of our study, therefore, lies in the attempt to trace the articulation of discourse positions across different sites and levels within the system, from national debates and activities to institutional practices and student subjectivities. 'The undoubted value of these analyses (of discourses) lies in their attempts to problematize policy through several of its 'levels' or 'dimensions' or 'moments of activity and effect' (Ball and Shilling, 1994:2). The use of polarizing categories such as elite/mass, standard/non-standard, access/quality, for example, and the emergence of condensation symbols such as enterprise or quality, provide a way of exploring the interconnections and contradictions between discursive practices at different levels.

We cannot here trace through more than a few of these interconnections. We have highlighted others in the text. One example is the notion of maturity as central to access discourse. Mature students are labelled as a distinct and separate category in all discourse positions, whether implicitly ridiculed or idealized. The age of maturity, for statistical recording, appears now to be routinized at over 21 for undergraduate entry. It is the way in which this arbitrary age and its label 'mature' has come to be contrasted with the notion of 'standard entry' which is fascinating. Such a wide and diverse group as all those over the age of 21 are seen as either a threat to notions of quality and excellence or valorized as illustrative of up-skilling, lifelong learning, or second chance education. This age division, as we have shown, constitutes one key element in the separation of discourse positions. Particularly in research reports, age is often conflated with the labels non-standard or non-traditional, despite evidence that the majority of over-21-year-old entrants have standard qualifications (again the meaning of 'standard' varies) and very little evidence as to their origins in non-participating social groups. This ambiguity is clearly evidenced and reinforced in the discursive practices of admissions tutors. The strength of the age categorization is shown in their differential selection processes and the justificatory accounts of these. Commonly, admissions tutors used age in crucial dividing practices and altered their selection mechanisms to take account of its supposed meaning and effects. The educational identities of the entrants we interviewed were also partly constituted by such national discourses and institutional practices. The majority provided us with life stories explaining their 'difference', their changing subjectivities which now encompassed studenthood. Maturity is not polarized with the category immaturity; that couplet is never used. Instead it contrasts with standard or with normal, and so by implication is abnormal. It is this abnormality, understood in ways framed by the national discourse and validated by the admissions process in institutions, which our interviewees had absorbed and which we asked them to account for.

The second example of interconnections is that of the student as a consumer and higher education as a market; concepts stemming not from a history of elite selection but from a more recent language of 'marketization', the commodification of education as a consumption good to be purchased by the discerning and self-interested consumer. We noted in Chapter 2 some ambiguities in this portrayal of the market and the important ways in which controls over it have been introduced at national level. A seeming near consensus round the necessity for students' loans and continuous rhetoric by politicians linking higher education with international competitiveness and the production of useful commercial research, illustrate the framing of the legitimacy of public and private expenditure in the 1990s. However, the individualization and privatization of financial responsibility has also led students to be constructed as investors and as stakeholders in their own and the nation's economic prosperity. Thus the apparent consensus hides an important tension between the discourse of consumption and that of investment.

Critical policy research unpacking the operation of education markets and the choices of consumers is more advanced for the compulsory education sector than in higher education. Current consumers are categorized in fairly limited ways, as Chapter 4 has shown. Institutions undertake limited market research, but rarely if ever within the critical framework being explored here. What they do do, as Chapter 5 illustrates, is to respond to changes in funding and its accompanying government rhetoric. They position themselves within a range of higher education markets and in doing so manage the demand from different groups of students/consumers, altering tactics at times of student expansion or consolidation. What Gerwitz *et al.* (1995) called the glossification of image production is clearly apparent. The use of a very few key words in mission statements conveys position within a historical status hierarchy and so presents a claim to a particular type of student consumer. Market position is also encapsulated in the provision of particular sorts of courses (by subject, mode or level for example), but there is a lack of formal and detailed control by central administration (except in terms of the numbers of entrants) over the behaviour of admissions tutors. Control over consumer choices, i.e., which students apply where, exercised through the discursive practices of the institution as a whole, appears to provide informal control over the nature of the selection process. In the absence of explicit policies or interventions, institutional discourse becomes a more significant site of struggle. The way applicants are spoken about determines how they are treated and so becomes the *de facto* means of intervention. The discourse of different disciplines provides rationales for resistance or inertia by admissions tutors. Interviews with students (although only from the new universities) provided us with supporting evidence that indeed the expectations/aspirations of consumers had been controlled and channelled. Their choice of an institution had been partly based on their perception of the status of that institution and their own position as reflecting/endorsing that status or not. As Bowe *et al.* (1994) argued, different forms of education carry different social meanings, and the consumption strategies of different consumers will reflect these meanings, often irrespective of formal qualifications for entry.

How does our account of the shifting, changing, conflictual nature of the discourse of access link with our initial question concerning its relationship to the emergence of a mass system? We have argued that the two discourses are intimately and inevitably connected, though should not be conflated. What does a mass system mean in terms of numbers, types of entrants, the nature of higher education itself and the meaning of equity? Though frequently defined in terms of numbers, most writers argue a mass system means far more than this. Mass can be seen to imply that students reflect the composition of society, that they come from all parts of it, that they are normal, ordinary, not special and different. The use of the binary polarization elite/mass reinforces this understanding through the processes we outlined in Chapter 2. But how appropriate is it to use the term mass in this sense about the system in England and Wales in the mid-1990s? We have spent some time detailing the discourse of differentiation, of the separation of normal from abnormal students within differing discourse positions, the legitimating processes used in a selective system. We have also demonstrated the ambiguities in statistical records. The institutionalization of certain qualifications as the ones to be counted frame the questions that can be asked. Are only full-time first-degree entrants counted? What about sub-degree entrants and part-time students? Mature students are ignored when the age participation rates are based on 18- to 19-year-olds. What social classifications are valorized through national and institutional data collection and so used in studies to claim or refute the widening of access? If we are talking (as we are) about a process, what time sequence is used? If time series data are almost impossible to compare (as they are) what can we say about the complexities of such a process? This ambiguity of evidence, as we have argued earlier, is useful to many players in the field. It can be manipulated to support differing discourse positions and institutional strategies.

An alternative approach is to use the term mass as a shorthand label illustrating educational changes which reflect and reinforce wider societal changes. Scott (1995:168) for example, argued that mass higher education could not be encapsulated as a single, totalizing idea, but is one of a range of multiple modernizations of the late twentieth century, articulating with changes in the nature of the state, the economy, in scientific thinking and academic cultures. However, within higher education institutions, he argued, it manifests the following attributes: a shift from courses to credit, departments to frameworks, subject-based teaching to student-centred learning and from a knowledge-based to a competency-based curriculum. On this basis the question then becomes, which parts of the system have adopted a mass culture and which remain outside? What gives certain institutions the power to resist all four of the above changes? We suggest it is the discourse of academic excellence, framed in particular ways to articulate with access on merit. Brown and Scase (1994) support this interpretation by providing detailed evidence of the selective incorporation by institutions of the changes outlined by Scott. A competency-based curriculum, they suggested, is only necessary when key aspects of middle-class socialization cannot be taken for granted. Its implementation is likely to be a sign of low status. The more prestigious institutions remain the cultural possession of the traditionally advantaged.

A mass system, then, is unlikely to be a uniform system. Scott (1995:37) suggested that in many countries binary systems, when unified, develop into stratified systems. What interests us in particular is the basis of this differentiation/restratification process. Will a historical status pattern be reinforced discursively by an emphasis upon the particular nature of academic knowledge; one which stresses the generation of knowledge and so the unique research-based nature of higher education? Or will the restratification be based upon the nature of the student intake to institutions, in terms both of qualifications and social selectivity? Will the key be input or output? Or will these two quite differing processes interact with and reinforce each other?

Will post binaryism just mean more of the same: a search for new and more sophisticated forms of hierarchy in which the old universities continue to attract, albeit in larger numbers traditional students recruited by a combination of social origins and academic performance? Or will it create greater convergence within the system, bringing greater numbers of non-traditional students to all institutions and so transforming their social character and in the process producing changes in course structures, pedagogy and forms of assessment?

(Smith, *et al.*, 1993:317)

Our understanding of the situation would not support this second scenario, that non-traditional students are a catalyst which will bring unifying change. Nor do we think there are only two options open. Differentiation may take place along a range of factors from historical reputation to local employer needs. What Chapter 2 demonstrated was the range of alternative discourse positions that might feed into a differentiation process. The market, for example, is a deliberately ambiguous term, given concrete meanings within particular discursive practices, such as those embodied in mission statements or specific compact arrangements, research contracts, or the recruitment practices of prestigious employers.

An understanding of contemporary discourse positions, a weighing up of their likely influence over future trends must, as we have said earlier, take account of the ways in which resources are allocated, both to institutions and individuals, where the power to allocate such resources lies, and how it has been legitimized. The institutionalization of student loans, the returning of the responsibility for funding to the individual, has been justified partly on the basis of the wish to introduce a mass system, and by the framing of the future as one where an expansion in opportunities for individuals, necessary for collective economic well-being, can only be available on the basis of self-finance. The debates are primarily about the form this self-finance will take. But though some notion of a consumer is implicit in all the discourse positions, the social selectivity assumed in most of them often remains hidden. A more explicit acknowledgement of this social selectivity is, surprisingly, demonstrated by HEFCE:

It seems that the old universities' core teaching activity remains primarily the initial education of school leavers with A levels. The new universities and many colleges of H.E. have significantly more entrants without A levels, and a student population made up of more older, ethnic minority, part-time and disabled students than the old universities.

(HEFCE, 1996a:25)

Brown and Scase suggested that 'the celebratory paradigm of widening access' (1994:165) is mistaken; that academic selectivity is still largely based on social selectivity; a view supported by Ainley (1994) who linked institutional differentiation to the nature of the knowledge on offer and the cultural capital required for entry. How that cultural capital has been concretized in qualification routes and admissions systems has been one of our central questions. Definitions of merit, the line between the deserving and the undeserving, has been renegotiated in several access positions. An institutionalization of a national credit framework, if it occurs, encompassing NVQs, GNVQs, A levels and other qualifications, is one attempt to alter the hierarchy of merit built into the qualifying system, but currently none of these alternatives has the discursive power of A levels. They remain the gold standard, the normal method of entry, the signifier of both individual and institutional worth, the predictor of quality output.

Quite contradictory scenarios concerning the future of a mass system can be legitimately portrayed by leading academics in the professional press. For example Duke (1994:ii), when writing about the growth of part-time students (an important segment of a mass system, and one which is largely self-financed), envisaged a time when 'going to university will become a normal part of adult living rather than something to finish before starting to be grown up.' In contrast Woodrow (1996:6), focusing largely upon full-time students, is more pessimistic:

> A mass system of higher education is not for the masses. In a period when recession and regressive economic policies have widened the gap between rich and poor, we have not succeeded in tackling under representation caused by socio-economic status. The virtual extinction of discretionary awards, changes in social security, the sharp decline in the real value of grants, and the unresolved shambles of student loan schemes have increasingly shifted responsibility for funding on to students and their families. This has resulted in a system of access by ability to pay.

Garner and Imeson (1996) supported Woodrow. They suggested that the cost of higher education for mature students had, by these measures, finally become too high.

We do not wish to predict future patterns. We have outlined the options, the contestations and the strengths of particular positions as we see them. There may be continuing retrenchment, a drawing-back from expansion. 'It is time to consider whether we now need consolidation, more expansion or more emphasis upon quality' (Gillian Shepherd, *Education and Training Parliamentary Monitor*, 1996:6). The polarization is an important one. Other players are positioning themselves, organizing elite groupings, claiming legitimacy for enhanced funding via the research assessment exercise or top-up fees and for their version of exclusive excellence. Others campaign instead for funding for part-time students and resourcing for lifelong learning. Discourse positions are made manifest in a range of institutional practices supported by a variety of inclusionary and exclusionary discursive accounts. Are these practices and accounts idiosyncratic, diverse across institutions and departments, or systematic enough to lead to new forms of restratification? Is it inevitable that institutional hierarchies will be based upon a narrow selectivity of student inputs, or will output be more significant?

The terms of reference of the Dearing Inquiry into higher education and in particular the framing of the context within which they are to focus their discussions illustrate the multiple nature of current discourses. The committee is to,

> make recommendations on how the purposes, shape, structure, size and funding of higher education, including support for students, should develop to meet the needs of the United Kingdom over the next 20 years, recognising that higher education embraces teaching, learning, scholarship and research
>
> (*Education and Training Parliamentary Monitor*, 1996)

They are to look carefully at available government resources, the needs of individuals and the future labour market, standards of awards, employment skills, the need for basic, applied and strategic research, student support, value for money and cost-effectiveness. These terms and the huge list of contextual factors which accompany them, and which are deemed to be crucial to their deliberations, represent a personal justification for our study. We had anticipated the vast majority, and provide an account of the competing discourses and discursive practices through which they have been made manifest over the past 30 years.

Appendix 1: Alternative Entry to Higher Education Project: Summary Information

The authors of this book came together in 1991 to undertake the Alternative Entry to Higher Education Project which was set up to explore the meaning in the growth in numbers of entrants to higher education who did not use the qualification routes of two A levels or equivalent vocational qualifications.

The project was funded by the Council for National Academic Awards, the Employment Department Training, Education and Enterprise Division, the Further Education Unit and the Unit for the Development of Adult Continuing Education. These organizations have since been reorganized, recast or merged with other bodies (see Abbreviations).

The research team was Sue Webb, (project coordinator), Pat Davies, Pat Green, Anne Thompson and Jenny Williams, with Peter Weller, Tessa Lovell and Soraya Shah. Gareth Parry was one of the key initiators of the study and the project director for the first phase of the work.

The study focused on a range of data at different levels in the system, including national data, institutional data and data gathered from admissions tutors and students. Different populations were sampled across these levels and a range of methods were used. These are summarized in Table 1, opposite.

Table 1   Research Sample 1991–93

Types of institutions	'New' universities	'Old' universities	Colleges of higher education	Total
Numbers of institutions	7	3	3	13
Numbers of alternative and Access entrants*	2707	477	741	3925
Questionnaire responses	813	119	213	1145
Numbers of interviews with students	92	0	0	92
Numbers of interviews with admissions tutors	28	0	0	28

* Indicates entrants to first year, full-time undergraduate degrees from UK and European Union.

In addition, a case study of all entrants to one 'new' university was conducted. The sample included entrants to all courses at undergraduate level (pre-degree and degree) and all modes of attendance (full- and part-time).

Table 2   First year full-time degree entrants

	Institution						
(i) Entry to seven 'new' universities (1991) (percentages)	1	2	3	4	5	6	7
Alternative entrants	13.3	24.6	12.2	8.9	4.9	10.4	14.1
Access entrants	5.3	7.0	2.9	1.6	5.2	4.7	7.6
Two A levels and vocational equivalent	81.4	68.4	84.9	89.5	89.9	84.9	78.3
N =	1100	1892	2995	2692	2215	2699	2482

	Institution		
(ii) Entry to three 'old' universities (1992) (percentages)	1	2	3
Alternative entrants	4.8	6.1	0.9
Access entrants	3.5	0.9	3.4
Two A levels and vocational equivalent	91.7	93.0	95.7
N =	1089	4002	2287
(iii) Entry to three colleges of higher education (1992) (percentages)	1	2	3
Alternative entrants	19.5	9.3	10.7
Access entrants	1.5	5.9	5.5
Two A levels and vocational equivalent	79.9	84.8	83.8
N =	1187	1607	1521

Table 3 Institutional case study – 1991 Entry qualifications on different pathways (percentages)

Pathway	2+ A levels	BTEC NC/ND	Alternative and Access
Full-time degree	71.5	6.8	21.7
Part-time degree	59.6	16.2	24.2
Full-time sub-degree	24.4	28.8	46.8
Part-time sub-degree	63.3	19.9	16.8

Appendix 2: Summary National Data

Table 1 Students enrolled in higher education by sex, 1965/6 to 1995/6

| | Thousands | | | | |
	M	F	All	% F	% P/T
1965/6	306	127	433	29.3	28.4
1970/1	416	205	621	33.0	26.4
1975/6	470	264	734	36.0	29.8
1980/1	524	303	827	36.6	35.3
1985/6	553	384	937	40.1	25.3
1988/9	582	448	1,030	43.5	37.5
1989/90	605	489	1,094	44.7	37.0
Increase 1965/6 to 1989/90	98%	285%	153%		
1994/5	788	779	1,567	49.7	31.3
1995/6 (prov.)	795	830	1,625	51.0	31.9
Increase 1994/5 to 1995/6	0.9%	6.5%	3.7%		

Source: 1965/6 to 1989/90 DES 1991c, Table 27, p. 30; 1994/5 – HESA 1996a; 1995/6 – HESA 1996b.
See notes at the end of this Appendix.

Table 2 First year, UK domiciled students: qualification aim, mode of study, sex and age group, 1994/5

| | First degree | | | | Other undergraduate | | | |
| | F/T | | P/T | | F/T | | P/T | |
	M	F	M	F	M	F	M	F
Under 21	96,393	98,078	1,007	709	14,370	11,072	3,007	2,128
21–24	21,426	15,291	3,433	3,043	4,582	3,669	5,691	6,005
25–29	9,817	7,730	4,695	5,438	2,423	2,449	6,375	8,458
30 and over	11,009	13,479	13,599	16,991	3,231	4,946	18,468	29,960
Unknown	195	168	247	263	101	136	609	1,149
Total	138,840	134,746	22,981	26,444	24,707	22,272	34,150	47,700
Totals, F/T, P/T	273,586		49,425		46,979		81,850	
Totals, First degree; other undergraduate	323,011				128,829			
Total, UK students	451,840							

Source: HESA, 1996a, Tables 1b and 1f.
See notes at the end of this Appendix.

Table 3 First year, UK domiciled students: qualification aim, sex and subject area, 1994/5

Subject Area	First degree		Other undergraduate		All undergraduate	
	M	F	M	F	Total	% F
Medicine and Dentistry	3,019	3,102	33	37	6,191	50.7
Subjects Allied to Medicine	4,058	14,184	1,829	12,725	32,796	82.0
Biological Sciences	7,144	10,556	955	1,101	19,756	59.0
Veterinary Science	175	285	–	–	460	62.0
Agriculture and Related Subjects	1,194	1,144	1,009	693	4,040	45.5
Physical Sciences	12,148	6,441	1,187	695	20,471	34.9
Mathematical and Computer Sciences	14,852	4,760	6,837	2,158	28,607	24.2
Engineering and Technology	24,978	4,001	10,187	1,550	40,716	13.6
Architecture, Building and Planning	7,523	1,673	3,520	767	13,483	18.1
Social, Economic and Political Studies and Law	17,409	21,735	2,369	5,348	46,861	57.8
Business and Administrative Studies	17,160	15,944	14,571	15,294	62,969	49.6
Librarianship and Information Science	1,656	2,357	294	519	4,826	59.6
Languages	5,870	13,429	1,828	2,852	23,979	67.9
Humanities	5,255	5,941	1,000	1,533	13,729	54.4
Creative Arts and Design	8,013	10,868	2,603	2,840	24,324	56.4
Education	4,606	11,958	2,186	5,498	24,248	72.0
Combined	29,030	34,164	4,298	6,478	73,970	54.9
Not known	–	–	59	160	219	73.1
Total	164,090	162,542	54,765	60,248	441,645	50.4

Source: HESA, Personal communication, 1 July 1996.
See notes at the end of this Appendix.

Table 4 First year, UK domiciled students: age group and highest qualification on entry, 1994/5

Highest qualification on entry	Age group				Total	
	Under 21	21–24	25+	Unknown	Number	%
(a) First degree						
HE qualification	5,996	9,968	21,419	87	37,470	11.5
A/AS levels and SCE Highers	150,066	12,631	13,840	189	176,726	54.1
GNVQ/GSVQ/NVQ/SVQ Level 3	280	59	75	1	415	0.1
ONC/OND (incl. BTEC and SCOTVEC)	10,592	4,208	4,919	31	19,750	6.0
Foundation Course	2,816	855	1,587	9	5,267	1.6
Accredited Access Course	296	2,333	8,578	7	11,214	3.4
Unaccredited Access Course	70	212	609	1	892	0.3
A level equivalent (incl. Int. Bac.)	591	233	1,604	–	2,428	0.7
GNVQ/GSVQ/NVQ/SVQ Level 2	48	32	122	1	203	0.1
GNVQ/GSVQ/NVQ/SVQ Level 1	22	11	25	–	58	–
GCSE/O level/SCE O grades	793	1,197	7,619	1	9,610	2.9
Other UK qualifications	1,027	1,163	3,980	30	6,200	1.9
Other EC/overseas qualifications	767	909	1,547	34	3,257	1.0
No qualification required	1	29	34	–	64	–
No formal qualification	347	796	3,494	19	4,656	1.4
Not known/not completed	24,249	9,574	14,266	333	48,422	14.8
Total	197,961	44,210	83,718	743	326,632	99.8
(b) Other undergraduate						
HE qualification	1,129	4,751	19,454	210	25,535	22.2
A/AS levels and SCE Highers	11,709	2,270	3,533	42	17,554	15.3
GNVQ/GSVQ/NVQ/SVQ Level 3	190	65	90	1	346	0.3
ONC/OND (incl. BTEC and SCOTVEC)	8,027	2,912	3,713	57	14,709	12.8
Foundation Course	313	154	330	2	799	0.7
Accredited Access Course	64	266	958	6	1,294	1.1
Unaccredited Access Course	19	15	66	–	100	0.1
A level equivalent (incl. Int. Bac.)	150	99	305	1	555	0.5
GNVQ/GSVQ/NVQ/SVQ Level 2	54	56	142	2	254	0.2
GNVQ/GSVQ/NVQ/SVQ Level 1	20	11	44	–	75	0.1

Table 4 Cont'd

Highest qualification on entry	Age group				Total	
	Under 21	21–24	25+	Unknown	Number	%
GCSE/O level/SCE						
O grades	1,106	1,026	3,081	19	5,232	4.6
Other UK qualifications	630	1,106	6,365	37	8,138	7.1
Other EC/overseas qualifications	299	394	1,023	26	1,742	1.5
No qualification required	1	1	3	–	5	–
No formal qualification	397	848	3,908	36	5,189	4.5
Not known/not completed	6,085	5,309	20,327	1,765	33,486	29.1
Total	30,193	19,283	63,342	2,195	115,013	100.1
(c) First degree and other undergraduate						
All qualifications	228,154	63,493	147,060	2,938	441,645	
%	51.7	14.4	33.3	0.7	100.1	

Source: HESA, Personal communication, 1 July 1996.
See notes at the end of this Appendix.

Table 5 First year, UK domiciled students: qualification aim, sex and entry qualifications

Highest qualification on entry	First degree		Other undergraduate	
	M	F	M	F
HE qualification	20,438	17,032	10,357	15,178
A/AS levels and SCE Highers	86,435	90,291	9,582	7,972
GNVQ/GSVQ/NVQ/SVQ Level 3	196	219	172	174
ONC/OND (incl. BTEC and SCOTVEC)	11,684	8,066	9,611	5,098
Foundation Course	2,523	2,744	432	367
Accredited Access Course	4,584	6,630	528	766
Unaccredited Access Course	417	475	56	44
A level equivalent (incl. Int. Bac.)	940	1,488	235	320
GNVQ/GSVQ/NVQ/SVQ Level 2	105	98	146	108
GNVQ/GSVQ/NVQ/SVQ Level 1	30	28	39	36
GCSE/O level/SCE O grades	4,598	5,012	2,033	3,199
Other UK qualifications	3,072	3,128	3,307	4,831
Other EC/overseas qualifications	1,593	1,664	835	907
No qualification required	35	29	4	1
No formal qualification	2,493	2,163	2,551	2,638
Not known/not completed	24,947	23,475	14,877	18,609
Total	164,090	162,542	54,765	60,248

Source: HESA, Personal communication, 1 July 1996.
See notes at the end of this Appendix.

Table 6 First year, UK domiciled students: qualification aim by ethnic group

Highest qualification on entry	White	Ethnic group									Info. refused	Info. not yet sought	Info. not known/ completed
		Black Caribbean	Black African	Black other	Indian	Pakistani	Bangla-deshi	Chinese	Asian Other	Other			
(a) First degrees													
HE qualification	28,152	604	835	243	979	570	117	230	419	461	1,972	2,864	24
A/AS levels and SCE Highers	134,755	850	1,061	415	4,630	2,078	544	1,311	1,511	2,017	5,453	21,844	257
GNVQ/GSVQ/NVQ/SVQ Level 3	300	5	6	2	31	15	6	5	3	4	17	21	–
ONC/OND (incl. BTEC and SCOTVEC)	13,987	429	627	163	1,037	554	178	161	258	281	989	1,060	26
Foundation Course	3,712	97	158	38	88	42	11	56	65	93	307	599	1
Accredited Access Course	7,839	482	364	137	171	131	49	35	73	204	615	1,074	40
Unaccredited Access Course	584	43	61	7	20	17	3	5	10	22	85	35	–
A level equivalent (incl. Int. Bac.)	1,902	25	42	18	24	20	8	8	40	32	176	128	5
GNVQ/GSVQ/NVQ/SVQ Level 2	139	3	13	2	7	2	3	1	1	4	11	17	–
GNVQ/GSVQ/NVQ/SVQ Level 1	37	3	1	1	2	2	–	1	1	–	2	8	–
GCSE/O level/SCE O grades	8,179	140	139	149	86	69	13	39	118	76	334	264	4
Other UK qualifications	4,475	153	158	31	143	98	54	26	54	106	410	482	10
Other EC/overseas qualifications	1,712	28	309	23	40	26	6	31	111	105	317	539	10
No qualification required	53	1	–	–	4	2	–	2	1	–	–	1	–
No formal qualification	3,110	159	240	63	88	59	24	32	66	143	414	256	2
Not known/not completed	28,039	507	544	166	1,530	746	138	285	445	586	3,205	12,065	166
Total 326,632	236,975	3,529	4,558	1,458	8,880	4,431	1,154	2,228	3,176	4,134	14,307	41,257	545
% 100.1	72.6	1.0	1.4	0.4	2.7	1.4	0.4	0.7	1.0	1.3	4.4	12.6	0.2

(b) Other undergraduate

														Total
HE qualification	18,036	373	480	132	464	214	65	139	191	296	1,901	3,229	15	
A/AS levels and SCE Highers	13,197	183	198	73	579	318	80	177	157	200	870	1,510	12	
GNVQ/GSVQ/NVQ/SVQ Level 3	245	12	5	3	30	7	1	5	5	10	11	12	–	
ONC/OND (incl. BTEC and SCOTVEC)	10,801	317	301	104	752	375	91	147	157	241	780	633	10	
Foundation Course	579	16	25	5	19	14	7	8	9	13	54	50	–	
Accredited Access Course	819	101	79	24	25	20	8	5	9	20	111	71	2	
Unaccredited Access Course	63	6	6	1	3	3	–	–	3	6	3	8	–	
A level equivalent (incl. Int. Bac.)	303	8	14	7	11	9	1	8	8	15	71	100	–	
GNVQ/GSVQ/NVQ/SVQ Level 2	193	6	10	1	5	6	2	–	2	4	15	10	–	
GNVQ/GSVQ/NVQ/SVQ Level 1	47	3	4	–	2	1	–	–	1	–	2	15	–	
GCSE/O level/SCE O grades	3,798	110	104	39	106	66	14	19	50	57	370	498	1	
Other UK qualifications	6,269	163	121	44	136	64	39	23	32	75	710	462	–	
Other EC/overseas qualifications	1,007	15	176	14	30	29	4	19	25	58	232	127	6	
No qualification required	5	–	–	–	–	–	–	–	–	–	–	–	–	
No formal qualification	2,845	158	182	40	94	56	19	60	54	94	699	882	6	
Not known/not completed	15,559	379	399	120	535	223	41	121	112	294	2,840	10,544	2,319	
Total	73,766	1,850	2,104	607	2,789	1,405	372	731	815	1,383	8,669	18,151	2,371	115,013
%	64.1	1.6	1.8	0.5	2.4	1.2	0.3	0.6	0.7	1.2	7.5	15.8	2.1	99.8

(c) First degree and other undergraduate
All qualifications

														Total
Total	310,741	5,379	6,662	2,065	11,669	5,836	1,526	2,959	3,991	5,517	22,976	59,408	2,916	441,645
%	70.4	1.2	1.5	0.5	2.6	1.3	0.3	0.7	0.9	1.2	5.2	13.5	0.7	100.0

Source: HESA, Personal communication, 1 July 1996.
See notes at the end of this Appendix.

Notes to tables

Data in Table 2 are taken from HESA 1996 which is based on the final data collection return from institutions in July 1995 for the 1994/5 academic year (total first year, UK domiciled students on first degree and other undergraduate programme = 451,840).

Data in Tables 3–6 are taken from a personal communication from HESA based on the first data collection returns from institutions in December 1995 for the 1994/5 academic year (total first year, UK domiciled students on first degree and other undergraduate programmes = 441,645).

The difference of 10,195 students between the two sets of data is accounted for by this time difference.

In Tables 4, 5 and 6 the following grouping has been used to aggregate the data:

Higher education level qualifications:
01   Higher degree of UK institution
02   Postgraduate diploma or certificate, excluding PGCE
03   PGCE
11   First degree of UK institution
12   Graduate of EU institution
13   Graduate of other overseas institution
14   GNVQ/GSVQ Level 5
15   NVQ/SVQ Level 5
16   Graduate equivalent qualification not elsewhere specified
21   OU credit(s)
22   Other credits from UK HE institution
23   Certificate or diploma of education (i.e., non-graduate initial teacher training qualification)
24   HNC or HND (including BTEC and SCOTVEC equivalents)
25   Dip. HE
26   GNVQ/GSVQ Level 4
27   NVQ/SVQ Level 4
28   Professional qualifications

A/AS levels and SCE highers
31   GCE 'A' level (with no 'AS' levels)
32   SCE 'Higher' and CSYS
33   SCE 'Higher' with no CSYS
34   Mixed GCE 'A' and SCE 'Higher' and/or CSYS
35   Mixed GCE 'A' and GCE 'AS' qualifications
36   GCE 'AS' qualifications only

GNVQ/GSVQ/NVQ/SVQ Level 3
37   GNVQ/GSVQ Level 3
38   NVQ/SVQ Level 3

ONC/OND (including BTEC and SCOTVEC)
   41   ONC and OND (including BTEC and SCOTVEC equivalents)

Foundation course
   43   Foundation course

Accredited Access course
   44   Accredited Access course

Un-accredited Access course
   45   Un-accredited Access course

A level equivalent (including International Baccalaureate)
   39   A level equivalent qualification not elsewhere specified
   42   International Baccalaureate

GNVQ/GSVQ/NVQ/SVQ Level 2
   51   GNVQ/GSVQ Level 2
   52   NVQ/SVQ Level 2

GNVQ/GSVQ/NVQ/SVQ Level 1
   53   GNVQ/GSVQ Level 1
   54   NVQ/SVQ Level 1

GCSE/O level/SCE O grades
   55   GCSE/'O' level qualifications only; SCE O grades and Standard grades.

Other UK qualifications
   61   Other UK qualification

Other EC/overseas qualifications
   62   Other EC qualification
   63   Other overseas qualification (non-EC)

No qualification required
   91   No qualification required for entry

No formal qualification
   98   Student has no formal qualification

Not known/completed
   99   Not known
   ( )   Not completed

References

Abbott, P. and Sapsford, R. (1987) *Women and Social Class*. London, Tavistock.

Acker, S. (1980) Women, the other academics, in Equal Opportunities Commission, *Equal Opportunities in Higher Education*, Report of and EOC/SRHE conference at Manchester Polytechnic, Manchester, EOC.

Adams, A. (1996) Women returners and fractured identities, in N. Charles and F. Hughes-Freeland (eds) *Practising Feminism*. London, Routledge.

Advisory Council for Adult and Continuing Education (1979) *Towards Continuing Education*. Leicester, ACACE.

Ainley, P. (1994) *Degrees of Difference*. London, Lawrence & Wishart.

Allen, C. (1992) Widening participation in higher education: a PCFC perspective, *Journal of Access Studies*, 7(1): 33–41.

Avis, J. (1991) Not so radical after all? Access, credit levels and the learner, *Journal of Access Studies*, 6(1): 40–51.

Babbidge, S. and Leyton, M. (1993) Selecting Access students for higher education – gone fishin'?, *Journal of Access Studies*, 8(2): 212–19.

Ball, C. (1984) Defective partnership – or triple alliance, in D. Urwin (ed.) *Fitness for Purpose. Essays in higher education by Christopher Ball*. Guildford, SRHE and NFER-Nelson.

Ball, C. (1988) *Raising the Standard: Wider access to higher education*. London, RSA.

Ball, C. (1989) *Widening Access to Higher Education*. London, RSA.

Ball, C. (1990) *More Means Different: Widening access to higher education*. London, RSA.

Ball, S.J. (1986) Streaming and mixed ability and social class, in R. Rogers (ed.) *Education and Social Class*. London, Falmer Press.

Ball, S.J. (1990a) *Politics and Policy Making in Education*. London, Routledge.

Ball, S.J. (ed.) (1990b) *Foucault and Education: Disciplines and knowledge*. London, Routledge.

Ball, S.J. (1993) Educational markets, choice and social class: the market as a class strategy, *British Journal of Sociology of Education*, 14(1): 3–19.

Ball, S.J. (1994a) *Educational Reform*. Buckingham, Open University Press.

Ball, S.J. (1994b) Researching inside the state: issues in the interpretation of elite interviews, in D. Halpin and B. Troyna (eds) *Researching Education Policy: Ethical and methodological issues*. London, Falmer Press.

Ball, S.J. (1994c) Some reflections on policy theory: a brief response to Hatcher and Troyna, *Journal of Educational Policy*, 9(2): 171–82.

Ball, S.J. and Shilling, C. (1994) At the crossroads: education policy studies, *British Journal of Education Studies*, 42(1): 1–5.

Banton, M. (1970) The concept of racism, in S. Zubaida, (ed.) *Race and Racialism*. London, Tavistock.

Bargh, C., Scott, P. and Smith, D. (1994) *Access and Consolidation: The impact of reduced student intakes on opportunities for non-standard applicants.* Leeds: Centre for Policy Studies in Education, University of Leeds.

Barnett, R. (1992) *Improving Higher Education, Total Quality Care.* Buckingham, SRHE and Open University Press.

Becher, A. (1990) *Academic Tribes and Territories.* Milton Keynes, SRHE and Open University Press.

Beloff, M. (1995) Why we need a university elite, *The Times*, 19 August.

Benn, R. and Burton, R. (1995) Targeting: is Access hitting the bull's eye?, *Journal of Access Studies*, 10(1): 7–19.

Benn, R. and Fieldhouse, R. (1993) Government policies on university expansion and wider access: 1945–51 and 1985–91 compared, *Studies in Higher Education*, 18(3): 299–313.

Bhat, A., Carr-Hill, R. and Ohri, S. (The Radical Statistics Race Group) (1988) *Britain's Black Population. A new perspective.* Aldershot, Gower.

Bhavani, K. and Phoenix, A. (1994) Shifting identities shifting racisms, *Feminism and Psychology*, 4(1): 5–18.

Bird, J., Yee, W. and Myler, A. (1992) *Widening Access to Higher Education for Black People.* Bristol, Bristol Polytechnic and Employment Department.

Bird, J., Yee, W.C., Sheibani, A. and Myler, A. (1992) Rhetorics of Access: realities of exclusion? Black students into higher education, *Journal of Access Studies*, 7(2): 146–63.

Blackburn, R.M. and Jarman, J. (1993) Changing inequalities in access to British universities, *Oxford Review of Education*, 19(2): 197–215.

Boehm, R. (1995) University Access for Aboriginal students: a Canadian case study, *Journal of Access Studies*, 10(1): 87–93.

Bourdieu, P. (1977) *Reproduction in Education, Society and Culture.* London, Sage.

Bourner, T. and Hamed, M. (1987a) Degree results in the public sector of higher education: comparative results for A level entrants and non-A level entrants, *Journal of Access Studies*, 2(1): 25–41.

Bourner, T. and Hamed, M. (1987b) *Non-standard Entry Students: Entry qualifications and degree performance*, CNAA Development Services Publication 10. London, CNAA.

Bourner, T., Reynolds, A., Hamed, M. and Barnett, R. (1991) *Part-time Students and their Experience of Higher Education.* Buckingham, SRHE and Open University Press.

Bowe, R., Ball, S.J. and Gewirtz, S. (1994) Parental choice, consumption and social theory: the operation of micro markets in education, *British Journal of Educational Studies* 42(1): 38–52.

Brah, A. (1993) Difference, diversity, differentiation: process of racialisation and gender, in J. Wrench and J. Solomos (eds) *Racism and Migration in Western Europe.* Oxford, Berg.

Brennan, J.L. (1986) Student learning and the 'capacity to benefit': the performance of non-traditional students in public sector higher education, *Journal of Access Studies*, 1(2): 23–32.

Brennan, J.L. and McGeevor, P.A. (1985) *CNAA Graduates: Their experiences and values twelve months after graduation.* CNAA Development Services, London, CNAA.

Britton, C. and Baxter, A. (1994) Mature students' routes into higher education, *Journal of Access Studies*, 9(2): 215–28.

Brown, A. (1992) *Higher Education Admission Policies in Action: Implications for GNVQ as a progression route into higher education.* Guildford, Department of Education Studies, University of Surrey.

Brown, A. and Bimrose, J. (1993) Admissions to higher education: current practice and future policy, *Journal of Access Studies*, 8(2): 154–69.

Brown, P. (1995) Cultural capital and social exclusion: some observations on recent trends in education, employment and the labour market, *Work, Employment and Society*, 9(1): 29–51.

Brown, P. and Scase, R. (1994) *Higher Education and Corporate Realities: Class, culture and the decline of graduate careers.* London, UCL Press.

Budgen, N. (1995) *Wolverhampton Express and Star*, 31 August.

Bulmer, M. (1986) Race and ethnicity, in R.G. Burgess (ed.) *Key Variables in Social Investigation.* London, Routledge and Kegan Paul.

Bush, D.M. and Simmons, R.G. (1981) Socialisation processes over the life course, in M. Rosenberg and R.H. Turner (eds) *Social Psychology: Sociological perspectives.* New York, Basic Books.

Centre for Contemporary Cultural Studies Education Group (1981) *Unpopular Education.* London, Hutchinson.

Clark, S. (1995) Access and admissions: current bottlenecks and the transition to a democratic higher education, *Journal of Access Studies*, 10(2): 137–55.

Coats, M. (1994) *Women's Education.* Buckingham, SHRE and Open University Press.

Coffield, F. (1995) Introduction and overview, in F. Coffield (ed.) *Higher Education in a Learning Society.* Durham, School of Education, University of Durham.

Commission for Racial Equality (1988) *Medical School Admissions: Report of a formal investigation into St. George's Hospital Medical School.* London, CRE.

Committee for Education (1963) *Higher Education: Report of the committee appointed by the Prime Minister under the chairmanship of Lord Robbins 1961–63* (The Robbins Report) Cmnd 2154. London, HMSO.

Committee of Vice Chancellors and Principals (1995) *Learning for Change – Building a new university system for a new century.* London, CVCP.

Committee of Vice Chancellors and Principals (1996) Survey of student finances, summary, in *Network*, 29.

Confederation of British Industry (1989) *Towards a Skills Revolution. Report of the Vocational Education and Training Task Force.* London, CBI.

Confederation of British Industry (1994) *Thinking Ahead. Ensuring the expansion of higher education into the 21st century.* London, CBI.

Connell, I. and Galaskinski, D. (1996) 'Missioning democracy: work in progress', unpublished.

Connelly, B. (1991) Access or access: a framework of interpretation, *Journal of Access Studies*, 6(2): 135–46.

Connolly, C. (1994) Shades of discrimination: university entry data 1990–92, in S. Haselgrove (ed.) *The Student Experience.* Buckingham, SRHE and Open University Press.

Corrigan, P. (1992) The Politics of Access Courses in the 1990s, *Journal of Access Studies*, 7(1): 19–32.

Council for National Academic Awards CNAA (1978) *Opportunities in Higher Education for Mature Students.* London, CNAA.

Council for National Academic Awards CNAA (1987) *CNAA Handbook 1988*. London, CNAA.

Council for National Academic Awards (1992) *Access Courses to Higher Education: A consolidated bulletin on the framework of national arrangements for the negotiation of Access Courses in England, Wales and Northern Ireland*. London, CNAA.

Croft, S. and Beresford, P. (1992) The politics of participation, *Critical Social Policy*, 35: 20–44.

Dale, R. (1989) *The State and Education Policy*. Buckingham, Open University Press.

Dale, R. (1994) Applied education politics or political sociology of education, in D. Halpin and B. Troyna (eds) *Researching Education Policy: Ethical and methodological issues*. London, Falmer Press.

Davies, B. and Harre, R. (1990) Positioning: conversation and the production of selves, *Journal for the Theory of Social Behaviour*, 20(1): 43–63.

Davies, P. (1986) 'The admission of mature students to higher education: two institutional case studies', unpublished MSc dissertation. University of Surrey.

Davies, P. (1994) Fourteen years on, what do we know about Access Students? Some reflections on national statistics, *Journal of Access Studies*, 9(1): 145–60.

Davies, P. (1995a) Response or resistance. Access students and government policy on admissions, *Journal of Access Studies*, 10(1): 2–80.

Davies, P. (1995b) HESA: the answer to all our problems?, *Higher Education Review*, 28(1): 66–72.

Davies, P. (ed.) (1995c) *Adults in Higher Education – International perspectives on access and participation*. London, Jessica Kingsley.

Davies, P. (1996) Noise rather than numbers: access to higher education for adults in three European countries, *Comparative Education*, 32(1): 111–23.

Davies, P. and Parry, G. (1993) *Recognising Access. An account of the formation and implementation of the National Framework for the Recognition of Access Courses*. Leicester, NIACE.

Davies, P. and Yates, J. (1987) The progress of former Access students in higher education, *Journal of Access Studies*, 2(1): 7–12.

Davies, P., Williams, J., Webb, S., Green, P. and Thompson, A. (1994) Mission possible? Institutional factors in patterns of alternative entry to higher education, *Scottish Journal of Adult and Continuing Education*, 1(2): 18–28.

Dawson, E. (1994) Increasing student numbers and Access initiatives in higher education: how does the public perceive these changes?, *Journal of Access Studies*, 9(1): 154–62.

Dearing, R. (1996a) *Review of Qualifications for 16–19 Year Olds: Full report*. Hayes, SCAA.

Dearing, R. (1996b) *Review of Qualifications for 16–19 Year Olds: Appendices*. Hayes, SCAA.

Department of Education and Science (DES) (1972) *Education: A framework for expansion*, White Paper, Cmnd 5174. London, HMSO.

Department of Education and Science (DES) (1978a) 'Special courses in preparation for entry to higher education', Letter to Chief Education Officers, 2 August.

Department of Education and Science (DES) (1978b) *Higher Education in the 1990s: A discussion document*. London, HMSO.

Department of Education and Science (DES) (1985a) *Academic Validation in Public Sector Higher Education* (The Lindop Report). Cmnd 9501. London, HMSO.

Department of Education and Science (DES) (1985b) *The Development of Higher Education in the 1990s*. London, HMSO.

Department of Education and Science (DES) (1987) *Higher Education: Meeting the challenge*, Cmnd 114. London, HMSO.

Department of Education and Science (DES) (1988a) *Student Numbers in Higher Education – Great Britain 1975 to 1986.* Statistical Bulletin 8/88. London, HMSO.

Department of Education and Science (DES) (1988b) *Advancing A Levels* (The Higginson Report). London, HMSO.

Department of Education and Science (DES) (1988c) *Mature Students in Higher Education 1975–1986.* Statistical Bulletin 11/88. London, DES.

Department of Education and Science (DES) (1989) *Shifting the Balance of Public Funding of Higher Education to Fees.* A consultative paper. London, DES.

Department of Education and Science (DES) (1991a) *Mature Students in Higher Education 1975 to 1988.* Statistical Bulletin 2/91. London, DES.

Department of Education and Science (DES) (1991b) *Higher Education: A New Framework*, Cmnd 1541. London, HMSO.

Department of Education and Science (DES) (1991c) *UK Education Statistics.* London, HMSO.

Department for Education (DfE) (1992a) *Mature Students in Higher Education – Great Britian 1980–1990.* Statistical Bulletin 18/92. London, DfE.

Department for Education (DfE) (1992b) 'Developments in Course Provision: Access Courses, Foundation Years, Franchising and Semester Organization', Letter to local authorities and to all institutions of higher education in the UK, 19 August.

Department for Education (DfE) (1994a) *Mature Students in Higher Education – Great Britain 1982–1992.* Statistical Bulletin 16/94. London, DfE.

Department for Education (DfE) (1994b) *Statistics of Education Students in Further and Higher Education in Former Polytechnics, Former PCFC Establishments and Colleges in the FE Sector 1993/94.* London, DfE.

Department for Education (DfE) (1995) *Education Facts and Figures.* London, DfE.

Department for Education (DfE) and OFSTED (1993) *The Government's Expenditure Plans 1993/4 to 1995/6*, Cmnd 2210. London, HMSO.

Department for Education and Employment (DfEE) (1995) *Lifetime Learning. A consultation document.* Sheffield, DfEE.

Department of Employment (DoE) (1981) *A New Training Initiative: a consultative document.* London, HMSO.

Department of Employment (DoE) (1984) *Training for Jobs*, Cmnd 9135. London, HMSO.

Department of Employment (DoE) (1990) *The Skills Link.* Sheffield, TEED.

Department of Employment (DoE) with the DES (1986) *Working Together: Education and training*, Cmnd 9823. London, HMSO.

Diamond, J. and Kearney, A. (1990) Access courses: a new orthodoxy?, *Journal of Further and Higher Education*, 14(1): 128–38.

Diamond, J. and Kearney, A. (1994) The politics of Access recognition, *Journal of Access Studies*, 9(1): 139–45.

Donald, J. (1979) Green Paper: Noise of Crisis, *Screen Education*, 30.

Duckenfield, M. and Stirner, P. (1992) *Learning Through Work.* Sheffield, Employment Department.

Duke, C. (1992) *The Learning University. Towards a new paradigm?* Buckingham, SRHE and Open University Press.

Duke, C. (1994) Part and parcel of the credit revolution, *THES*, 30 September, ii–iii.

Dwyer, P.J. (1995) Foucault, docile bodies and post-compulsory education in Australia, *British Journal of Sociology of Education*, 16(4): 46–7.

Earwaker, J. (1991) Boo to the barbarians, *THES*, 29 March.

Edelman, M. (1977) *Political Language: Words that succeed and policies that fail.* London, Academic Press.

Education and Training Parliamentary Monitor (1996) Dearing Enquiry: membership and terms of reference, March.

Edwards, R. (1991) The politics of meeting learner needs: power, subject, subjection, *Studies in the Education of Adults*, 23(1): 85–97.

Edwards, R. (1993) *Mature Women Students. Separating or connecting family and education.* London, Taylor and Francis.

Egerton, M. and Halsey, A.H. (1993) Trends by social class and gender in access to higher education in Britain, *Oxford Review of Education*, 29(2): 183–95.

Epstein, D. (1993) *Changing Classroom Cultures.* Stoke on Trent, Trentham.

Evans, J. and Crivello, L. (1995) Do we need to teach numeracy, literacy and other academic skills in higher education?, *Journal of Access Studies*, 10(2): 156–72.

Evans, N. (1988) *The Assessment of Prior Experiential Learning.* CNAA Development Services Publication no. 17. London, CNAA.

Fairclough, N. (1989) *Language and Power.* Harlow, Longman.

Fairclough, N. (1993) Critical discourse analysis and the marketisation of public discourse: the universities, *Discourse and Society*, 4:2.

Finch, J. (1986) *Research and Policy: The uses of qualitative methods in social and educational research.* London, Falmer Press.

Finn, D., Grant, N. and Johnson, R. (1978) Social democracy, education and the crisis in cultural studies, in CCCS *On Ideology.* London, Hutchinson.

Forman, N. (1996) *Times Higher Education Supplement*, 1 March, 17.

Foucault, M. (1977) *The Archaeology of Knowledge.* London, Tavistock.

Foucault, M. (1979) On governmentality, *Ideology and Consciousness*, 6:5–22.

Foucault, M. (1980) Power/knowledge, in C. Gordon (ed.) *Michael Foucault: Power/ Knowledge: Selected interviews and other writings 1972–1977.* Sussex, Harvester Press.

Foucault, M. (1986) Disciplinary power and subjection, in S. Lukes (ed.) *Power. Readings in social and political theory.* Oxford, Basil Blackwell.

Foucault, M. (1989) *The Archaeology of Knowledge.* London, Routledge.

Freire, P. (1972) *Pedagogy of the Oppressed.* Harmondsworth, Penguin.

Fulton, O. (ed.) (1981) *Access to Higher Education.* Guildford, SRHE.

Fulton, O. and Ellwood, S. (1989) *Admissions to Higher Education. Policy and practice.* Sheffield, Training Agency.

Further Educaiton Unit (1987) *Access to Further and Higher Education: A discussion document.* London, FEU.

Gale, T.C. and McNamee, P.J. (1995) Alternative pathways to traditional destinations: higher education for disadvantaged Australians, *British Journal of Sociology of Education*, 16(4): 437–50.

Gallacher, J. and Wallis, W. (1993) '*The Performance of Students with Non-traditional Qualifications in Higher Education*', an unpublished report to SCOTVEC. Glasgow, Glasgow Caledonian University.

Gallagher, A., Richards, N. and Locke, M. (1993) *Mature Students in Higher Education: How Institutions can Learn from Experience.* Centre for Institutional Studies Commentary Series no. 40. University of East London.

Garner, L. and Imeson, R. (1996) More bricks in the wall: the ending of the older students' allowance and the new 16 hour rule: has the cost of higher education for mature students finally got too high?, *Journal of Access Studies* 11(1): 97–110.

Garnsey, E. (1978) Women's work and theories of social stratification, *Sociology*, 12(2): 223–44.

Gee, J.P. and Lankshear, C. (1995) The new work order: critical language awareness and 'fast capitalism', *Texts in Discourse Studies in the Cultural Politics of Education*, 16(1): 5–19.

Gewirtz, S., Ball, S.J. and Bowe, R. (1995) *Markets, Choice and Equity in Education*. Buckingham, Open University Press.

Gilroy, P. (1987) *There Ain't No Black in the Union Jack*. London, Hutchinson.

Gramsci, A. (1971) *Selections from the Prison Notebooks*, edited by Q. Hoare and G. Nowell-Smith. New York, International Publishers.

Griffiths, M. (1995) Making a difference: feminism, post-modernism and methodology of education research, *British Education Research Journal*, 21:2.

Hacking, I. (1991) How should we do the history of statistics? in G. Burchell, C. Gordon and P. Miller (eds) *The Foucault Effect: Studies in governmental rationality*. Hemel Hempstead, Harvester Wheatsheaf.

Hall, S. (1990) Cultural identity and diaspora, in J. Rutherford (ed.) *Identity – Community, Culture, Difference*. London, Lawrence & Wishart.

Halpin, D. and Troyna, B. (eds) (1994) *Researching Education Policy: Ethical and methodological issues*. London, Falmer Press.

Halsey, A.H. (ed.) (1988) *British Social Trends Since 1900*. London, Macmillan Press.

Hammersley, M. (1994) Ethnography, policy making and practice in education, in D. Halpin and B. Troyna (eds) *Researching Education Policy: Ethical and methodological issues*. London, Falmer Press.

Harrison, R. (1993) Disaffection and access, in J. Calder (ed.) *Disaffection and Diversity*. London, Falmer Press.

Hartley, D. (1995) The 'MacDonaldization' of higher education: food for thought, *Oxford Review of Education*, 21(4): 409–23.

Hatcher, R. and Troyna, B. (1994) The 'policy cycle': a Ball by Ball account, *Journal of Educational Policy*, 9(2): 155–70.

Heath, A.F., Mills, C. and Roberts, J. (1992) Towards meritocracy? Some recent evidence on an old problem, in C. Crouch and A. Heath (eds) *Social Research and Social Reform*. Oxford, Oxford University Press.

HEFCE (Higher Education Funding Council for England) (1993) *Strategic Plans and Financial Forecasts*. Circular 17/93, Bristol: HEFCE.

HEFCE (1994) *Profiles of Higher Education Institutions*. Bristol, HEFCE.

HEFCE (1995) *Higher Education in Further Education Colleges: Funding the relationship*. Bristol, HEFCE.

HEFCE (1996a) *Widening Access to Higher Education*. A Report by the HEFCE's Advisory Group on Access and Participation. Bristol, HEFCE, ref. M 9/96.

HEFCE (1996b) *Policy Statement on Equal Opportunities in Quality Assessment*. Bristol, HEFCE.

HEQC (Higher Education Quality Council) (1994) *Learning from Audit*. London, HEQC.

HEQC (1996) *Draft Guidelines on Quality Assurance: Entry to higher education*. London, HEQC.

HESA (Higher Education Statistical Agency) (1995) *HESA Data Report. Students in higher education institutions*. Cheltenham, HESA.

HESA (1996a) *Students in Higher Education Institutions 1994–5.* Reference Volume. Cheltenham, HESA.

HESA (1996b) 'Student Enrolments on Higher Education Courses at Publicly Funded Higher Education Institutions in the United Kingdom for the Academic Year 1995–96'. Press release 30 April. Cheltenham, HESA.

HESA (1996c) *Entry Qualifications in Higher Education.* Research Datapack 2. Cheltenham, HESA.

Hollinshead, B. and Griffiths, J. (1990) *Mature Students: Marketing and admissions policy.* London, CNAA.

Hollway, W. (1989) *Subjectivity and Method in Psychology,* London, Sage.

Hughes, C. and Tight, M. (1995) The myth of the learning society, *British Journal of Educational Studies,* 43(3): 290–304.

Jackson, R. (1988) *Manpower Planning in Higher Education.* Chevening Discussion Papers.

Jackson, R. (1995) Private cash will restore autonomy, *THES,* 8 December.

James, D. (1995) Mature studentship in higher education: beyond a 'species' approach, *British Journal of Sociology of Education,* 16(4): 451–66.

Jenkins, S. (1995) *Accountable to None: The Tory nationalisation of Britain.* London, Hamish Hamilton.

Johnes, J. (1992) The potential effects of wider access in higher education degree quality, *Higher Education Quarterly,* 45(1): 88–107.

Johnes, J. and Taylor, J. (1990) *Performance Indicators in Higher Education.* Buckingham, SRHE and Open University Press.

Johnson, S. (1994) 'Women in transition: the expectations and reality of higher education', paper presented at the SRHE Student Experience conference, University of York.

Judd, J., Abrams, F. and Castle, S. (1996) *Independent on Sunday,* 25 February, 17.

Kedourie, E. (1988) *Diamonds into Glass,* Policy Study no. 89, London, Centre for Policy Studies.

Keen, C. and Higgins, T. (1992) *Adults' Knowledge of Higher Education.* Cheltenham, HEIST/PCAS.

Keep, E. (1996) Economic demand for higher education: a sound foundation for further expansion?, *Higher Education Quarterly,* 50(2): 89–109.

Kelly, T. (1990) *Developing Wider Access to Universities. Project report.* Leeds, Bradford and Leeds Universities (for the DES).

Kenway, J. (1990) Education and the Right's discursive policies, in S.J. Ball (ed.) *Foucault and Education.* London, Routledge.

Lal, D. (1989) *Nationalised Universities,* Policy Study no. 103, London, Centre for Policy Studies.

Lather, P. (1991) *Getting Smart: Feminist research and pedagogy with/in the post modern.* London, Routledge.

Leicester, M. (1993) Anti-racist Access?, *Journal of Access Studies,* 8(2): 220–4.

Lemelin, R.E. (ed.) (1994) Issues in Access to Higher Education, Conference proceedings, International Access Conference, University of South Maine, USA.

Lennon, K. (1995) Gender and knowledge, *Journal of Gender Studies,* 4(2): 133–43.

Leonard, M. (1994) Transforming the household: mature women students and access to higher education, in S. Davies, C. Lubelska and J. Quinn (eds) *Changing the Subject. Women in Higher Education.* London, Taylor and Francis.

Letwin, S.R. (1992) *The Anatomy of Thatcherism.* London, Fontana.

Lieven, M. (1989) Access courses after ten years: a review, *Higher Education Quarterly*, 43: 160–74.

Liggett, E. (1982) The universities and mature student entry, *Adult Education*, 55(2): 125–36.

Little, A. and Robbins, D. (1981) Race Bias, in D.W. Piper (ed.) *Is Higher Education Fair?* Buckingham, SRHE and Open University Press.

Lyon, E. (1988) Unequal opportunities: black minorities and access to higher education, *Journal of Further and Higher Education*, 12(3): 21–37.

McFadden, M.G. (1995) 'Second chance' education: settling old scores, *Journal of Access Studies*, 10(1): 40–59.

McGivney, V. (1993) *Women, Education and Training. Barriers to access, informal starting points and progression routes.* Leicester, NIACE.

Mackay, L., Scott, P. and Smith, D. (1995) Changing environment of UK Higher Education, *Higher Education Management*, 7(2): 193–205.

Maclure, M. (1994) Language and discourse: the embrace of uncertainty, *British Journal of Sociology of Education*, 15(2): 283–300.

Marsh, C. and Blackburn, R.M. (1992) Class differences in access to higher education, in R. Burrows and C. Marsh (eds) *Consumption and Class Divisions and Change.* London, MacMillan.

Marshall, J.D. (1990) Foucault and educational research, in S.J. Ball (ed.) *Foucault and Education.* London, Routledge.

Mason, R. (1987) The logic of non-standard entry, *Journal of Further and Higher Education*, 11(3).

Maynard, L. (1992) Are mature students a problem? *Journal of Access Studies* 7(1): 106–11.

Metcalf, H. (1993) *Non-traditional Students' Experience of Higher Education: A review of the literature.* CVCP Briefing, London, Policy Studies Institute.

Miles, S. and Middleton, C. (1995) Girls' education in the balance: the ERA and inequality, in L. Dawtrey, J. Holland and M. Hammer (eds) *Equality and Inequality in Educational Policy*, Clevedon, Multilingual Matters.

Miller, P. and Rose, N. (1993) Governing economic life, in M. Game and T. Johnson (eds) *Foucault's New Domains.* London, Routledge.

Ministry of Education (1960) *Grants to Students* (The Anderson Report), Cmnd 1051. London, HMSO.

Mirza, H.S. (1992) *Young, Female and Black.* London, Routledge.

Mirza, H. (1993) The social construction of black womanhood in British educational research: towards a new understanding, in M. Arnot and K. Weiler, (eds) *Feminism and Social Justice in Education.* London, Falmer Press.

Modood, T. (1992) *Not Easy Being British: Colour, culture and identity.* Stoke on Trent, Trentham and Runnymede Trust.

Modood, T. (1993) The number of ethnic minority students in British higher education: some grounds for optimism, *Oxford Review of Education*, 19(2): 167–82.

Modood, T. and Shiner, M. (1994) *Ethnic Minorities and Higher Education: Why are there differential rates of entry?* London, Policy Studies Institute in collaboration with UCAS, PSI Publishing.

Molloy, S. and Carroll, V. (1992) *Progress and Performance in Higher Education.* CNAA Project Report 34. London, CNAA.

Morgan, P. (1990) *Breaking the Academic Mould.* London, BTEC Strategic Seminar Paper.

National Advisory Body for Local Authority Higher Education (1984) *A Strategy for Higher Education in the Late 1980s and Beyond.* London, NAB.

National Institute of Adult Continuing Education (1989) *Adults in Higher Education: Policy discussion paper.* Leicester, NIACE.

National Institute of Adult Continuing Education (1993) *Adult Higher Education: A vision. A policy discussion paper.* Leicester, NIACE.

Neave, G. and van Vught, F. (eds) (1991) *The Changing Relationship Between Government and Higher Education in Western Europe.* Oxford, Pergamon.

Opacic, S. (1994) The student learning experience in the mid 1990s, in S. Haselgrove, (ed.) *The Student Experience.* Buckingham, Open University Press.

Parry, G. (1986) From patronage to partnership, *Journal of Access Studies,* 1(1).

Parry, G. (1989) Marketing and mediating the higher education boundary, in O. Fulton *Access and Institutional Change.* Buckingham, Open University Press.

Parry, G. (1995) England, Wales and Northern Ireland, in P. Davies (ed.) *Adults in Higher Education. International perspectives in access and participation.* London, Jessica Kingsley.

Parry, G. (1996) Access education in England and Wales 1973–1994: from second chance to third wave, *Journal of Access Studies,* 11(1): 10–33.

Parry, G. and Davies, P. (1990) *Wider Access and the Professional Engineering Institutions.* London, CNAA.

Parry, G. and Wake, C. (eds) (1990) *Access and Alternative Futures for Higher Education.* London, Hodder and Stoughton.

Pascall, G. and Cox, R. (1993) *Women Returning to Higher Education.* Buckingham, SRHE and Open University Press.

PCAS (Polytechnics and Colleges Admissions Service) (1993) *Statistical Supplement to the PCAS Annual Report 1991–2.* Cheltenham, PCAS.

PCAS (1994) *Statistical Supplement to the PCAS Annual Report 1992–3.* Cheltenham, PCAS.

PCFC (Polytechnics and Colleges Funding Council) (1992) *Widening Participation in Higher Education: Report of a study of polytechnics and colleges of higher education in England.* Bristol, PCFC.

Peeke, G. (1994) *Mission and Change.* Buckingham, SRHE and Open University Press.

Peinovich, P. (1996) Conditions of openness to mature learners in English universities 1995: a view from the United States, *Journal of Access Studies,* 11(1): 59–75.

Percy, K. (1985) Adult learners in higher education, in C. Titmuss (ed.) *Widening the Field: Continuing Education in Higher Education.* Guildford, SRHE and NFER-Nelson.

Pickering, J. and Gardner, P. (1992) Access: a selector's perception, *Journal of Access Studies,* 7(2): 220–33.

Potter, J. and Wetherall, M. (1994) Analysing discourse, in A. Bryman and R.G. Burgess (eds) *Analysing Qualitative Data.* London, Routledge.

Raab, C.D. (1993) Education and the impact of the new right, in G. Jordan and N. Ashford (eds) *Public Policy and the Impact of the New Right.* London, Pinter.

Raab, C.D. (1994) Theorising governance and education, *British Journal of Educational Studies,* 42(1): 6–22.

Ranson, S. (1993) Markets of democracy for education, *British Journal of Educational Studies,* 41(4): 333–51.

Ranson, S. (1995) Public institutions for cooperative action: a reply to James Tooley, *British Journal of Educational Studies,* 43(1): 35–42.

Redpath, B. and Robus, N. (1989) *Mature Students' Incomings and Outgoings. A report of a survey by the Social Survey Division of OPCS on behalf of the DES.* London, HMSO.

Richards, H. (1996) Levy hangs in balance, *Times Higher Education Supplement,* 2 February.

Richardson, J.T.E. (1995) Mature students in higher education, *Studies in Higher Education,* 20(1): 5–17.

Robbins, D. (1993) The practical importance of Bourdieu's analysis of higher education, *Studies in Higher Education,* 18(2): 151–63.

Roberts, D. and Higgins, T. (1992) *Higher Education: The student experience.* Leeds, HEIST.

Robertson, D. (1994) *Choosing to Change: Extending access, choice and mobility in higher education.* Report of HEQC CAT Development Project. London, HEQC.

Robertson, D. (1995) Access, choice and mobility, *Access Network,* 3.

Rogers, R. (ed.) *Education and Social Class.* London, Falmer Press.

Salter, B. and Tapper, T. (1994) *The State and Higher Education.* Ilford, Woburn Press.

Schuller, T. (1991) Reassessing the future, in T. Schuller (ed.) *The Future of Higher Education.* Buckingham, SRHE and Open University Press.

Scott, J. (1992) Deconstructing equality versus difference: or the uses of post-structuralist theory for feminism, in L. McDowell and R. Pringle (eds) *Defining Women.* Cambridge, Polity Press.

Scott, P. (1995) *The Meanings of Mass Higher Education.* Buckingham, SRHE and Open University Press.

Scott, P. and Smith, D. (1995) *Access and Consolidation. The impact of steady state on opportunities for non-standard applicants to universities and colleges: A second report.* Leeds, Centre for Policy Studies in Education, University of Leeds.

Shah, S. (1994) Kaleidoscope people: locating the 'subject' of pedagogic discourse, *Journal of Access Studies,* 9(2): 257–70.

Singh, R. (1990) Ethnic minority experience in higher education, *Higher Education Quarterly,* 44(4): 344–59.

Skeggs, B. (1994) The constraints of neutrality: the 1988 Reform Act and feminist research, in D. Halpin and B. Troyna (eds) *Researching Education Policy: Ethical and methodological issues.* London, Falmer Press.

Skellington, R., Morris, P. and Gordon, P. (1992) *'Race' in Britain Today.* London, Sage.

Smith, D. and Saunders, M. (1991) *Other Routes: Part-time higher education policy.* Buckingham, SHRE and Open University Press.

Smith, D., Scott, P. and McKay, L. (1993) Mission impossible? Access and the dash for growth in British higher education, *Higher Education Quarterly* 47(4): 316–33.

Smith, D., Scott, P. and Bargh, C. (1995) Standard systems, non-standard students: the impact of consolidation on access to higher education, *Journal of Access Studies,* 10(2): 120–36.

Smithers, A. (1990) *The Vocational Route into Higher Education.* Manchester, University of Manchester.

Smithers, A. and Griffin, A. (1986) *The Progress of Mature Students.* Manchester, Joint Matriculation Board.

Smithers, A. and Robinson, P. (1989) *Increasing Participation in Higher Education.* London, British Petroleum Educational Services.

Smithers, A. and Robinson, P. (1995) *Post-18 Education: Growth, change and prospect.* London, Council for Industry and Higher Education.

Society for Research in Higher Education (1983) *Excellence in Diversity: The report on the Leverhulme Studies.* Guildford, SRHE.

Standing Conference on University Entrance (SCUE), Open College, PCAS (1992) *Successful Admissions: Tactics, procedures and responsibilities.* Manchester, Open College.

Stowell, M. (1992) Equal opportunities, access and admissions: tensions and issues for institutional policy, *Journal of Access Studies*, 7(2): 164–79.

Stuart, M. (1995) Education and self identity: a process of inclusion and exclusion, in M. Stuart and S. Thomson (eds) *Engaging with Difference: The 'other' in adult education.* Leicester, NIACE.

Stuart, M. and Thomson, S. (eds) (1995) *Engaging with Difference: The other in Adult Education.* Leicester, NIACE.

Tarsh, J. (1982) *The Correlation between A levels and Degree Performance.* Unit for Manpower Studies. London, DES.

Tasker, M. and Packham, D. (1994) Changing cultures? Government intervention in higher education 1987–93, *British Journal of Education Studies*, 42(2): 150–62.

Taylor, P. (1992) Ethnic group data and applications to higher education, *Higher Education Quarterly*, 46(4): 359–74.

Taylor, P. (1993) Minority ethnic groups and gender in access to higher education, *New Community*, 19(3): 425–40.

Thomas, K. (1990) *Gender and Subject in Higher Education.* Buckingham, Open University Press.

Thompson, A. and Parry, G. (1992) *Access Co-ordinators in Higher Education.* London, City University.

Tight, M. (1991) *Higher Education: A part-time perspective.* Buckingham, SRHE and Open University Press.

Tomlinson, S. (1983) Black women in higher education – case studies of university women in Britain, in L. Barton and S. Walker (eds) *Race, Class and Education.* Beckenham, Croom Helm.

Tooley, J. (1995) Markets or democracy for education? A reply to Stewart Ranson, *British Journal of Educational Studies*, 43(1): 21–33.

Trow, M. (1974) Problems in the transition from elite to mass higher education in Organisation for Economic Co-operation and Development. *Policies for Higher Education.* Paris, OECD.

Trow, M. (1989) The Robbins trap: British attitudes and the limits of expansion, *Higher Education Quarterly*, 43(1): 55–75.

Troyna, B. (1994) Critical social research and education policy, *British Journal of Education Studies*, 42(1): 70–84.

Troyna, B. and Vincent (1995) The discourses of social justice in higher education, *Discourse: Studies in the cultural politics of education*, 16:2.

Tuckett, A. (1990) A higher education system fit for adult learners, in G. Parry and C. Wake (eds) *Access and Alternative Futures for Higher Education.* London, Hodder and Stoughton.

Turner, R.H. (1960) Sponsored and contest mobility and the school system, *American Sociological Review*, xxv(5): 855–67.

Tysome, T. (1995) Consensus mars rival party plans, *THES*, 20 October.

UCAS (Universities and Colleges Admissions Service) (1994) *UCAS Annual Report 1993–94 Entry.* Cheltenham, UCAS.

UCAS (1995) *Statistical Bulletin. Access and foundation applicants.* Cheltenham, UCAS.

UDACE (Unit for the Development of Adult Continuing Education) (1985) *Helping Adults to Learn: a consultative document on educational guidance for adults.* Leicester, NIACE.

UDACE (1988) *Developing Access: A discussion paper.* Leicester, UDACE.

Universities Grants Committee (1984) *A Strategy for Higher Education into the 1990s.* London, UGC.

Universities Statistical Record (1994) *University Statistics 1993–94. Volume I – students and staff.* Cheltenham, USR.

Usher, R. and Bryant, I. (1989) *Adult Education as Theory, Practice and Research: The captive triangle.* London, Routledge.

Wagner, L. (1989) Access and standards: an unresolved (and unresolvable?) debate, in C. Ball and H. Eggins (eds) *Higher Education in the 1990s: New dimensions.* Milton Keynes, SRHE and Open University Press.

Wakeford, N. (1994) Becoming a mature student: the social risks of identification, *Journal of Access Studies*, 9(2): 241–56.

Warren Piper, D. (ed.) (1981) *Is Higher Education Fair?* Guildford, SRHE.

Webb, S. (1991) 'Shop-work: an ethnography of a large department store', unpublished PhD. thesis, University of Manchester.

Webb S., Davies, P., Green, P., Thompson, A. and Williams, J. (1994a) *Alternative Entry to Higher Education: Summary report.* Leicester, NIACE.

Webb, S., Davies, P., Williams, J., Green, P. and Thompson, A. (1994b) 'Alternative entry to higher education: final report', unpublished.

Webb, S., Davies, P., Williams, J., Green, P. and Thompson, A. (1994c) Access and alternative entrants to higher education: routes, tracks, triggers and choices, *Journal of Access Studies*, 9(2): 197–214.

Weil, S.W. (1993) Access: towards education or miseducation? Adults imagine the future, in M. Thorpe, R. Edwards and A. Hanson (eds) *Culture and Process of Adult Learning: A reader.* London, Routledge.

Wheeler, S. and Birtle, J. (1993) *A Handbook for Personal Tutors.* Buckingham, SRHE and Open University Press.

Whitty, G. (1989) The new right and the National Curriculum: state control or market forces, *Journal of Educational Policy*, 4(4): 329–41.

Willenborg, L.C.R.J., de Waal, A.G. and Keller W.J. (1995) 'Some methodological issues in statistical disclosure control', unpublished paper presented at the Second Cathy Mash Memorial Seminar at the Royal Statistical Society, November.

Williams, J., Davis, L. and Cocking, J. (1989) *Words or Deeds: A review of equal opportunity policies in higher education.* London, Commission for Racial Equality.

Willis, P.E. (1977) *Learning to Labour: How working class kids get working class jobs.* Farnborough, Saxon House.

Wilson, J.M. (1982) The accuracy of A level forecasts, *Educational Research*, 24(3): 216–22.

Woodley, A., Wagner, L., Slowey, M., Hamilton, M. and Fulton, O. (1987) *Choosing to Learn: Adults in education.* Buckingham, SRHE and Open University Press.

Woodrow, M. (1996) Access is not obsolete, *The Lecturer*, February.

Wright, P. (1991) Access or accessibility, *Journal of Access Studies*, 6(1): 6–16.

Wright, P. (1993) Enterprise and access, *Journal of Access Studies*, 8(1): 5–7.

Young, S. (1996) Academic profile at a touch of the button, *Times Educational Supplement*, 2 August.

Index

A levels
  academic traditionalist discourse of,
    29, 30, 31, 70
  as impediment to access, 36
  point scores as criteria for
    admission, 114–15
  as predictors of degree
    performance, 29, 70
  recoding in HESA data of, 57
  as route to higher education, 10
  treated as gold standard, 10, 26, 29,
    30, 36, 113–15
academic autonomy, 29, 30
academic research on access to higher
    education, 65–6, 155
  alternative entry project, 83–5
  concepts of gender, 75–6
  concepts of mature students,
    71–4
  concepts of 'race' and ethnicity,
    76–9
  concepts of social class, 79–83
  concepts of standard/non-standard
    and traditional/non-traditional,
    68–9
  concepts of student inputs and
    outputs, 69–71
  context of, 66–7
academic traditionalist discourse,
    28–32
  in admissions practice, 109
  link between entry qualifications
    and degree performance, 29,
    70

of non-standard students and
    quality, 30, 31–2, 116, 117
  and research on 'race' and
    ethnicity, 79
  in self-identity of alternative
    students, 146
  use of quantitative data, 48–9
Access courses
  compared with 'access', 42–3
  criticisms of, 76
  and ethnicity, 78–9
  in HESA data, 58
  quality of, 40
  as route to higher education, 11,
    127–8
  and social class, 81
  student grants and benefits, 12,
    81
  see also alternative and Access
    students
Access Courses Recognition Group
    (ACRG), 11
access movement discourse, 42–5
  in admissions practice, 109
  link between entry qualifications
    and degree performance, 70
  mature students as catalyst for
    change, 116
  and research on 'race' and
    ethnicity, 78, 79
  and research on social class, 82–3
  in self-identity of alternative
    students, 137, 146
  use of quantitative data, 49–50

accessibility
  alternative students' perceptions of,
    146–7
  strategies of, 95
accountability, 8
  quality assurance of Access courses,
    11
  quality monitoring, 96–8, 106
accreditation of prior learning (APL),
  11–12
ACRG (Access Courses Recognition
  Group), 11
admissions policy and practice
  ability to benefit as criteria in, 114,
    119
  alternative students' perceptions of,
    147, 148–9
  departmental and institutional
    policies, 110–11
  and discourse of admission, 109–12
  discourses affecting, 98–9
    expansion and consolidation, 6,
      7, 36, 109–10
    forms of management, 95–6, 101,
      105–6
    numbers and marketing, 9–10,
      93–5, 103–5, 122–5
    quality monitoring, 96–8, 106,
      116–17
  institutional comparison of student
    intakes, 99–102
  relationship between policy and
    practice, 110–12
  see also quantitative data
admissions tutors
  discursive practice of, 106–7, 109
    A levels perceived as gold
      standard, 113–15
    constructions of mature students,
      see mature students
    divisions between standard and
      non-standard students, 113,
      117–18, 133
    impact of drive for quality on,
      116–17
    perceptions of Access courses,
      127–8
  non-compliance with institutional
    policy, 111
  role and status of work, 96, 112

age participation index (API), 6
Ainley, P., 160
Allen, C., 97, 110
alternative and Access students
  educational identity on leaving
    school
    access denied, 132, 133–7, 142
    untapped potential, 132, 137–8,
      142
    wasted potential, 132–3, 138–40,
      142
  identity in higher education, 145–6,
    156
    education as investment, 149–51
    as non-standard or abnormal,
      148–9
    perceptions of institutions, 146–8,
      157
  institutional comparison of
    recruitment of, 99–102
  positioning and self-identity, 130–1,
    151–2
  shifting identities of, 140–1
    influence of education, 143–5
    influence of family, 145
    influence of work, 141–3
  social class of, 84–5
'Alternative Entry to Higher
  Education' project, 83–5, 130–1,
  162
Anderson Report, 5
API (age participation index), 6
APL (accreditation of prior learning),
  11–12
Authorized Validating Agencies
  (AVAs), 11

Ball, C., 35, 36
Ball, S.J., 28, 37, 154
Bargh, C., 68, 71, 110, 117, 118,
  121–2, 124
Barnett, R., 71
Beloff, M., 30
benefits, *see* social security benefits
Benn, R., 81, 82–3
Blackburn, R.M., 81–2
Bowe, R., 34
Brown, P., 158, 159–60
Budgen, Nicholas, 30
Burton, R., 81, 82–3

business management, influence on
    mission statements, 88, 92, 98
Business and Technology Council
    (BTEC), 10–11

categorizations, polarizing
    categorizations, 25–7, 42–3
choice, marketeers' concept of, 32,
    34
Clarke, S., 98
Coffield, F., 60
colleges of further education, *see*
    further education colleges
colleges of higher education
    development of, 4
    mission statements, 90
compacts, between higher and further
    education institutions, 4, 13, 94,
    105
completion rates, discourse of, 48
compliance, 20, 32, 35, 38
    non-compliance of admissions
        tutors, 111
condensation symbols, 25, 27, 45–6,
    153
    see also icon words
continuous student record (CSR), 57,
    97
courses
    entry and completion of, 48
    modular programmes, 13, 106
    structure and recruitment, 13, 100,
        101–2
credit systems, 39–41, 49, 59

Dawson, E., 123
Dearing Inquiry into higher
    education, 14–15, 35, 153, 154,
    155, 161
degree courses, *see* courses
degree performance, link with entry
    qualifications, 29, 31, 69–71,
    117
differentiation, 19–20, 32, 34–5, 38,
    41, 45, 109
    and hierarchies in higher
        education, 5, 37–8, 90–1, 158–60
    polarizing categorizations, 25–7
disabled people, recruitment of, 10
disciplines, *see* courses

discourse
    Foucault's concept of, 15, 16
    polarized categorizations in, 25–7
discourse approach
    application to higher education,
        15–21, 154–5
    applications of discourse analysis,
        15–21
    debates within, 2, 153–4
    strengths of, 153
discourse positions, 17–18, 27–8, 45
    and future of higher education,
        159–61
    use of quantitative data, 48–50, 64
    see also academic traditionalist
        discourse; access movement
        discourse; liberal meritocratic
        discourse; marketeer discourse;
        utilitarian trainer discourse
discursive practices, 18
    interconnections between, 155–7
    of liberal meritocrats, 39–40
    use of quantitative data, 48–50
    of utilitarian trainers, 36–7
    see also admissions policy and
        practice; admissions tutors;
        mission statements
distance learning, 13
dividing practices, *see* differentiation
Duke, C., 160

Earwaker, J., 91
economic discourse of higher
    education, 9, 35–6
    see also marketeer discourse
educational policy, discourse analysis
    of, 17
elite status of institutions
    academic traditionalist discourse of,
        29, 30, 31, 116–17
    as marketing strategy, 94
Ellwood, S., 97, 110
employment
    and identity of alternative students,
        134–5
    as trigger for entry to higher
        education, 141–3, 149
    in utilitarian trainer discourse, 35–8
Enterprise in Higher Education
    Initiative (EHE), 13, 36

equal opportunities policies, 88–9,
    102–3, 110
equity
    liberal meritocratic discourse of, 39,
        41
    marketeer discourse of, 33
    research on gender, 75–6
    research on 'race' and ethnicity,
        76–9
    research on social class, 79–83
    and under-represented groups in
        higher education, 10, 39, 41, 74
    utilitarian trainer discourse of, 37–8
ethnicity
    and educational identity of
        alternative students, 136
    quantitative data on, 51, 56, 77
    recruitment of ethnic groups, 10
    research on, 76–9

family, as trigger for entry to higher
    education, 145
fees, 5, 7, 33
FESR (Further Education Statistical
    Record), 51
FEU (Further Education Unit), 68
Forman, Nigel, 30
Forum for Access Studies (FAST), 14,
    42
Foucault, M., 15, 16, 154
foundation/year 0 courses, 13, 107
franchising, 13
Fulton, O., 97, 110
funding
    of further education, 8
    government control of higher
        education, 7–8
    in liberal meritocratic discourse,
        41
further education
    funding of, 8
    as trigger for entry to higher
        education, 143–5
further education colleges, links with
    higher education institutions, 4,
    13, 94, 105
Further Education Funding Council
    (FEFC), 8
Further Education Statistical Record
    (FESR), 51

Further Education Unit (FEU), 68
Further and Higher Education Act
    (1992), 8

Gallagher, A., 118
Gardner, P., 115, 118
Garner, L., 81, 82
gender
    and educational identity, 135–6,
        138
    research on, 75–6
    in utilitarian trainer discourse, 37
    see also women
General National Vocational
    Qualifications (GNVQs), 11
government
    influence on higher education, 7–8,
        14, 29, 32–4, 63, 93, 154
    use of quantitative data, 48
grants, *see* student grants
Griffiths, J., 94

Hall, S., 131–2
Halsey, A.H., 75
Hatcher, R., 153–4
HEFCs (Higher Education Funding
    Councils), 7, 89–90, 159
HEQC (Higher Education Quality
    Council), 11, 88, 97
HESA (Higher Education Statistical
    Agency), 54, 56–9, 97
higher education
    application of discourse approach
        to, 15–21, 154–5
    control of, 6–8
    data on entry and participation,
        see quantitative data
    demand and supply, 6–7, 93–5,
        103–5, 122–5
    expansion, consolidation and
        restratification of, 5–6, 36,
        109–10, 128, 157–60
    government influence on, 7–8, 14,
        29, 32–4, 63, 93, 154
    hierarchies and differentiation
        within, 5, 37–8, 90–1, 158–60
    'key players' and levels of power in,
        14, 154–5
    nature of, 3–6
    purposes of, 8–12

structure and organization of study
in, 12–14, 100, 101–2, 106
under-represented groups in, 10,
39, 41, 74
Higher Education Funding Councils
(HEFCs), 7, 89–90, 159
higher education institutions
discursive practices, 157
admissions, *see* admissions policy
and practice
case study, 102–7
collection and analysis of data,
52–3, 61, 63
comparisons of, 99–102
mission statements, 88–93, 98,
100, 102–3
strategic plans, 92–3
links with further education colleges
and schools, 4, 13, 94, 105
market position of, 63, 157
students' perceptions of, 146–8, 157
see also colleges of higher
education; polytechnics;
universities
Higher Education Quality Council
(HEQC), 11, 88, 97
higher education shops, 104
Higher Education Statistical Agency
(HESA), 54, 56–9, 97
Hollinshead, B., 94

icon words, 25, 32, 35, 38–9, 42, 45
in mission statements, 90–2, 100
see also condensation symbols
identity of alternative and Access
students, 130–1, 151–2
educational identity on leaving
school
access denied, 132, 133–7, 142
untapped potential, 132, 137–8,
142
wasted potential, 132–3, 138–40,
142
identity in higher education, 145–6,
156
education as investment, 149–50
as non-standard or abnormal,
148–9
perceptions of institutions, 146–8,
157

shifting identities, 140–1
influence of education, 143–5
influence of family, 145
influence of work, 141–3
Imeson, R., 81, 82
institutionalization, 20, 32, 35, 38,
41–2, 45
barriers to, 110–11
institutions, *see* higher education
institutions
interviews
of alternative and Access students,
118, 147
of mature students, 118, 119–21

Jackson, R., 33–4, 37
James, D., 73
Jarman, J., 81–2
Johnes, J., 69–70

Keep, E., 34
knowledge, Foucault's concept of,
16

Leverhulme Study, 53
liberal meritocratic discourse, 38–42,
49
and research on 'race' and
ethnicity, 79
and research on social class, 82
in self-identity of alternative
students, 138
use of quantitative data, 49
Lindop Report, 30
loans, *see* student loans

management
of access and admissions, 95–6,
101, 105–6
discourse in mission statements, 88,
92, 98
marketeer discourse, 32–5, 156–7
and identity of alternative students,
149
in mission statements, 88, 92
of quality, 117
and research on social class, 83
use of quantitative data, 49
marketing strategies, 92, 94–5, 104
Marshall, J.D., 19

MASNs (maximum aggregate student
    numbers), 93, 109, 114
mass system of education
    academic traditionalist discourse of,
        31–2
    implications of, 1
    marketeer discourse of, 35
    restratification of, 157–60
mature students
    access movement discourse of, 43–4
    admissions tutors' constructions of,
        156
        impact of supply and demand,
            122–5
        interviews, 118, 119–21
        motivation, 121
        normalization, 126–7
        perceived expense of, 125
        as returners, 126
    as catalyst for change in higher
        education, 116
    concepts in access research of, 71–4
    difficulties faced by, 43–4
    grants and allowances for, 12
    marketing and recruitment of, 9, 94
    as non-standard or abnormal, 70,
        119, 156
    perceptions of admissions process,
        120, 123, 148–9
    quantitative data on, 51, 60
    see also alternative and Access
        students
maximum aggregate student numbers
    (MASNs), 93, 109, 114
Miller, P., 66
mission statements, 88–93, 98, 100,
    102–3
'Model E' projection, 60–1
Modood, T., 78
modular degrees, 13, 106
motivation, of mature students, 121
mustering, 54

National Vocational Qualifications
    (NVQs), 11
new right, see marketeer discourse
newspapers, criticisms of access in, 24,
    26, 30–1
NIACE (National Institute of Adult
    Continuing Education), 39

normalization, 20, 32, 34–5, 38
    of non-standard students, 57, 126–7

occupation, and problems of
    researching class, 80
Opacic, S., 39
Open College Networks, 11, 104
Open University, 4
outreach strategies, 94, 104

Packham, D., 46
Parry, G., 6, 9, 11, 82, 96, 110
PCAS (Polytechnics and Colleges
    Admissions Service), 54
Peeke, G., 88, 92
Peinovich, P., 95, 110, 128
Pickering, J., 115, 118
policy
    discourse analysis of educational
        policy, 17
    equal opportunities policies, 88–9,
        102–3, 110
    mission statements, 88–93, 98, 100,
        102–3
    see also admissions policy and
        practice
polytechnics
    compared with universities, 4–5,
        30
    creation and development of, 4
    discourse of equal opportunity in,
        88–9
positions, see discourse positions
post-structuralist approach, 2, 153–4
postgraduate study, 13
power
    debate on state power, 153–4
    different levels in higher education
        of, 154–5
    Foucault's concept of, 16

qualifications
    credit systems, 39–41, 49, 59
    entry qualifications, 10–12, 68, 155,
        160
        quantitative data on, 51–2, 55–6,
            57–8
    relationship with degree
        performance, 29, 31, 69–71,
        117

see also A levels; vocational
    qualifications
qualitative research and data, 49, 76
quality, discourses of standards and,
    20, 30, 31–2, 116–17
quality assurance, 8
    of Access courses, 11
quality monitoring, 96–8, 106
quantitative data on participation in
    higher education, 47
    academic research, 53, 63–4
    before 1994/95, 50–3
    discursive use of, 48–50, 64
    post 1994/95
        HESA data collection and
            analysis, 54, 56–9
        UCAS data collection and
            analysis, 53, 54–6
    problems of, 51–3, 59–62, 101
    recent and current trends in
        collection and analysis, 62–4
    terminology of, 48

'race'
    and educational identity of
        alternative students, 136
    research on higher education and,
        76–9
    see also ethnicity
Ranson, S., 34
rationalization, 20, 32, 35, 41
recruitment, *see* admissions policy and
    practice
research, *see* academic research
returners
    educational identity of, 138
    mature students constructed as, 126
Robbins Report, 5, 6
Robertson, D., 39, 40–1, 43, 59, 96,
    112
Rose, N., 66

Salter, B., 27, 45, 48
Scase, R., 158, 159–60
schools
    and educational identity of
        alternative students, 132–40
    links with higher education
        institutions, 94, 105
Scott, P., 31, 69, 92, 158

selectivity
    discourses of, 29, 33, 36, 39
    social selectivity, 31, 159–60
    see also admissions policy and
        practice
skills, transfer from personal to public
    life, 37
Smith, D., 31, 69, 92–3, 98
social class
    of alternative entry students, 84–5,
        134, 138
    problems of quantitative data on,
        56, 80–4
    recruitment of lower socio-
        economic groups, 10
    relationship with gender, 76
    research on higher education and,
        79–83
    in utilitarian trainer discourse, 37–8
social justice, as aim of higher
    education, 9, 10
social security benefits, for students,
    12, 81
state
    models of power of, 153–4
    see also government
statistics, *see* quantitative data
Stowell, M., 97, 98
strategic plans, 92–3
structural approach to marketing, 94,
    104
structuralist approach, 2, 153–4
student grants, 5, 12, 33
    see also social security benefits
student loans, 12, 33, 159
students
    admissions, *see* admissions policy
        and practice
    as consumers, 34, 156–7
    discourses of selection of, 29, 33,
        36, 39
    qualifications of, *see* qualifications
    ratio of full-time to part-time, 13
    research on and concepts of
        difference between, 65, 74
    alternative entry project, 83–5
    gender, 75–6
    'race' and ethnicity, 76–9
    social class, 79–83
    research on experiences of, 71

standard/non-standard and
traditional/non-traditional,
68–9
definitions of, 68–9, 113
degree performance of, 70
differentiation in admissions
practice, 113, 117–18, 133
discourses of normality/
abnormality, 25, 26, 33, 36–7,
40, 43
non-standard as burden or
catalyst, 36, 71, 125, 159
normalization of non-standard,
57, 126–7
problems of quantitative data on,
51–2, 56, 57
role of age in perceptions of, 70,
119, 156
self-identity of alternative
students, 148–9
see also alternative and Access
students; mature students
subjects of study, *see* courses
subjects within discourses, 18

Tapper, T., 27, 45, 48
Tasker, M., 46
technical approach to marketing, 94,
104
Thompson, A., 96, 110
trainers, *see* utilitarian trainer
discourse
Troyna, B., 153–4
Tuckett, A., 124

UCAS (Universities and Colleges
Admissions Service), 53, 54–6, 97,
155

universities
compared with polytechnics, 4–5,
30
creation and development of,
3–4
discourse of equal opportunity in,
89
hierarchy of, 5, 37–8, 90, 91,
158–60
influence of, 27
students' perceptions of, 146,
147
utilitarian trainer discourse, 35–8
and identity of alternative students,
149
and research on social class, 83
use of quantitative data, 49

vocational qualifications
academic traditionalist criticisms of,
30
HESA data on, 57–8
as route to higher education,
10–11
utilitarian trainer discourse of, 36,
37
voucher system, 33, 49

Williams, J., 88–9
Williams, Peter, 88
women
influences on entry to higher
education, 138, 142–3
trends in participation in higher
education, 10, 75–6
and utilitarian trainer discourse of
skills, 37
Woodrow, M., 160